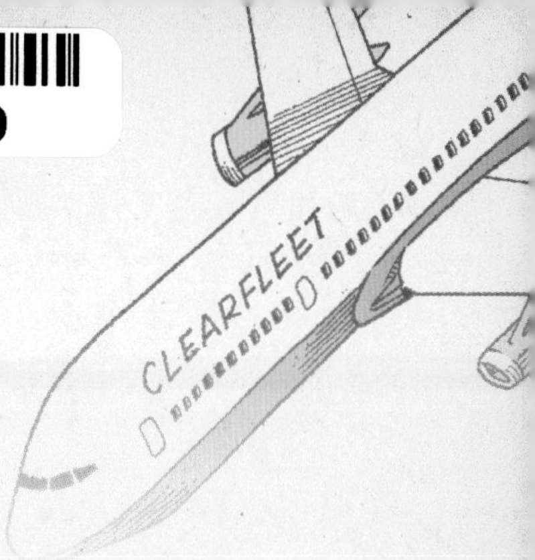
CLEARFLEET

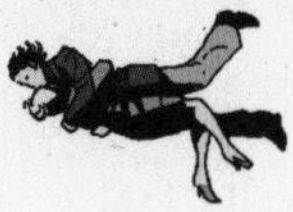

air

LETTERS FROM LOST COUNTRIES

LETTERS FROM LOST COUNTRIES

G. Willow Wilson Writer

M. K. Perker Artist

Chris Chuckry Colorist

Jared K. Fletcher Letterer

AIR created by Wilson and Perker

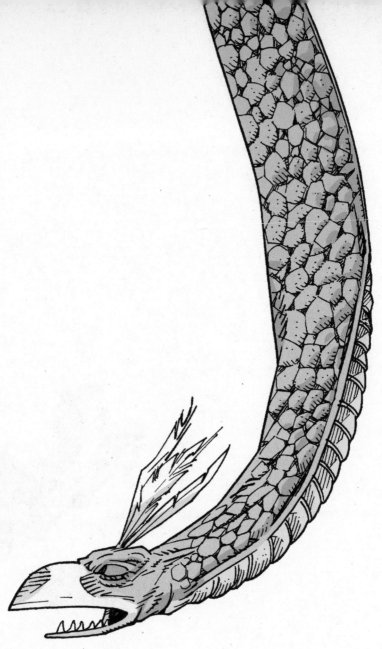

Karen Berger Senior VP-Executive Editor & Editor-original series
Pornsak Pichetshote Associate Editor-original series
Bob Harras Editor-collected edition
Robbin Brosterman Senior Art Director
Louis Prandi Art Director
Paul Levitz President & Publisher
Georg Brewer VP-Design & DC Direct Creative
Richard Bruning Senior VP-Creative Director
Patrick Caldon Executive VP-Finance & Operations
Chris Caramalis VP-Finance
John Cunningham VP-Marketing
Terri Cunningham VP-Managing Editor
Amy Genkins Senior VP-Business & Legal Affairs
Alison Gill VP-Manufacturing
David Hyde VP-Publicity
Hank Kanalz VP-General Manager, WildStorm
Jim Lee Editorial Director-WildStorm
Gregory Noveck Senior VP-Creative Affairs
Sue Pohja VP-Book Trade Sales
Steve Rotterdam Senior VP-Sales & Marketing
Cheryl Rubin Senior VP-Brand Management
Alysse Soll VP-Advertising & Custom Publishing
Jeff Trojan VP-Business Development, DC Direct
Bob Wayne VP-Sales

Cover illustration by M. K. Perker

AIR: LETTERS FROM LOST COUNTRIES
Published by DC Comics. Cover and compilation
Copyright © 2009 DC Comics. All Rights Reserved.

DC Comics, 1700 Broadway,
New York, NY 10019
A Warner Bros. Entertainment Company.
Printed in Canada.
Second Printing. ISBN: 978-1-4012-2153-9

SUSTAINABLE FORESTRY INITIATIVE
Certified Fiber Sourcing
www.sfiprogram.org

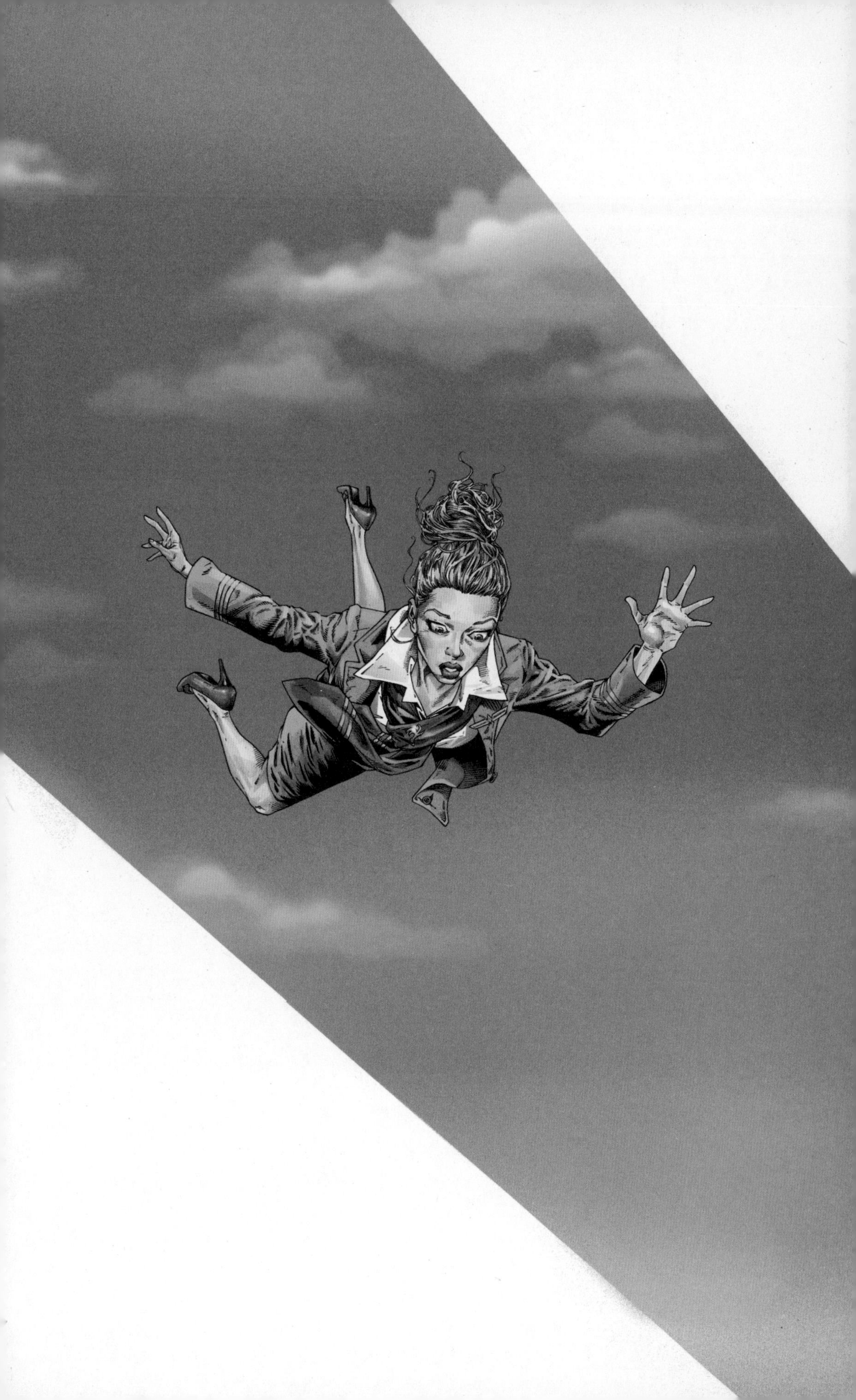

CHAPTER 1

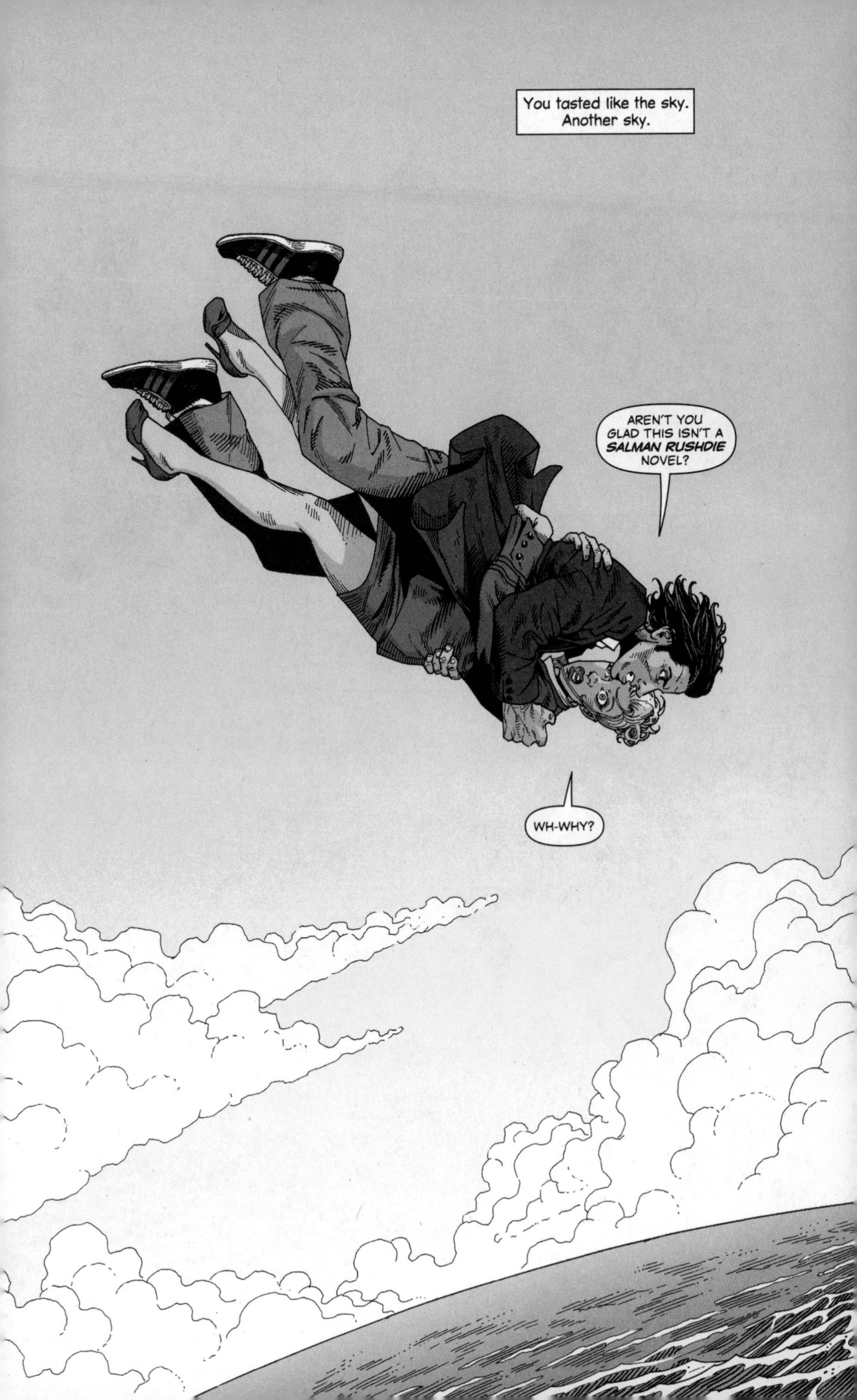
You tasted like the sky. Another sky.
AREN'T YOU GLAD THIS ISN'T A *SALMAN RUSHDIE* NOVEL?
WH-WHY?

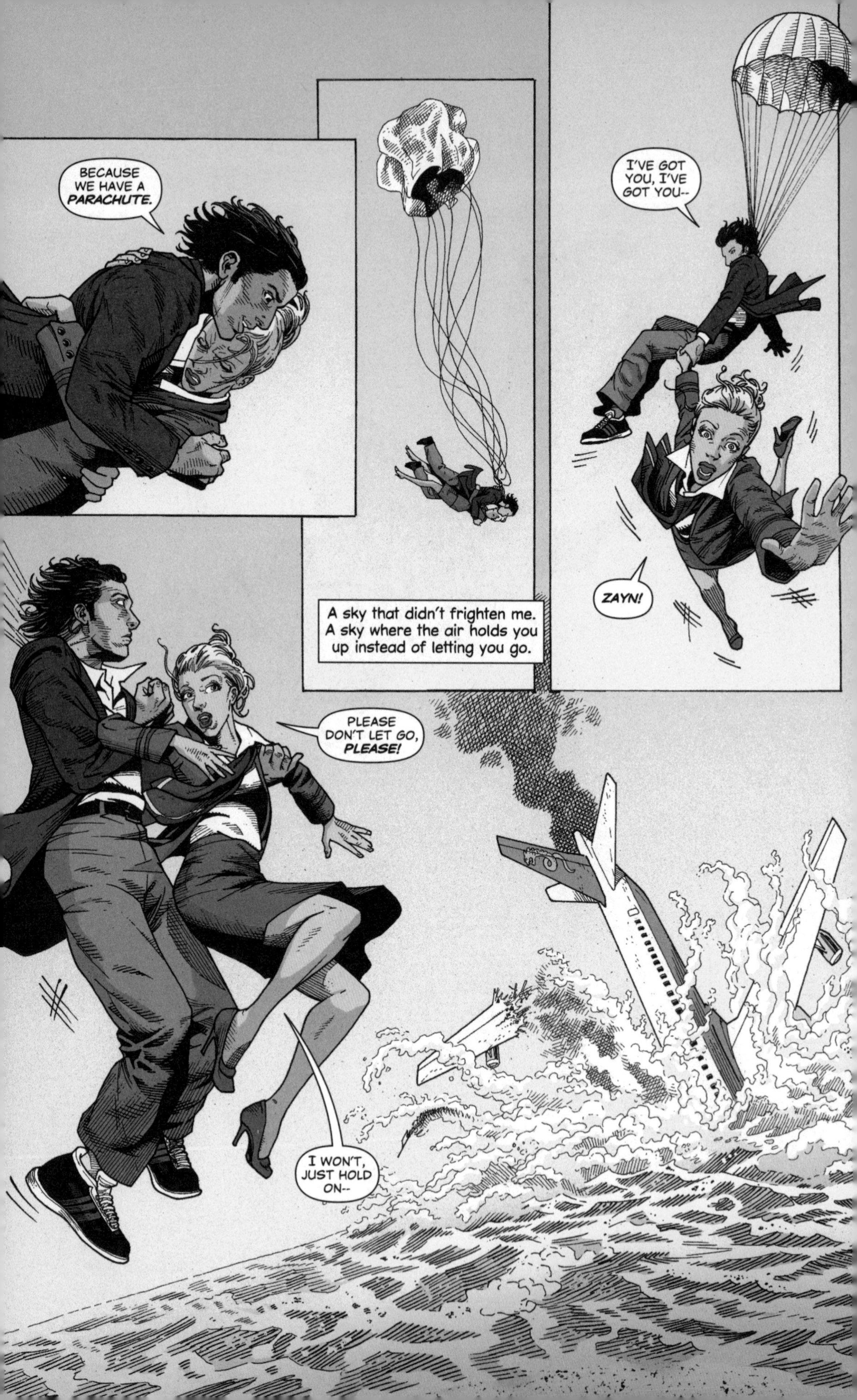

BECAUSE WE HAVE A PARACHUTE.
A sky that didn't frighten me. A sky where the air holds you up instead of letting you go.
I'VE GOT YOU, I'VE GOT YOU--
ZAYN!
PLEASE DON'T LET GO, PLEASE!
I WON'T, JUST HOLD ON--

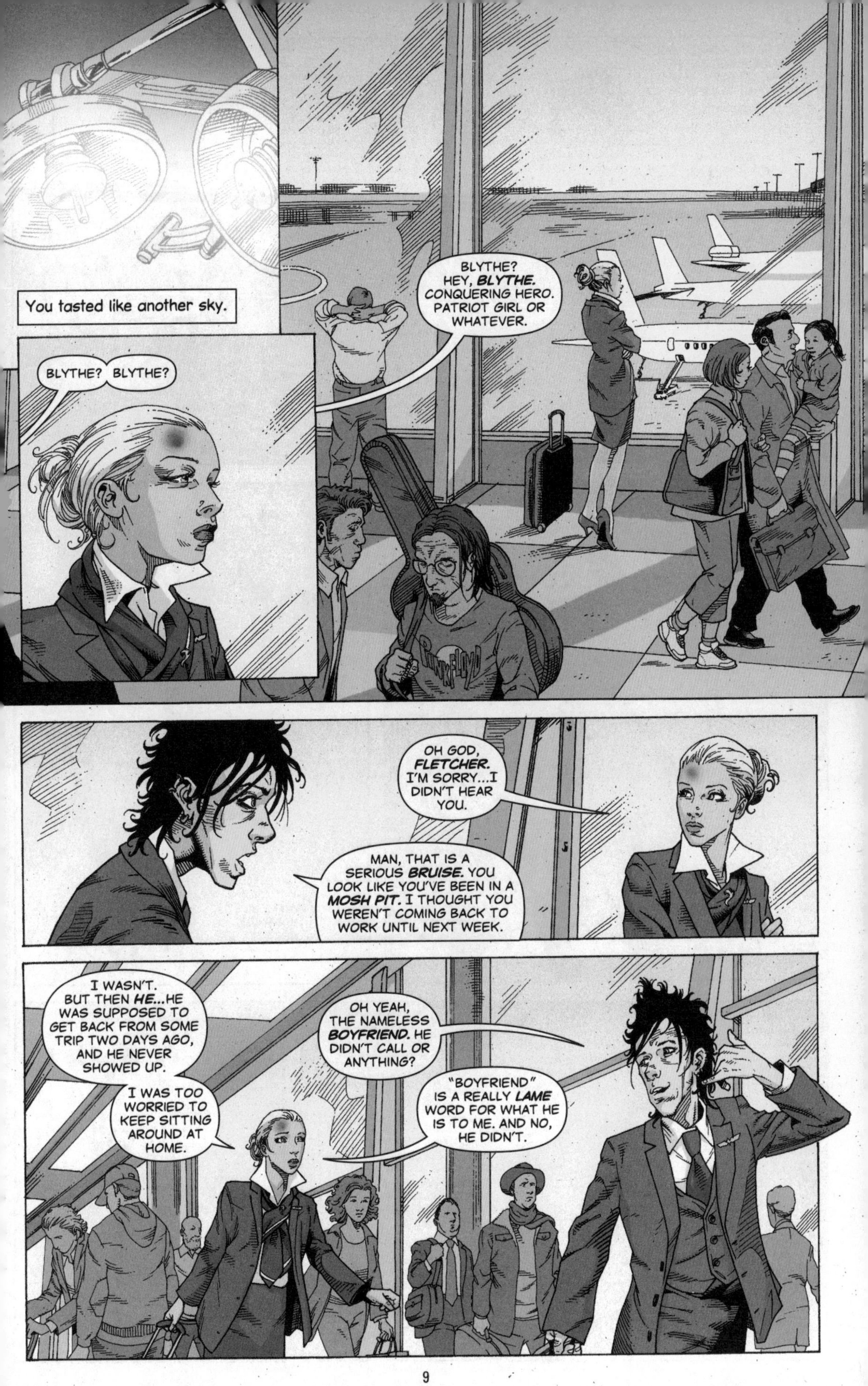
You tasted like another sky.
BLYTHE? HEY, BLYTHE. CONQUERING HERO. PATRIOT GIRL OR WHATEVER.
BLYTHE? BLYTHE?
OH GOD, FLETCHER. I'M SORRY...I DIDN'T HEAR YOU.
MAN, THAT IS A SERIOUS BRUISE. YOU LOOK LIKE YOU'VE BEEN IN A MOSH PIT. I THOUGHT YOU WEREN'T COMING BACK TO WORK UNTIL NEXT WEEK.
I WASN'T. BUT THEN HE...HE WAS SUPPOSED TO GET BACK FROM SOME TRIP TWO DAYS AGO, AND HE NEVER SHOWED UP.
I WAS TOO WORRIED TO KEEP SITTING AROUND AT HOME.
OH YEAH, THE NAMELESS BOYFRIEND. HE DIDN'T CALL OR ANYTHING?
"BOYFRIEND" IS A REALLY LAME WORD FOR WHAT HE IS TO ME. AND NO, HE DIDN'T.

OKAY THEN, *LOVER-BOY*? COMPANION IN THE *NIHILIST NIGHTMARE* THAT IS *LIFE*?

YOU'RE ON THE *MILAN* FLIGHT, RIGHT? OTHERWISE YOU'RE FOLLOWING ME FOR NOTHING.

YES, YES, I'M ON THE MILAN FLIGHT. I'M *COMING*--

GATES 140·141·142

ISTANBUL
BARCELONA
ATHENS
BELGRAD
LISBON
HAMBURG
PRAGUE
OSLO

BLYTHE? COME ON, WE HAVE TO *RUN*.

WAIT...JUST WAIT ONE SECOND...

BREAKING NEWS

...CARRYING HUMANITARIAN AID SUPPLIES TO *BANGLADESH*. RADIO CONTACT WITH THE PLANE WAS LOST OVER 72 HOURS AGO, BUT NO WRECKAGE HAS BEEN FOUND.

PASSENGERS ARE BELIEVED TO INCLUDE AMERICAN AND PAKISTANI AID WORKERS, AMONG THEM SARAH BROCK, JAVAD ARYANPUR--

OH GOD...

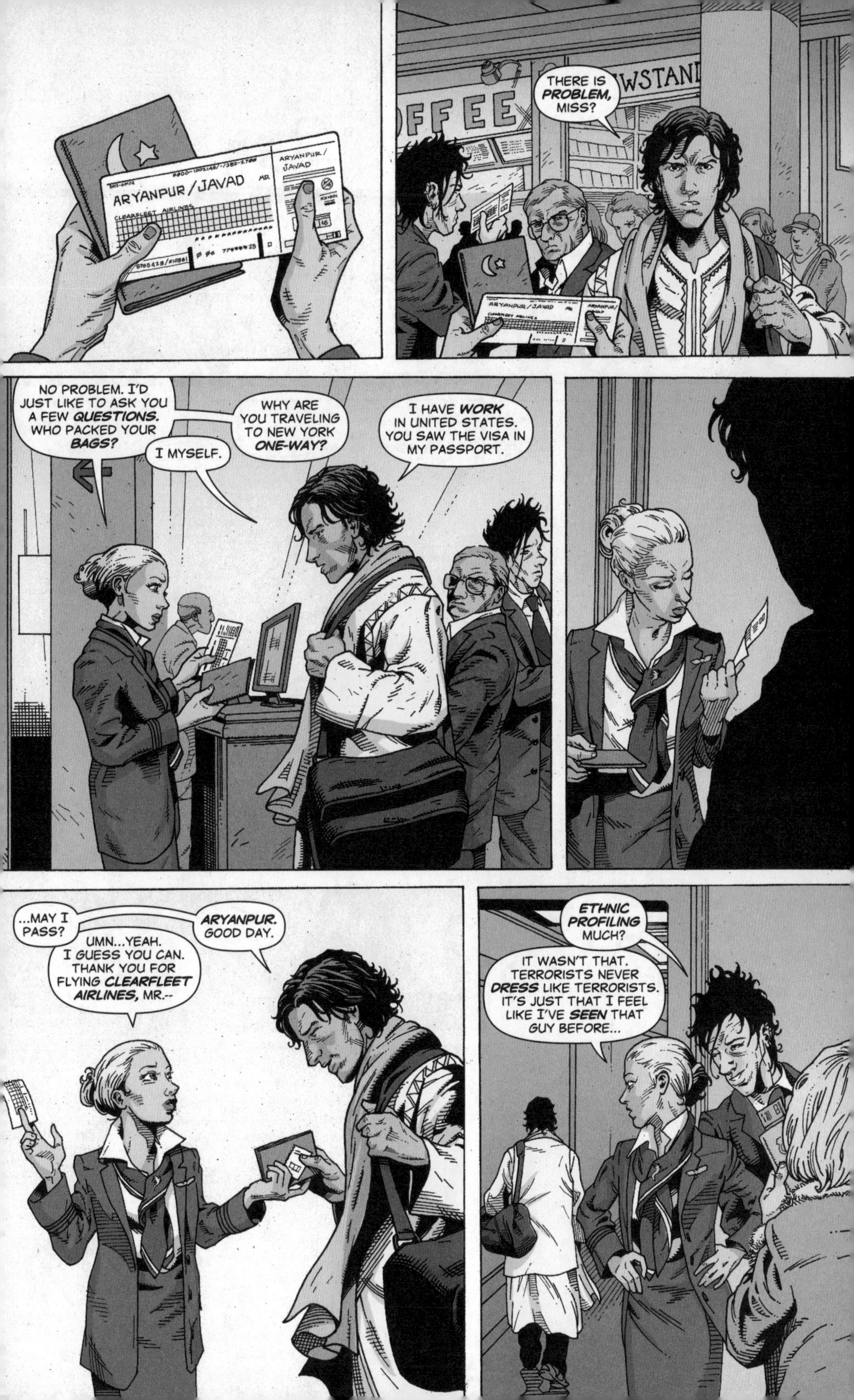

ARYANPUR/JAVAD MR
ARYANPUR/ JAVAD
CLEARFLEET AIRLINES
THERE IS PROBLEM, MISS?
NO PROBLEM. I'D JUST LIKE TO ASK YOU A FEW QUESTIONS. WHO PACKED YOUR BAGS?
I MYSELF.
WHY ARE YOU TRAVELING TO NEW YORK ONE-WAY?
I HAVE WORK IN UNITED STATES. YOU SAW THE VISA IN MY PASSPORT.
...MAY I PASS?
UMN...YEAH. I GUESS YOU CAN. THANK YOU FOR FLYING CLEARFLEET AIRLINES, MR.--
ARYANPUR. GOOD DAY.
ETHNIC PROFILING MUCH?
IT WASN'T THAT. TERRORISTS NEVER DRESS LIKE TERRORISTS. IT'S JUST THAT I FEEL LIKE I'VE SEEN THAT GUY BEFORE...

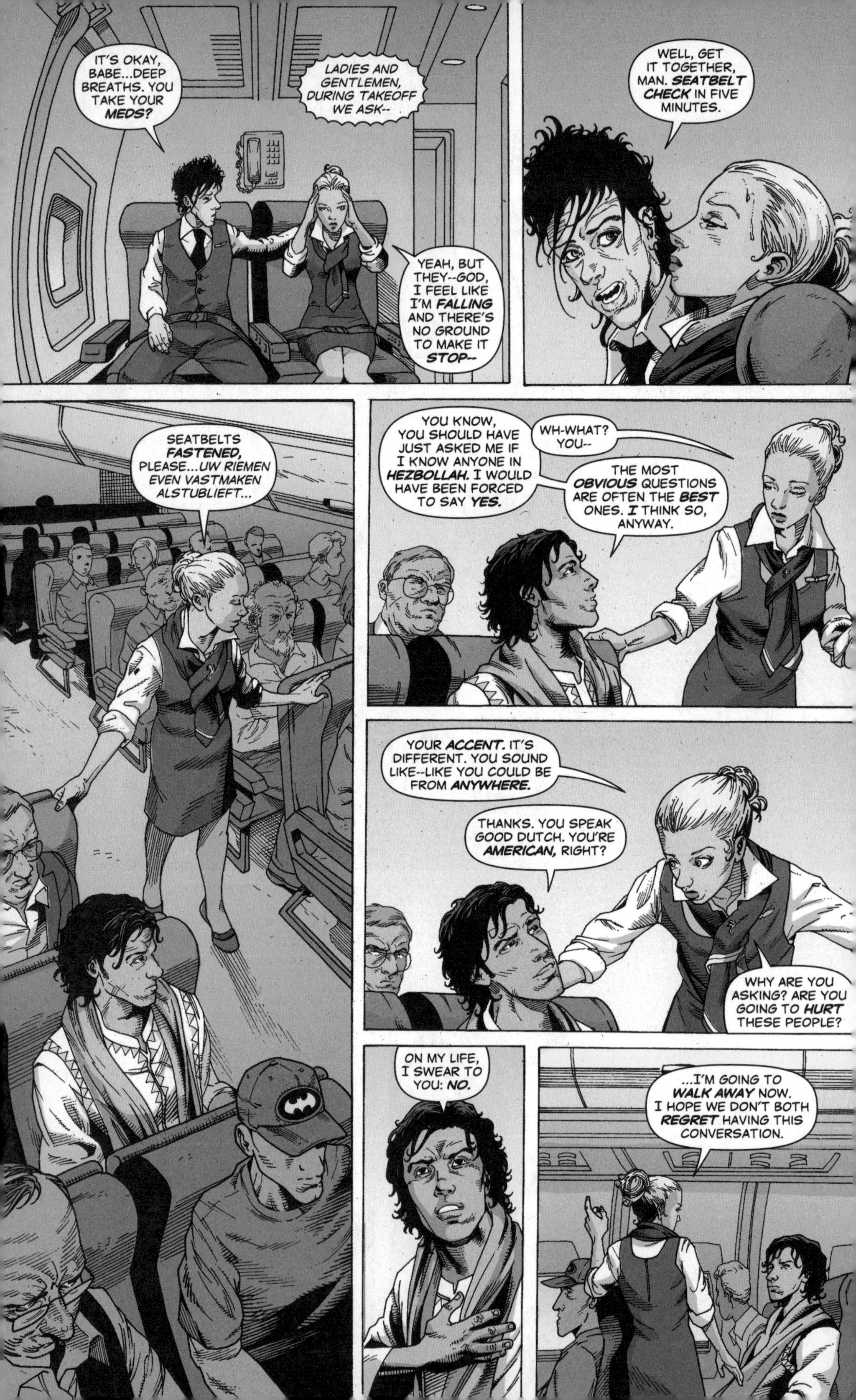
IT'S OKAY, BABE...DEEP BREATHS. YOU TAKE YOUR MEDS?
LADIES AND GENTLEMEN, DURING TAKEOFF WE ASK--
YEAH, BUT THEY--GOD, I FEEL LIKE I'M FALLING AND THERE'S NO GROUND TO MAKE IT STOP--
WELL, GET IT TOGETHER, MAN. SEATBELT CHECK IN FIVE MINUTES.
SEATBELTS FASTENED, PLEASE...UW RIEMEN EVEN VASTMAKEN ALSTUBLIEFT...
YOU KNOW, YOU SHOULD HAVE JUST ASKED ME IF I KNOW ANYONE IN HEZBOLLAH. I WOULD HAVE BEEN FORCED TO SAY YES.
WH-WHAT? YOU--
THE MOST OBVIOUS QUESTIONS ARE OFTEN THE BEST ONES. I THINK SO, ANYWAY.
YOUR ACCENT. IT'S DIFFERENT. YOU SOUND LIKE--LIKE YOU COULD BE FROM ANYWHERE.
THANKS. YOU SPEAK GOOD DUTCH. YOU'RE AMERICAN, RIGHT?
WHY ARE YOU ASKING? ARE YOU GOING TO HURT THESE PEOPLE?
ON MY LIFE, I SWEAR TO YOU: NO.
...I'M GOING TO WALK AWAY NOW. I HOPE WE DON'T BOTH REGRET HAVING THIS CONVERSATION.

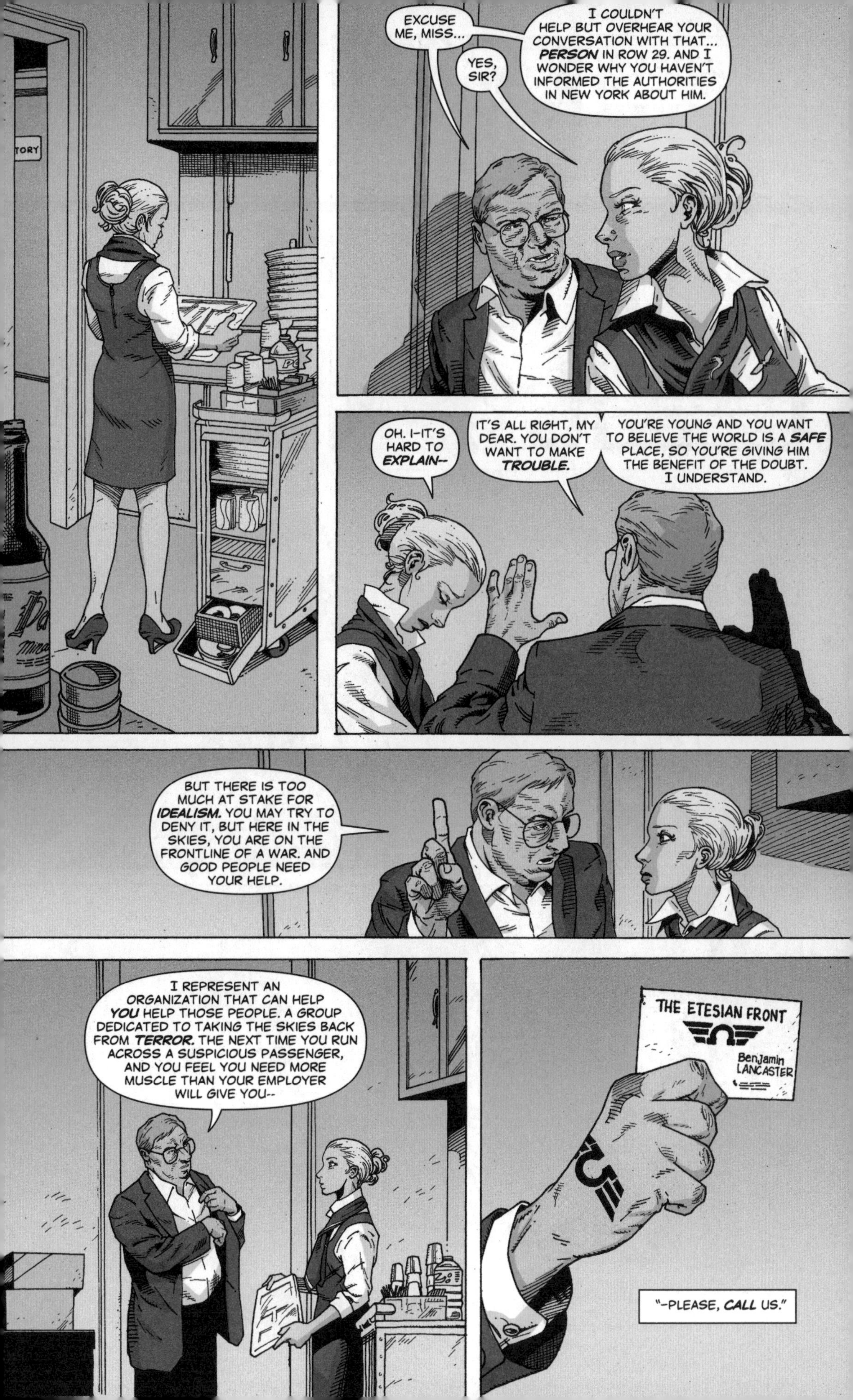
TORY
EXCUSE ME, MISS...
YES, SIR?
I COULDN'T HELP BUT OVERHEAR YOUR CONVERSATION WITH THAT... PERSON IN ROW 29. AND I WONDER WHY YOU HAVEN'T INFORMED THE AUTHORITIES IN NEW YORK ABOUT HIM.
OH. I-IT'S HARD TO EXPLAIN--
IT'S ALL RIGHT, MY DEAR. YOU DON'T WANT TO MAKE TROUBLE.
YOU'RE YOUNG AND YOU WANT TO BELIEVE THE WORLD IS A SAFE PLACE, SO YOU'RE GIVING HIM THE BENEFIT OF THE DOUBT. I UNDERSTAND.
BUT THERE IS TOO MUCH AT STAKE FOR IDEALISM. YOU MAY TRY TO DENY IT, BUT HERE IN THE SKIES, YOU ARE ON THE FRONTLINE OF A WAR. AND GOOD PEOPLE NEED YOUR HELP.
I REPRESENT AN ORGANIZATION THAT CAN HELP YOU HELP THOSE PEOPLE. A GROUP DEDICATED TO TAKING THE SKIES BACK FROM TERROR. THE NEXT TIME YOU RUN ACROSS A SUSPICIOUS PASSENGER, AND YOU FEEL YOU NEED MORE MUSCLE THAN YOUR EMPLOYER WILL GIVE YOU--
THE ETESIAN FRONT
Benjamin LANCASTER
"--PLEASE, CALL US."

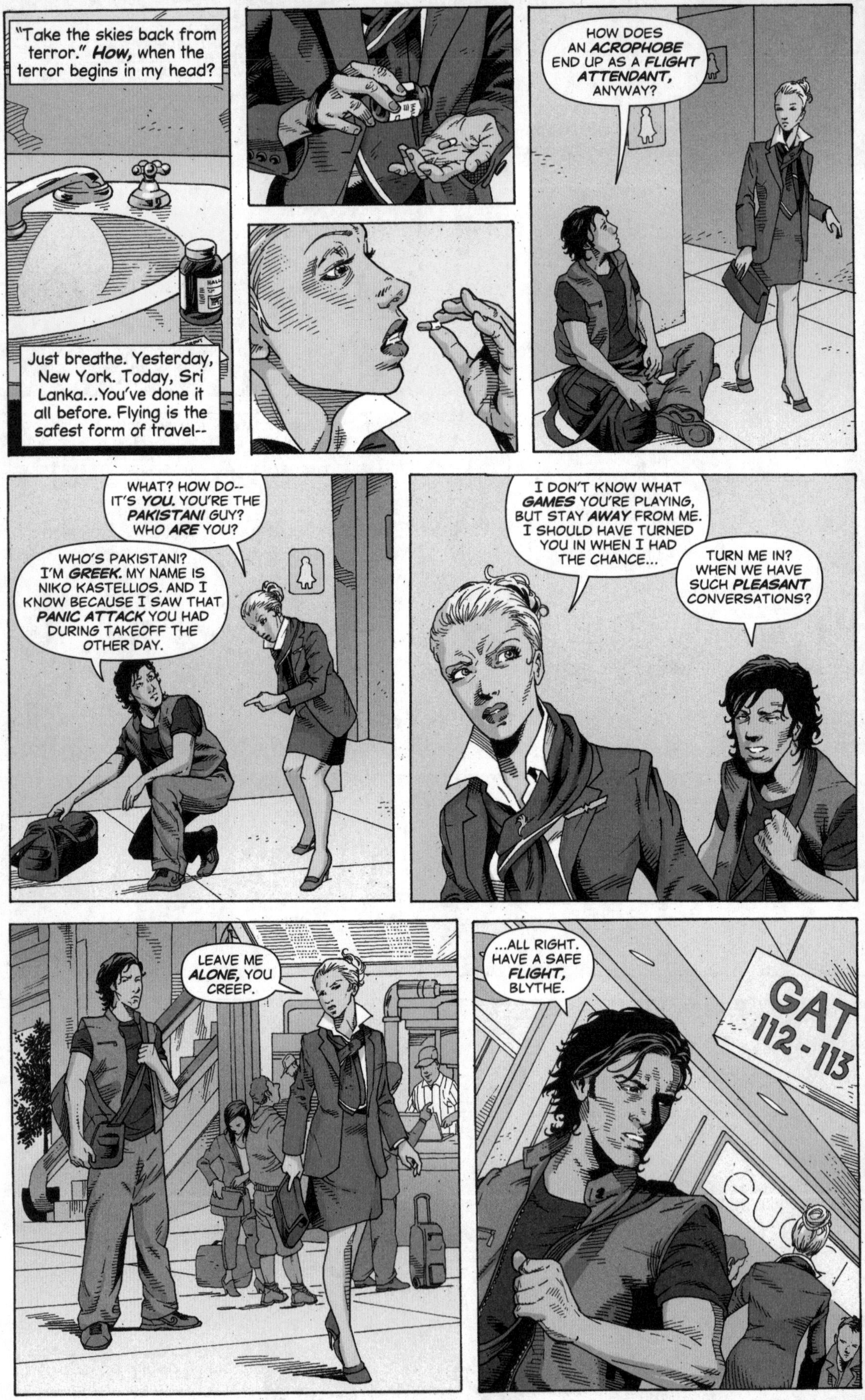
"Take the skies back from terror." How, when the terror begins in my head?
Just breathe. Yesterday, New York. Today, Sri Lanka...You've done it all before. Flying is the safest form of travel--
HOW DOES AN ACROPHOBE END UP AS A FLIGHT ATTENDANT, ANYWAY?
WHAT? HOW DO-- IT'S YOU. YOU'RE THE PAKISTANI GUY? WHO ARE YOU?
WHO'S PAKISTANI? I'M GREEK. MY NAME IS NIKO KASTELLIOS. AND I KNOW BECAUSE I SAW THAT PANIC ATTACK YOU HAD DURING TAKEOFF THE OTHER DAY.
I DON'T KNOW WHAT GAMES YOU'RE PLAYING, BUT STAY AWAY FROM ME. I SHOULD HAVE TURNED YOU IN WHEN I HAD THE CHANCE...
TURN ME IN? WHEN WE HAVE SUCH PLEASANT CONVERSATIONS?
LEAVE ME ALONE, YOU CREEP.
...ALL RIGHT. HAVE A SAFE FLIGHT, BLYTHE.
GAT
112 - 113

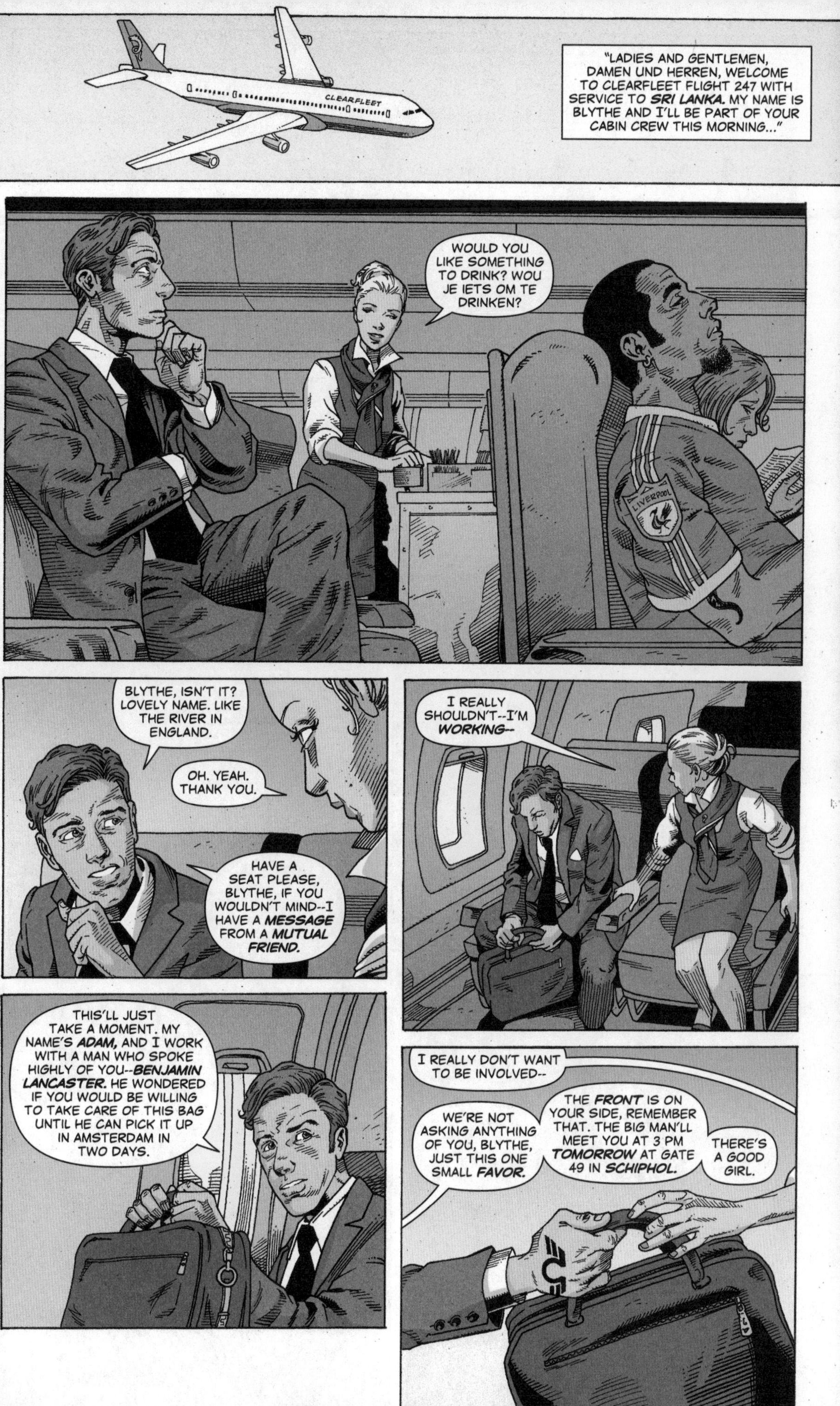

"LADIES AND GENTLEMEN, DAMEN UND HERREN, WELCOME TO CLEARFLEET FLIGHT 247 WITH SERVICE TO SRI LANKA. MY NAME IS BLYTHE AND I'LL BE PART OF YOUR CABIN CREW THIS MORNING..."
CLEARFLEET
WOULD YOU LIKE SOMETHING TO DRINK? WOU JE IETS OM TE DRINKEN?
LIVERPOOL
BLYTHE, ISN'T IT? LOVELY NAME. LIKE THE RIVER IN ENGLAND.
OH. YEAH. THANK YOU.
HAVE A SEAT PLEASE, BLYTHE, IF YOU WOULDN'T MIND--I HAVE A MESSAGE FROM A MUTUAL FRIEND.
I REALLY SHOULDN'T--I'M WORKING--
THIS'LL JUST TAKE A MOMENT. MY NAME'S ADAM, AND I WORK WITH A MAN WHO SPOKE HIGHLY OF YOU--BENJAMIN LANCASTER. HE WONDERED IF YOU WOULD BE WILLING TO TAKE CARE OF THIS BAG UNTIL HE CAN PICK IT UP IN AMSTERDAM IN TWO DAYS.
I REALLY DON'T WANT TO BE INVOLVED--
WE'RE NOT ASKING ANYTHING OF YOU, BLYTHE, JUST THIS ONE SMALL FAVOR.
THE FRONT IS ON YOUR SIDE, REMEMBER THAT. THE BIG MAN'LL MEET YOU AT 3 PM TOMORROW AT GATE 49 IN SCHIPHOL.
THERE'S A GOOD GIRL.

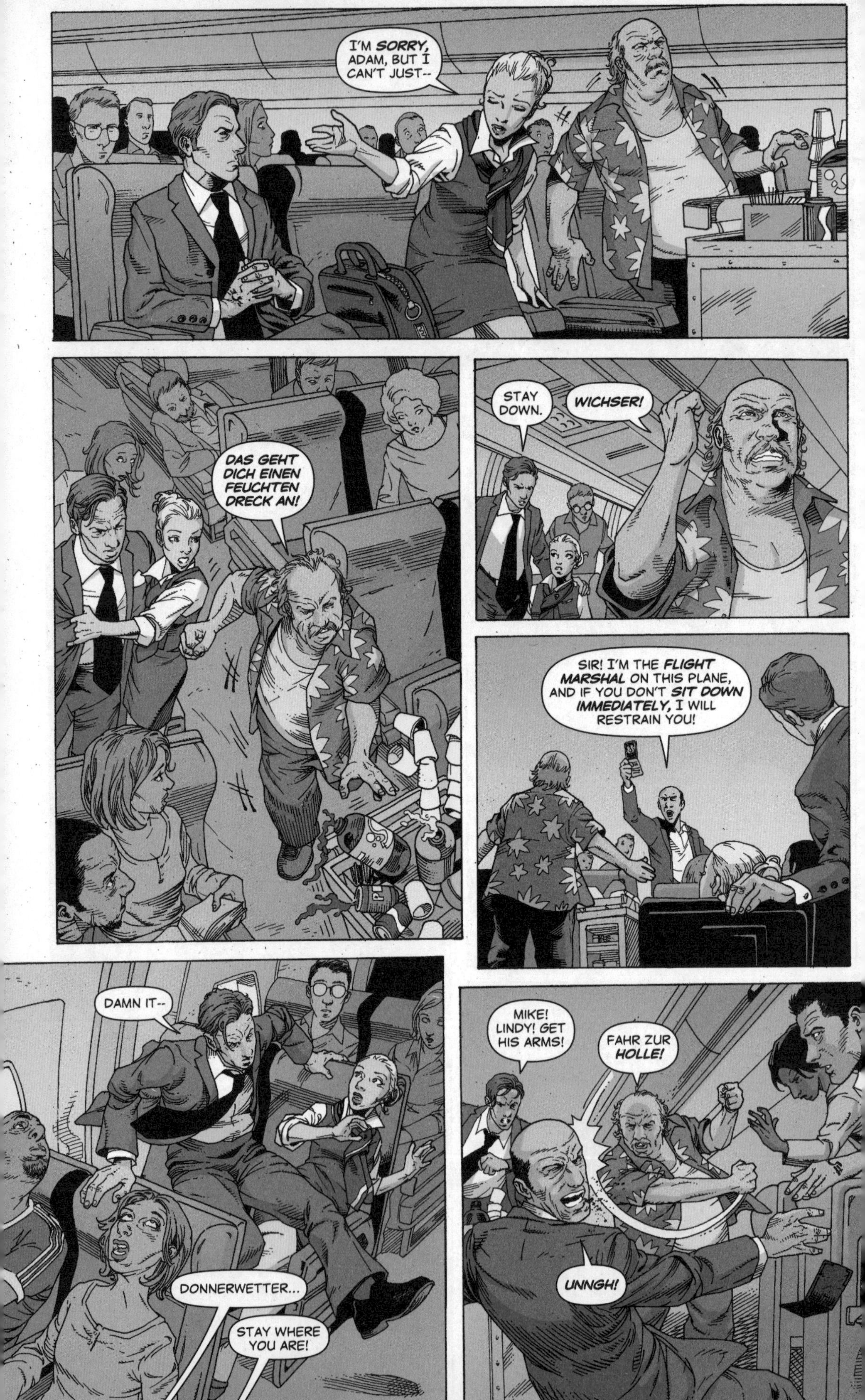
I'M SORRY, ADAM, BUT I CAN'T JUST--
DAS GEHT DICH EINEN FEUCHTEN DRECK AN!
STAY DOWN.
WICHSER!
SIR! I'M THE FLIGHT MARSHAL ON THIS PLANE, AND IF YOU DON'T SIT DOWN IMMEDIATELY, I WILL RESTRAIN YOU!
DAMN IT--
DONNERWETTER...
STAY WHERE YOU ARE!
MIKE! LINDY! GET HIS ARMS!
FAHR ZUR HOLLE!
UNNGH!

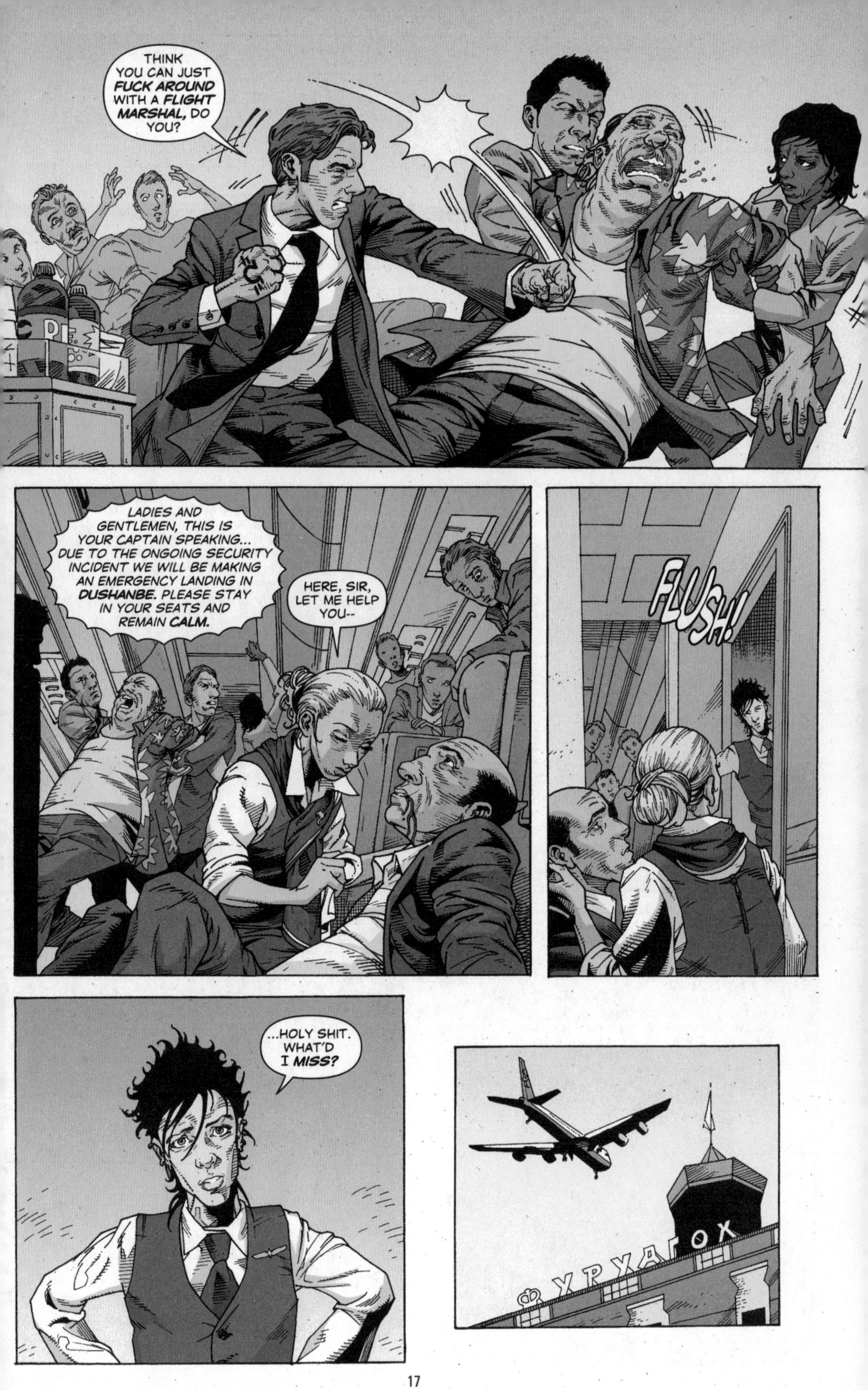
THINK YOU CAN JUST FUCK AROUND WITH A FLIGHT MARSHAL, DO YOU?
LADIES AND GENTLEMEN, THIS IS YOUR CAPTAIN SPEAKING... DUE TO THE ONGOING SECURITY INCIDENT WE WILL BE MAKING AN EMERGENCY LANDING IN DUSHANBE. PLEASE STAY IN YOUR SEATS AND REMAIN CALM.
HERE, SIR, LET ME HELP YOU--
FLUSH!
...HOLY SHIT. WHAT'D I MISS?

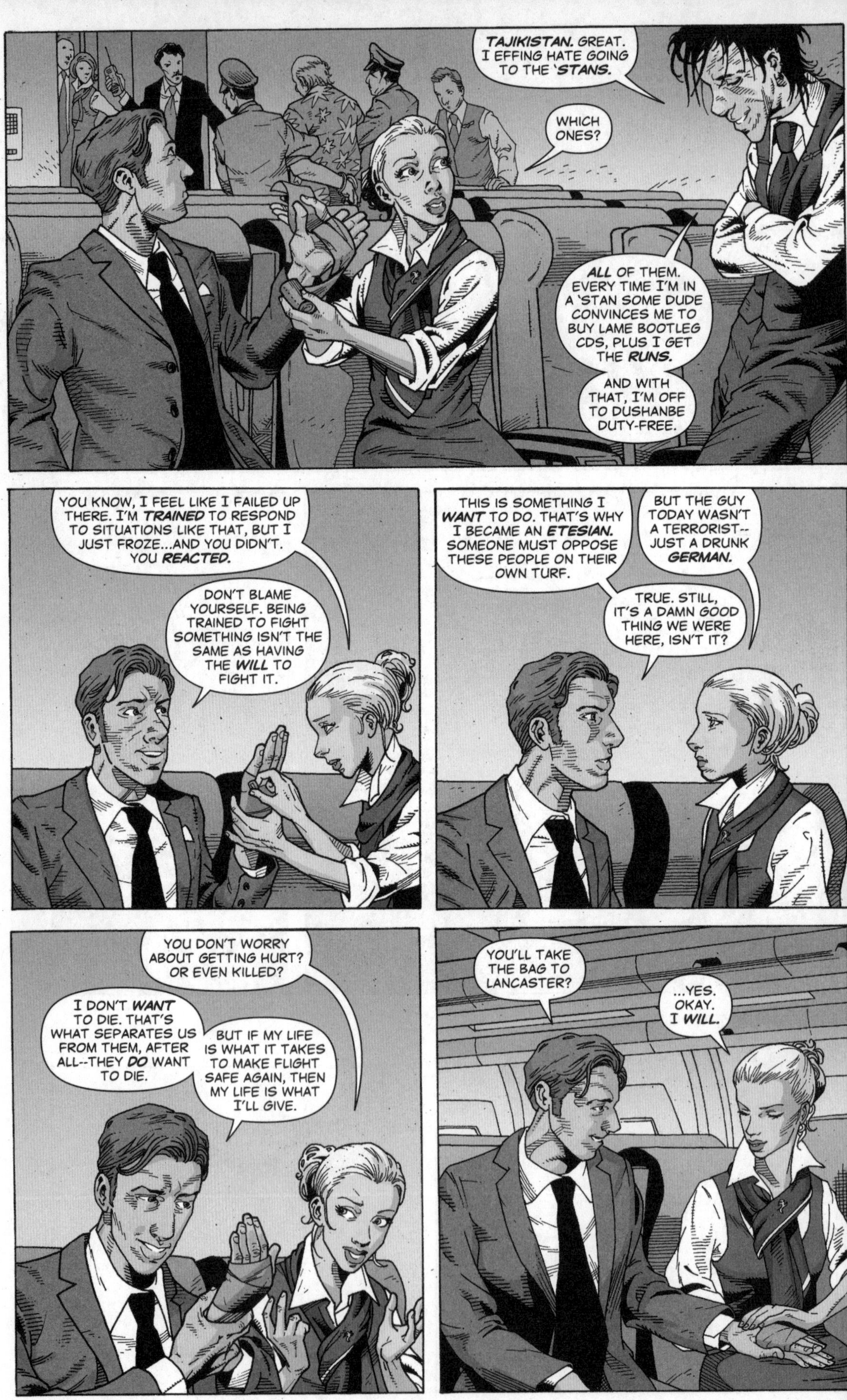
TAJIKISTAN. GREAT. I EFFING HATE GOING TO THE 'STANS.
WHICH ONES?
ALL OF THEM. EVERY TIME I'M IN A 'STAN SOME DUDE CONVINCES ME TO BUY LAME BOOTLEG CDS, PLUS I GET THE RUNS.
AND WITH THAT, I'M OFF TO DUSHANBE DUTY-FREE.
YOU KNOW, I FEEL LIKE I FAILED UP THERE. I'M TRAINED TO RESPOND TO SITUATIONS LIKE THAT, BUT I JUST FROZE...AND YOU DIDN'T. YOU REACTED.
DON'T BLAME YOURSELF. BEING TRAINED TO FIGHT SOMETHING ISN'T THE SAME AS HAVING THE WILL TO FIGHT IT.
THIS IS SOMETHING I WANT TO DO. THAT'S WHY I BECAME AN ETESIAN. SOMEONE MUST OPPOSE THESE PEOPLE ON THEIR OWN TURF.
BUT THE GUY TODAY WASN'T A TERRORIST-- JUST A DRUNK GERMAN.
TRUE. STILL, IT'S A DAMN GOOD THING WE WERE HERE, ISN'T IT?
YOU DON'T WORRY ABOUT GETTING HURT? OR EVEN KILLED?
I DON'T WANT TO DIE. THAT'S WHAT SEPARATES US FROM THEM, AFTER ALL--THEY DO WANT TO DIE.
BUT IF MY LIFE IS WHAT IT TAKES TO MAKE FLIGHT SAFE AGAIN, THEN MY LIFE IS WHAT I'LL GIVE.
YOU'LL TAKE THE BAG TO LANCASTER?
...YES. OKAY. I WILL.

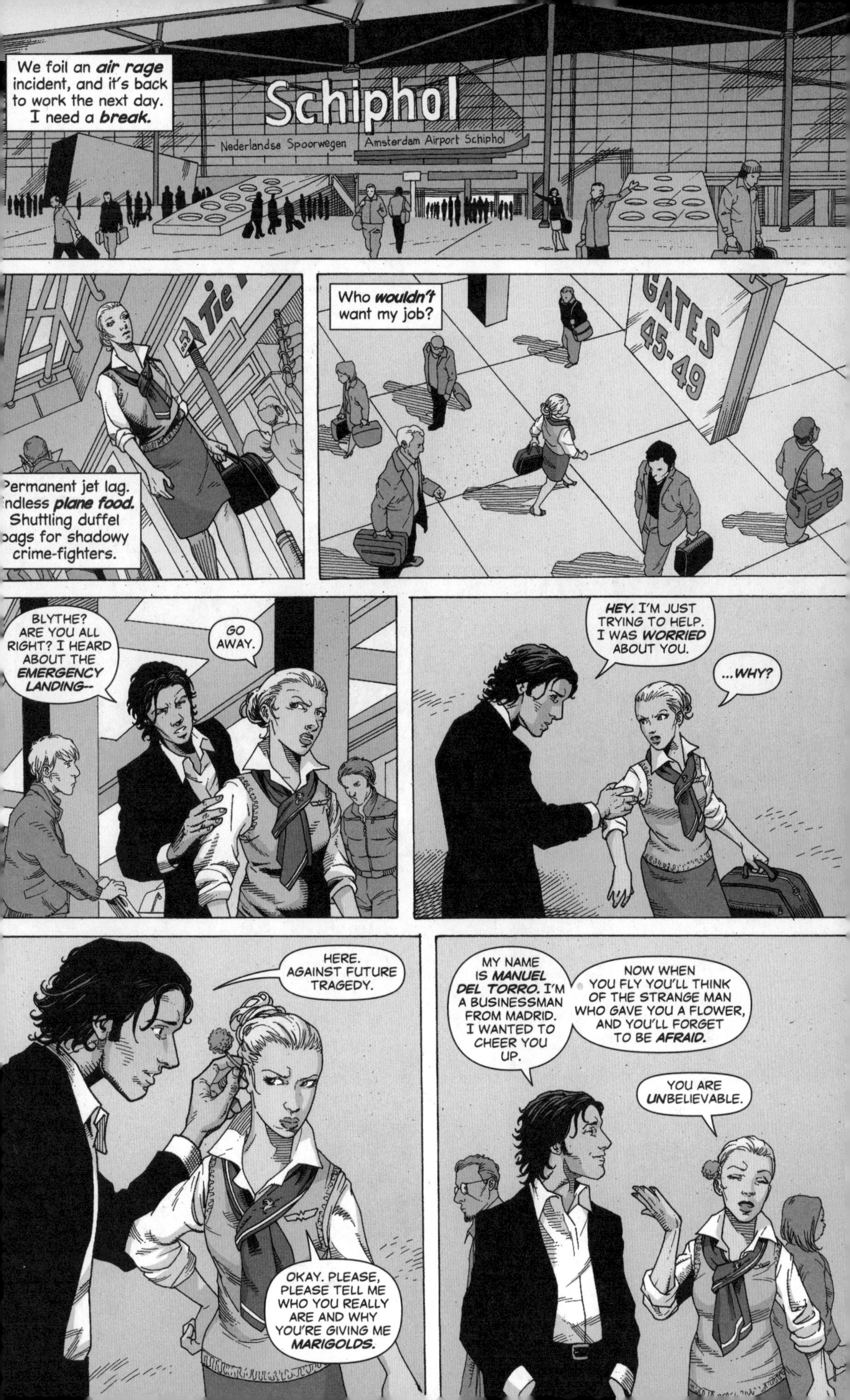

We foil an *air rage* incident, and it's back to work the next day. I need a *break.*
Schiphol
Nederlandse Spoorwegen
Amsterdam Airport Schiphol
Permanent jet lag. Endless *plane food.* Shuttling duffel bags for shadowy crime-fighters.
Who *wouldn't* want my job?
GATES 45-49
BLYTHE? ARE YOU ALL RIGHT? I HEARD ABOUT THE *EMERGENCY LANDING--*
GO AWAY.
HEY. I'M JUST TRYING TO HELP. I WAS *WORRIED* ABOUT YOU.
...WHY?
HERE. AGAINST FUTURE TRAGEDY.
OKAY. PLEASE, PLEASE TELL ME WHO YOU REALLY ARE AND WHY YOU'RE GIVING ME *MARIGOLDS.*
MY NAME IS *MANUEL DEL TORRO.* I'M A BUSINESSMAN FROM MADRID. I WANTED TO CHEER YOU UP.
NOW WHEN YOU FLY YOU'LL THINK OF THE STRANGE MAN WHO GAVE YOU A FLOWER, AND YOU'LL FORGET TO BE *AFRAID.*
YOU ARE *UN*BELIEVABLE.

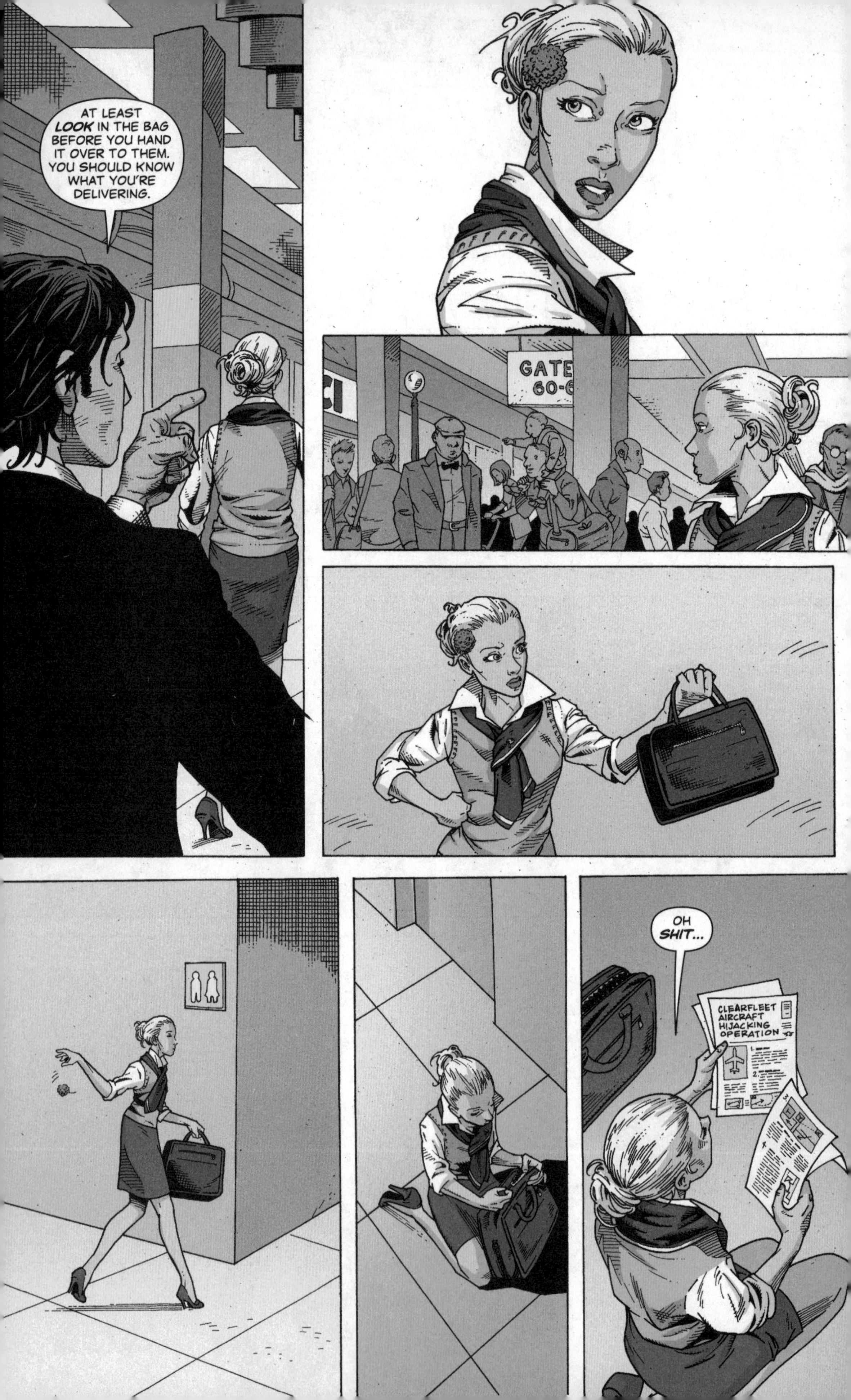
AT LEAST LOOK IN THE BAG BEFORE YOU HAND IT OVER TO THEM. YOU SHOULD KNOW WHAT YOU'RE DELIVERING.
GATE 60-6
OH SHIT...
CLEARFLEET AIRCRAFT HIJACKING OPERATION

I'M DISAPPOINTED IN YOU, BLYTHE. *VERY* DISAPPOINTED. I WAS HOPING WE COULD *TRUST* YOU.

I-I DIDN'T-- I DIDN'T MEAN TO--

DID YOU THINK WE WEREN'T *WATCHING* YOU? FOLLOWING YOUR MOVEMENTS, YOUR CONVERSATIONS? DIDN'T YOU REALIZE THIS WAS A *TEST*?

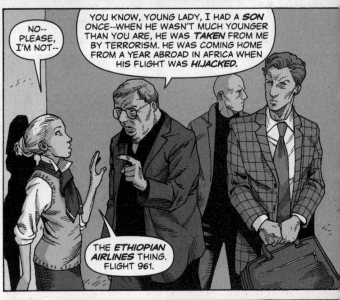

NO-- PLEASE, I'M NOT--

YOU KNOW, YOUNG LADY, I HAD A *SON* ONCE--WHEN HE WASN'T MUCH YOUNGER THAN YOU ARE, HE WAS *TAKEN* FROM ME BY TERRORISM. HE WAS COMING HOME FROM A YEAR ABROAD IN AFRICA WHEN HIS FLIGHT WAS *HIJACKED.*

THE *ETHIOPIAN AIRLINES* THING. FLIGHT 961.

YOU KNOW IT, THEN. SO YOU KNOW WHY THE *ETESIAN FRONT* MUST OPERATE IN WAYS THAT ARE SOMETIMES BRUTAL.

I'M REALLY, REALLY SORRY.

I'M AFRAID AN APOLOGY WILL NOT BE *ENOUGH.*

OH NO. NOT FOR THIS.

FOR *THIS.*

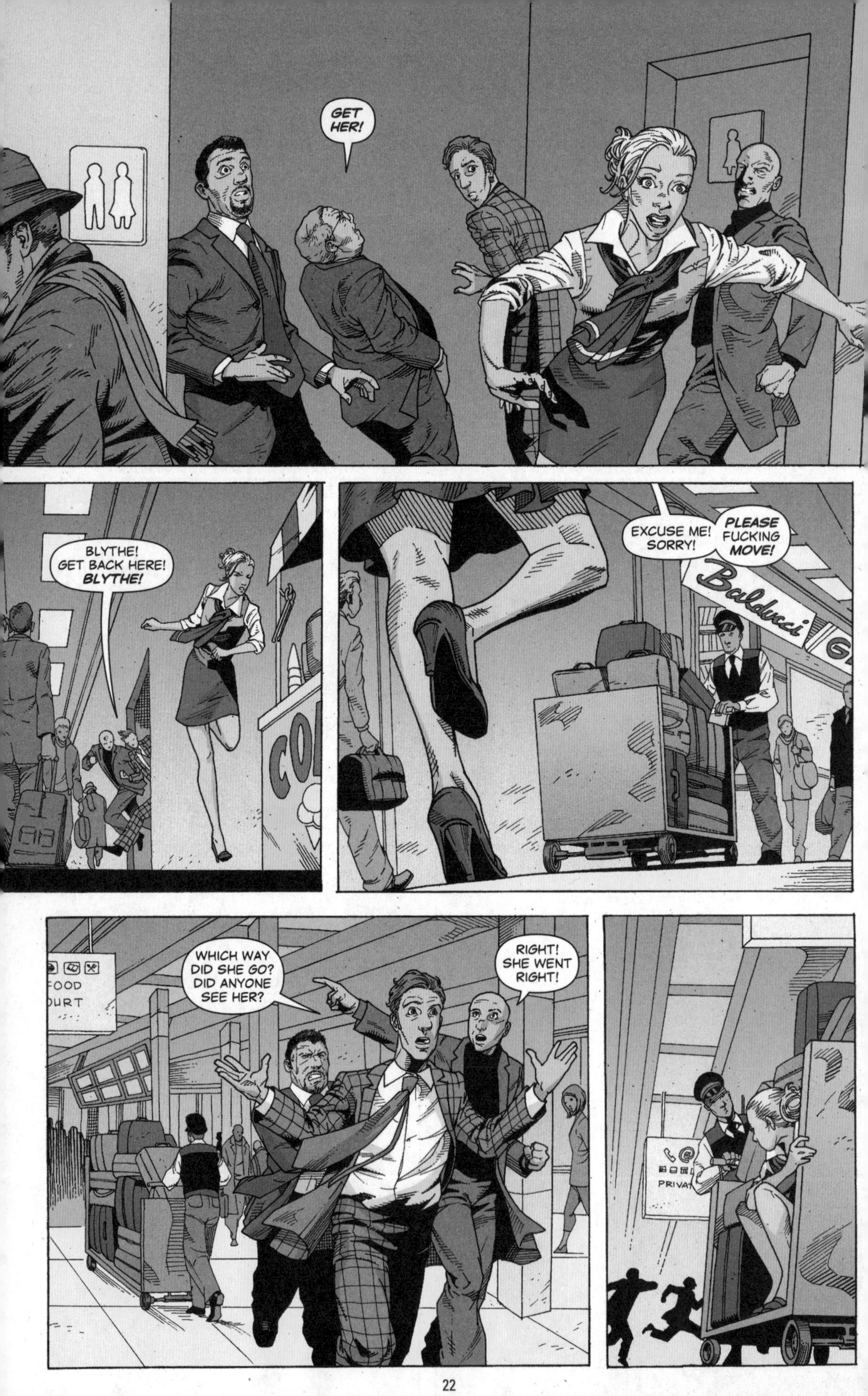
GET HER!
BLYTHE! GET BACK HERE! BLYTHE!
EXCUSE ME! SORRY!
PLEASE FUCKING MOVE!
Balducci
WHICH WAY DID SHE GO? DID ANYONE SEE HER?
RIGHT! SHE WENT RIGHT!

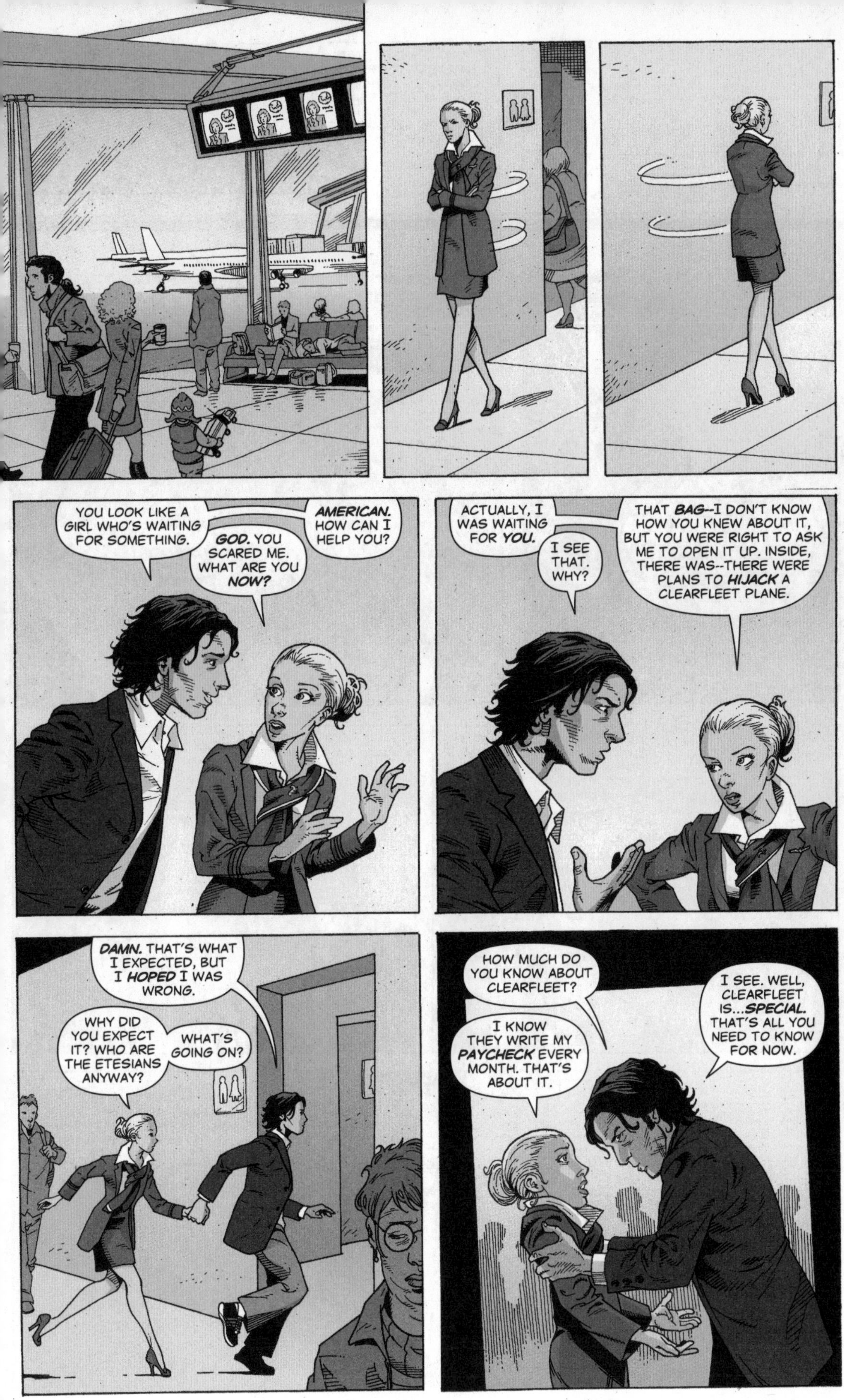

YOU LOOK LIKE A GIRL WHO'S WAITING FOR SOMETHING.
AMERICAN. HOW CAN I HELP YOU?
GOD. YOU SCARED ME. WHAT ARE YOU NOW?
ACTUALLY, I WAS WAITING FOR YOU.
I SEE THAT. WHY?
THAT BAG--I DON'T KNOW HOW YOU KNEW ABOUT IT, BUT YOU WERE RIGHT TO ASK ME TO OPEN IT UP. INSIDE, THERE WAS--THERE WERE PLANS TO HIJACK A CLEARFLEET PLANE.
DAMN. THAT'S WHAT I EXPECTED, BUT I HOPED I WAS WRONG.
WHY DID YOU EXPECT IT? WHO ARE THE ETESIANS ANYWAY?
WHAT'S GOING ON?
HOW MUCH DO YOU KNOW ABOUT CLEARFLEET?
I KNOW THEY WRITE MY PAYCHECK EVERY MONTH. THAT'S ABOUT IT.
I SEE. WELL, CLEARFLEET IS...SPECIAL. THAT'S ALL YOU NEED TO KNOW FOR NOW.

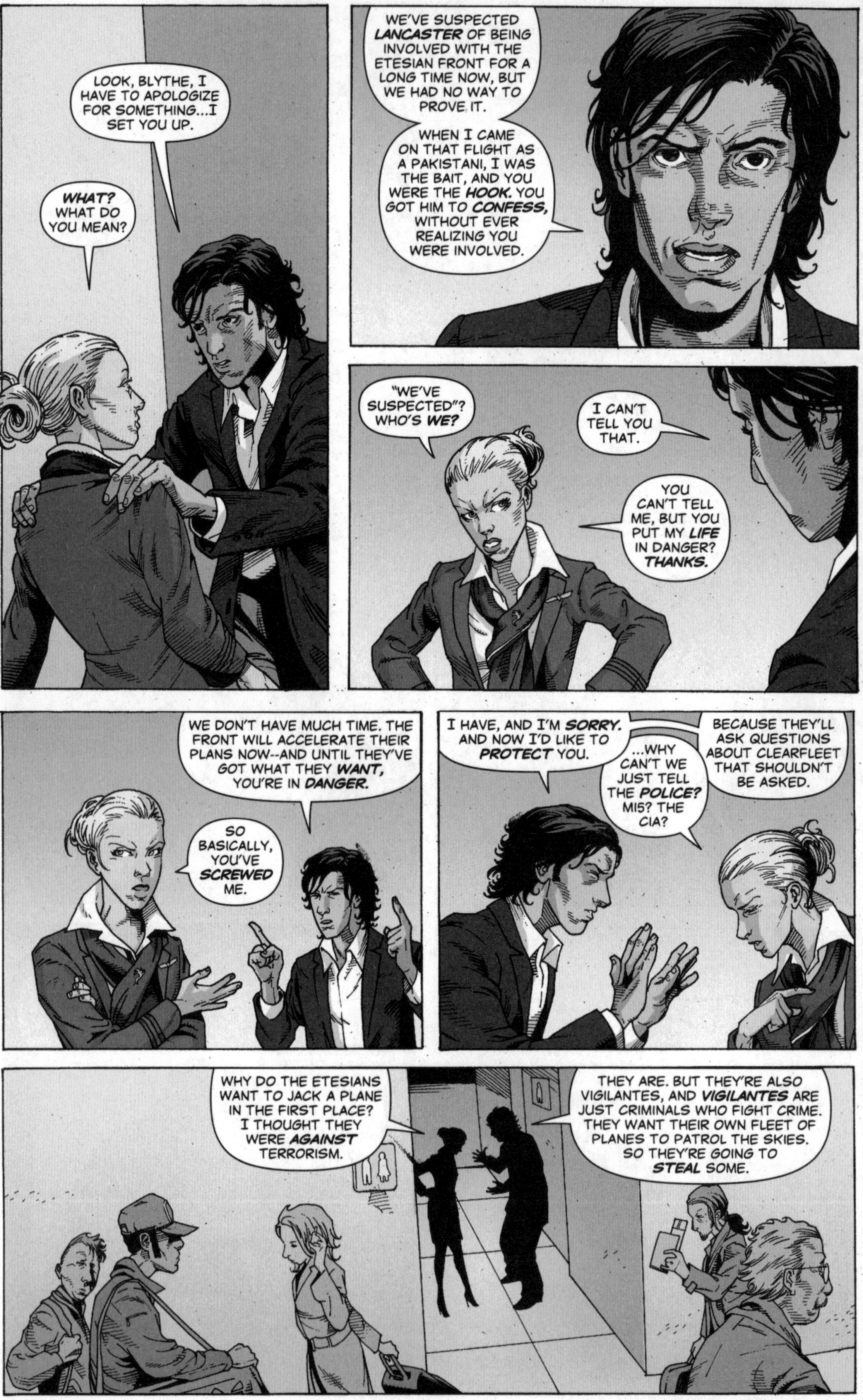
LOOK, BLYTHE, I HAVE TO APOLOGIZE FOR SOMETHING...I SET YOU UP.
WHAT? WHAT DO YOU MEAN?
WE'VE SUSPECTED LANCASTER OF BEING INVOLVED WITH THE ETESIAN FRONT FOR A LONG TIME NOW, BUT WE HAD NO WAY TO PROVE IT.
WHEN I CAME ON THAT FLIGHT AS A PAKISTANI, I WAS THE BAIT, AND YOU WERE THE HOOK. YOU GOT HIM TO CONFESS, WITHOUT EVER REALIZING YOU WERE INVOLVED.
"WE'VE SUSPECTED"? WHO'S WE?
I CAN'T TELL YOU THAT.
YOU CAN'T TELL ME, BUT YOU PUT MY LIFE IN DANGER? THANKS.
WE DON'T HAVE MUCH TIME. THE FRONT WILL ACCELERATE THEIR PLANS NOW--AND UNTIL THEY'VE GOT WHAT THEY WANT, YOU'RE IN DANGER.
SO BASICALLY, YOU'VE SCREWED ME.
I HAVE, AND I'M SORRY. AND NOW I'D LIKE TO PROTECT YOU.
...WHY CAN'T WE JUST TELL THE POLICE? MI5? THE CIA?
BECAUSE THEY'LL ASK QUESTIONS ABOUT CLEARFLEET THAT SHOULDN'T BE ASKED.
WHY DO THE ETESIANS WANT TO JACK A PLANE IN THE FIRST PLACE? I THOUGHT THEY WERE AGAINST TERRORISM.
THEY ARE. BUT THEY'RE ALSO VIGILANTES, AND VIGILANTES ARE JUST CRIMINALS WHO FIGHT CRIME. THEY WANT THEIR OWN FLEET OF PLANES TO PATROL THE SKIES. SO THEY'RE GOING TO STEAL SOME.

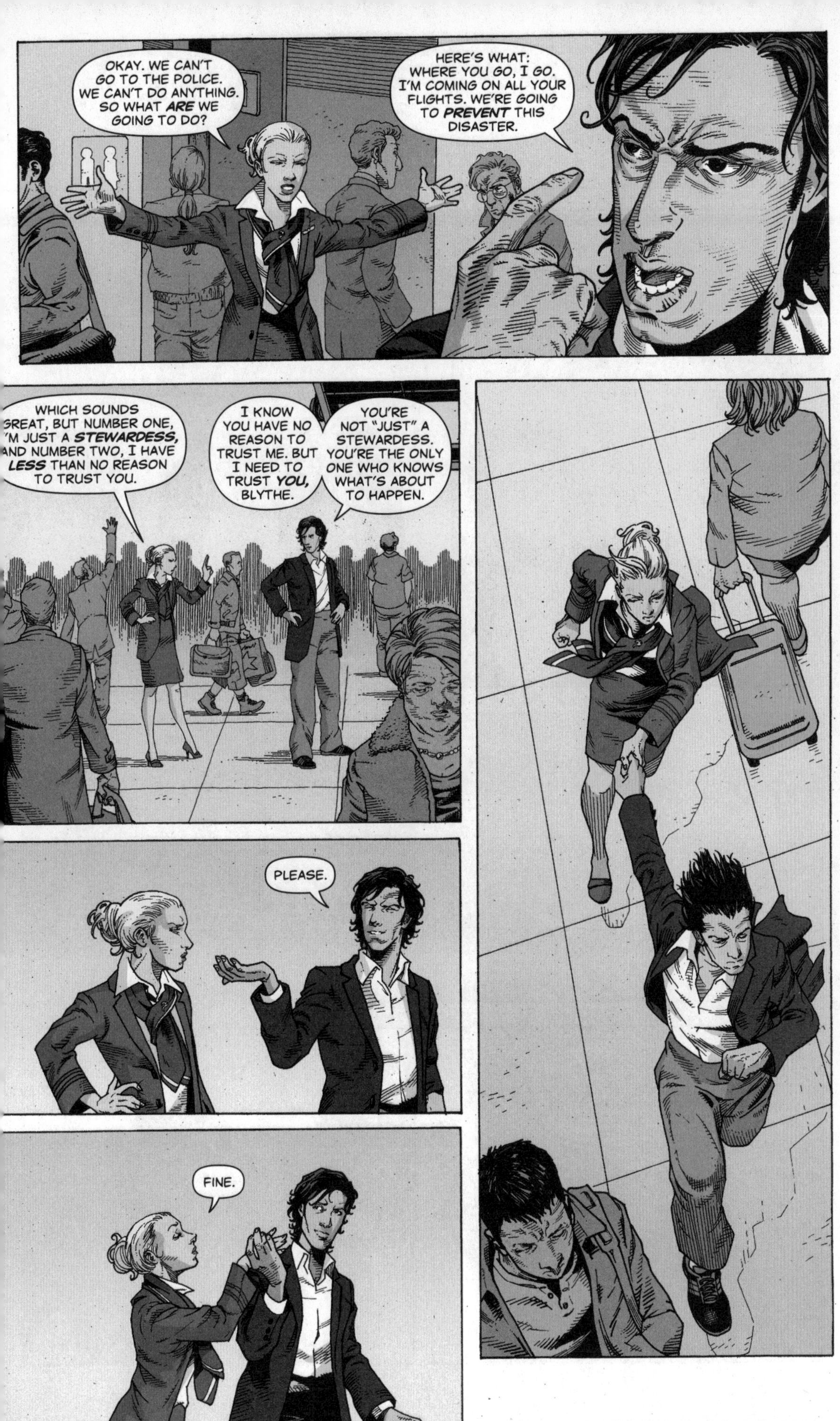
OKAY. WE CAN'T GO TO THE POLICE. WE CAN'T DO ANYTHING. SO WHAT ARE WE GOING TO DO?
HERE'S WHAT: WHERE YOU GO, I GO. I'M COMING ON ALL YOUR FLIGHTS. WE'RE GOING TO PREVENT THIS DISASTER.
WHICH SOUNDS GREAT, BUT NUMBER ONE, I'M JUST A STEWARDESS, AND NUMBER TWO, I HAVE LESS THAN NO REASON TO TRUST YOU.
I KNOW YOU HAVE NO REASON TO TRUST ME. BUT I NEED TO TRUST YOU, BLYTHE.
YOU'RE NOT "JUST" A STEWARDESS. YOU'RE THE ONLY ONE WHO KNOWS WHAT'S ABOUT TO HAPPEN.
PLEASE.
FINE.

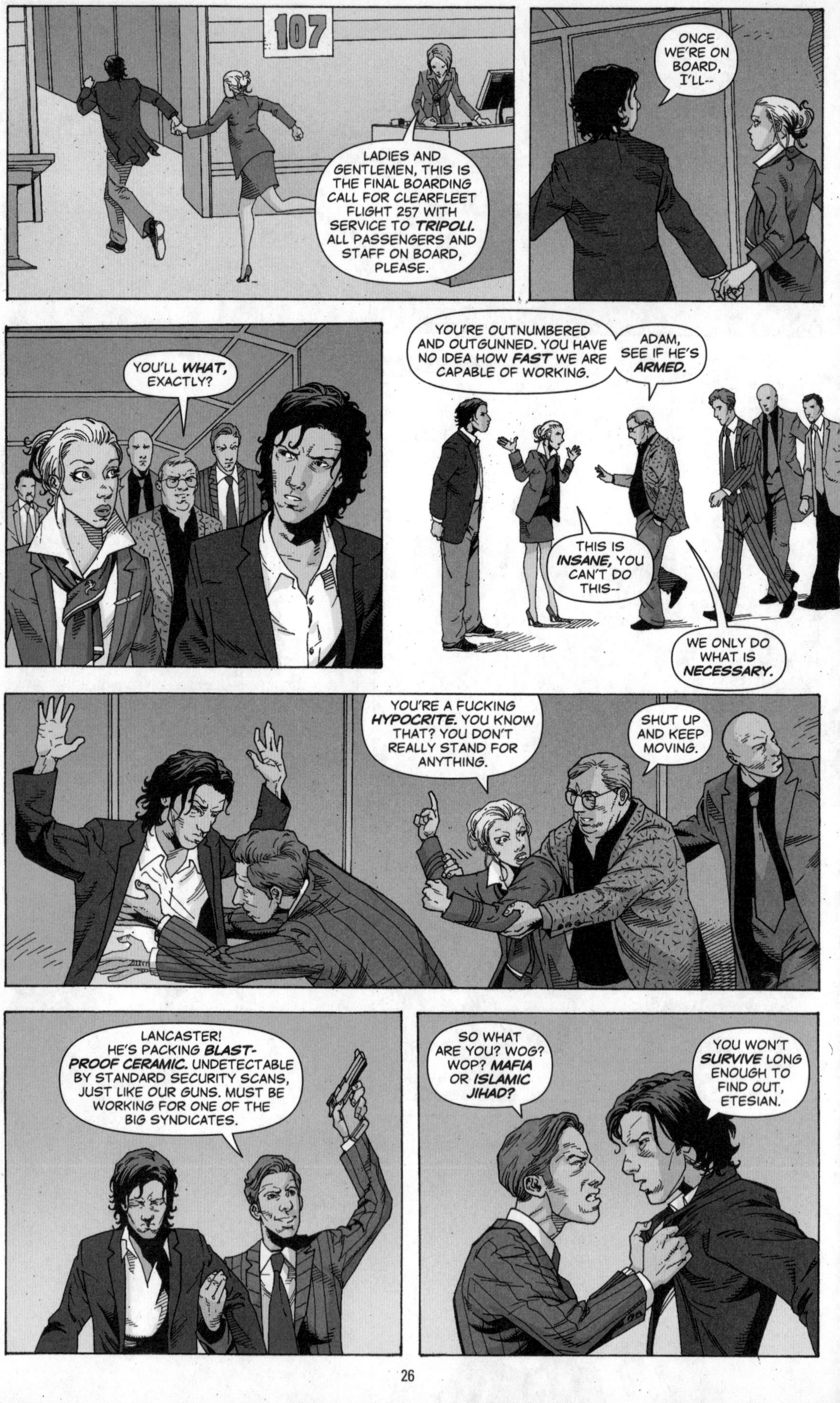

107
LADIES AND GENTLEMEN, THIS IS THE FINAL BOARDING CALL FOR CLEARFLEET FLIGHT 257 WITH SERVICE TO TRIPOLI. ALL PASSENGERS AND STAFF ON BOARD, PLEASE.
ONCE WE'RE ON BOARD, I'LL--
YOU'LL WHAT, EXACTLY?
YOU'RE OUTNUMBERED AND OUTGUNNED. YOU HAVE NO IDEA HOW FAST WE ARE CAPABLE OF WORKING.
ADAM, SEE IF HE'S ARMED.
THIS IS INSANE, YOU CAN'T DO THIS--
WE ONLY DO WHAT IS NECESSARY.
YOU'RE A FUCKING HYPOCRITE. YOU KNOW THAT? YOU DON'T REALLY STAND FOR ANYTHING.
SHUT UP AND KEEP MOVING.
LANCASTER! HE'S PACKING BLAST-PROOF CERAMIC. UNDETECTABLE BY STANDARD SECURITY SCANS, JUST LIKE OUR GUNS. MUST BE WORKING FOR ONE OF THE BIG SYNDICATES.
SO WHAT ARE YOU? WOG? WOP? MAFIA OR ISLAMIC JIHAD?
YOU WON'T SURVIVE LONG ENOUGH TO FIND OUT, ETESIAN.

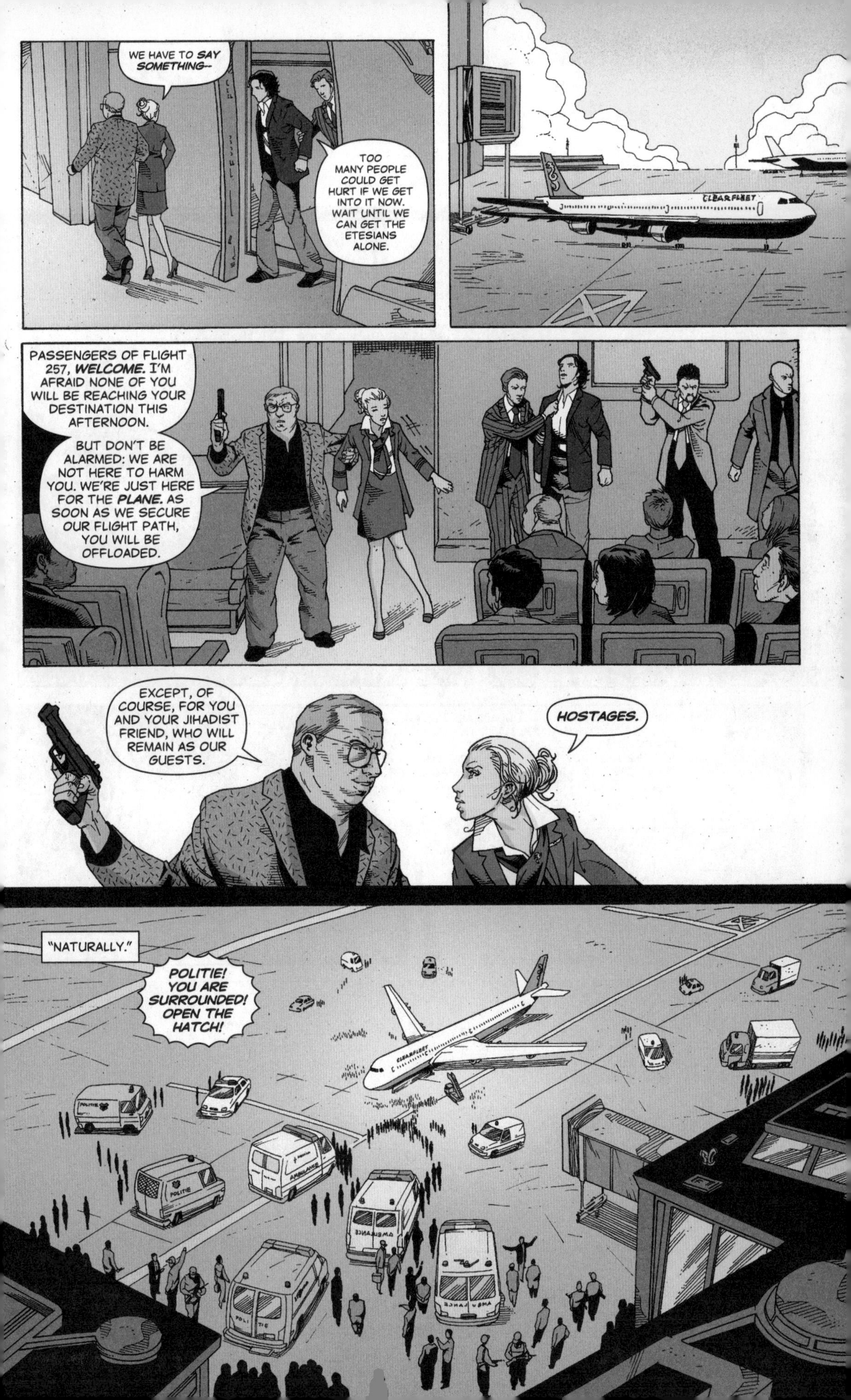
WE HAVE TO SAY SOMETHING--
TOO MANY PEOPLE COULD GET HURT IF WE GET INTO IT NOW. WAIT UNTIL WE CAN GET THE ETESIANS ALONE.
CLEARFLEET
PASSENGERS OF FLIGHT 257, WELCOME. I'M AFRAID NONE OF YOU WILL BE REACHING YOUR DESTINATION THIS AFTERNOON.
BUT DON'T BE ALARMED: WE ARE NOT HERE TO HARM YOU. WE'RE JUST HERE FOR THE PLANE. AS SOON AS WE SECURE OUR FLIGHT PATH, YOU WILL BE OFFLOADED.
EXCEPT, OF COURSE, FOR YOU AND YOUR JIHADIST FRIEND, WHO WILL REMAIN AS OUR GUESTS.
HOSTAGES.
"NATURALLY."
POLITIE! YOU ARE SURROUNDED! OPEN THE HATCH!
POLITIE
AMBULANCE

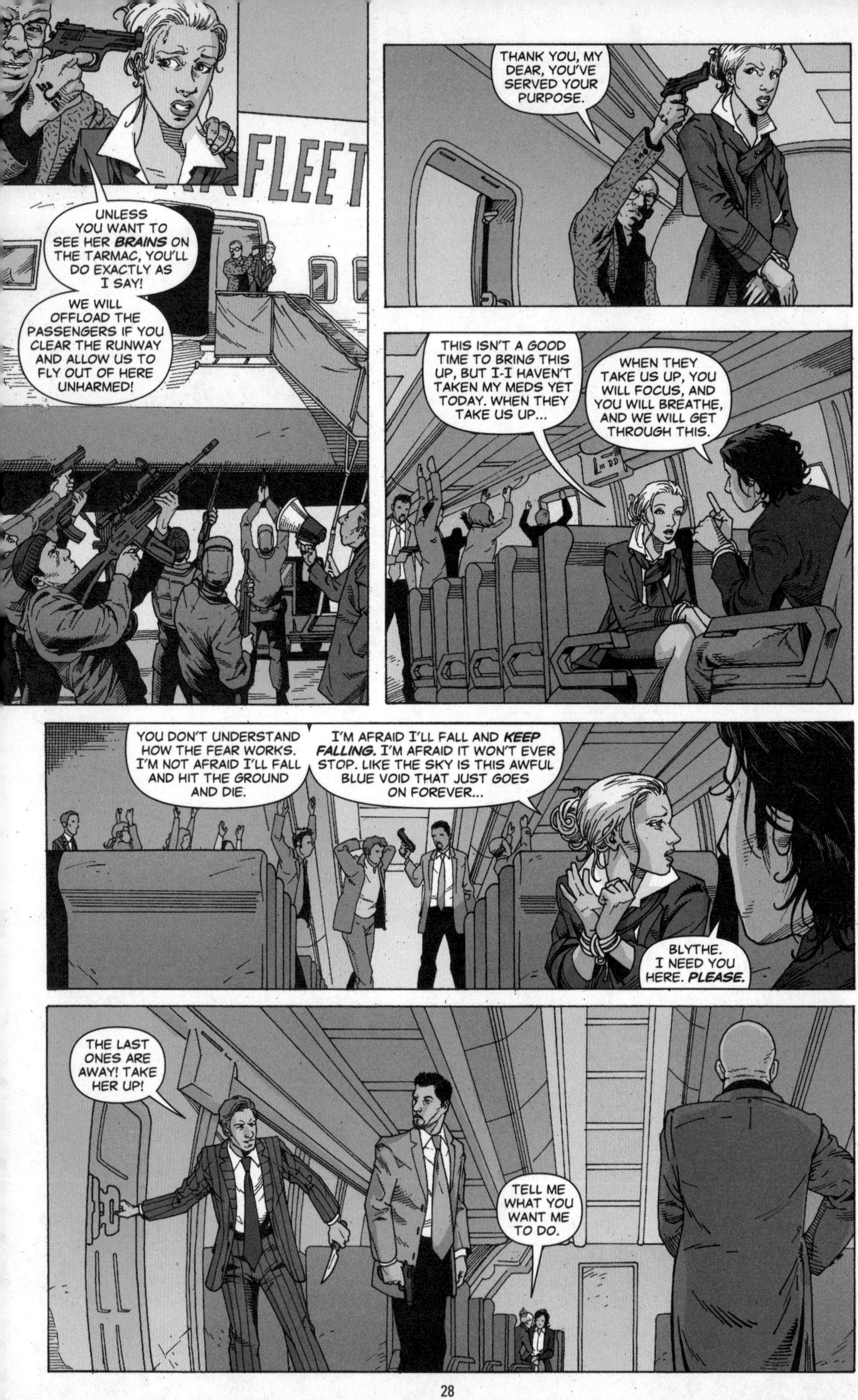
UNLESS YOU WANT TO SEE HER BRAINS ON THE TARMAC, YOU'LL DO EXACTLY AS I SAY!
WE WILL OFFLOAD THE PASSENGERS IF YOU CLEAR THE RUNWAY AND ALLOW US TO FLY OUT OF HERE UNHARMED!
FLEET
THANK YOU, MY DEAR, YOU'VE SERVED YOUR PURPOSE.
THIS ISN'T A GOOD TIME TO BRING THIS UP, BUT I-I HAVEN'T TAKEN MY MEDS YET TODAY. WHEN THEY TAKE US UP...
WHEN THEY TAKE US UP, YOU WILL FOCUS, AND YOU WILL BREATHE, AND WE WILL GET THROUGH THIS.
YOU DON'T UNDERSTAND HOW THE FEAR WORKS. I'M NOT AFRAID I'LL FALL AND HIT THE GROUND AND DIE.
I'M AFRAID I'LL FALL AND KEEP FALLING. I'M AFRAID IT WON'T EVER STOP. LIKE THE SKY IS THIS AWFUL BLUE VOID THAT JUST GOES ON FOREVER...
BLYTHE. I NEED YOU HERE. PLEASE.
THE LAST ONES ARE AWAY! TAKE HER UP!
TELL ME WHAT YOU WANT ME TO DO.

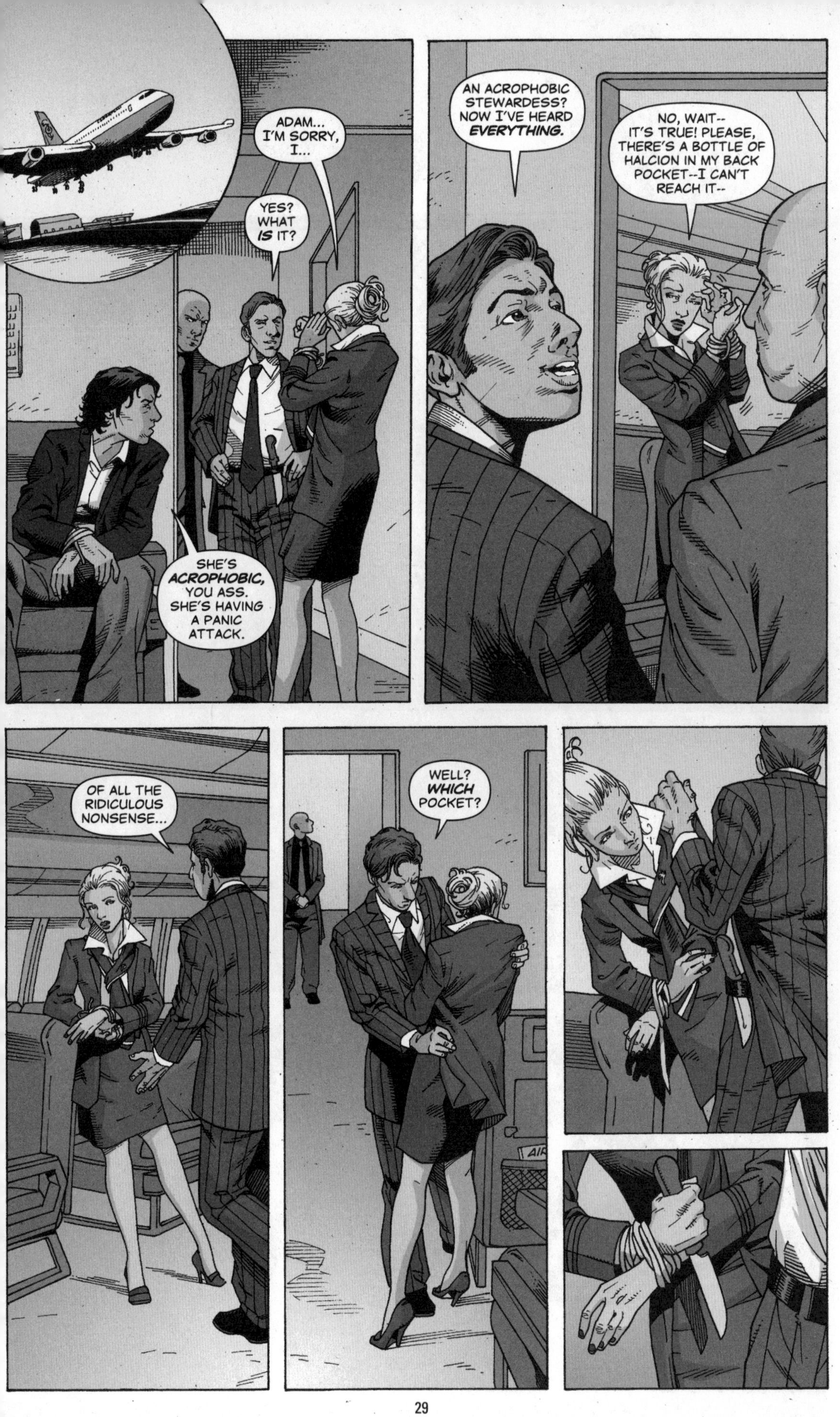
ADAM... I'M SORRY, I...
YES? WHAT *IS* IT?
SHE'S *ACROPHOBIC,* YOU ASS. SHE'S HAVING A PANIC ATTACK.
AN ACROPHOBIC STEWARDESS? NOW I'VE HEARD *EVERYTHING.*
NO, WAIT-- IT'S TRUE! PLEASE, THERE'S A BOTTLE OF HALCION IN MY BACK POCKET--I CAN'T REACH IT--
OF ALL THE RIDICULOUS NONSENSE...
WELL? *WHICH* POCKET?

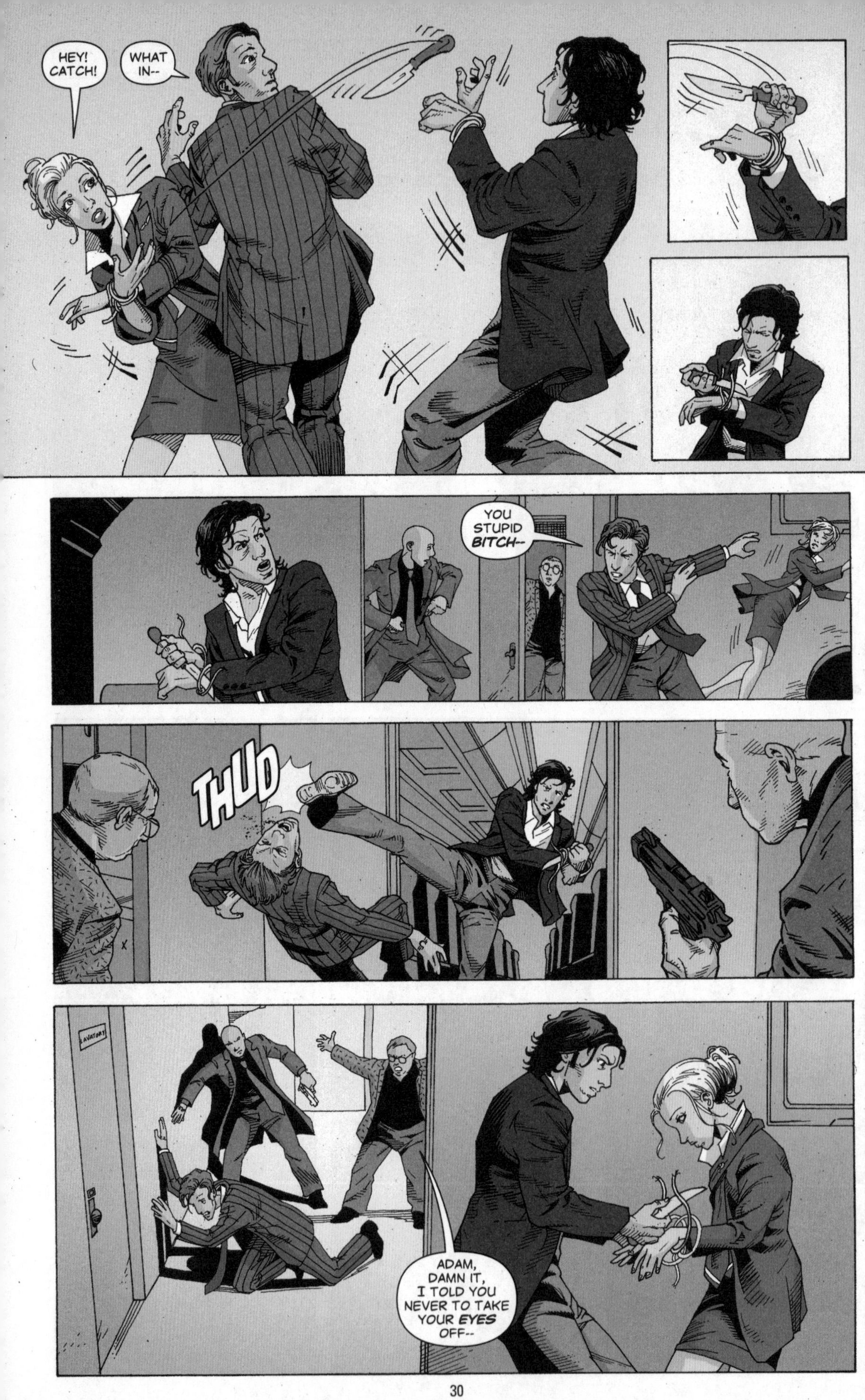
HEY! CATCH!
WHAT IN--
YOU STUPID BITCH--
THUD
LAVATORY
ADAM, DAMN IT, I TOLD YOU NEVER TO TAKE YOUR EYES OFF--

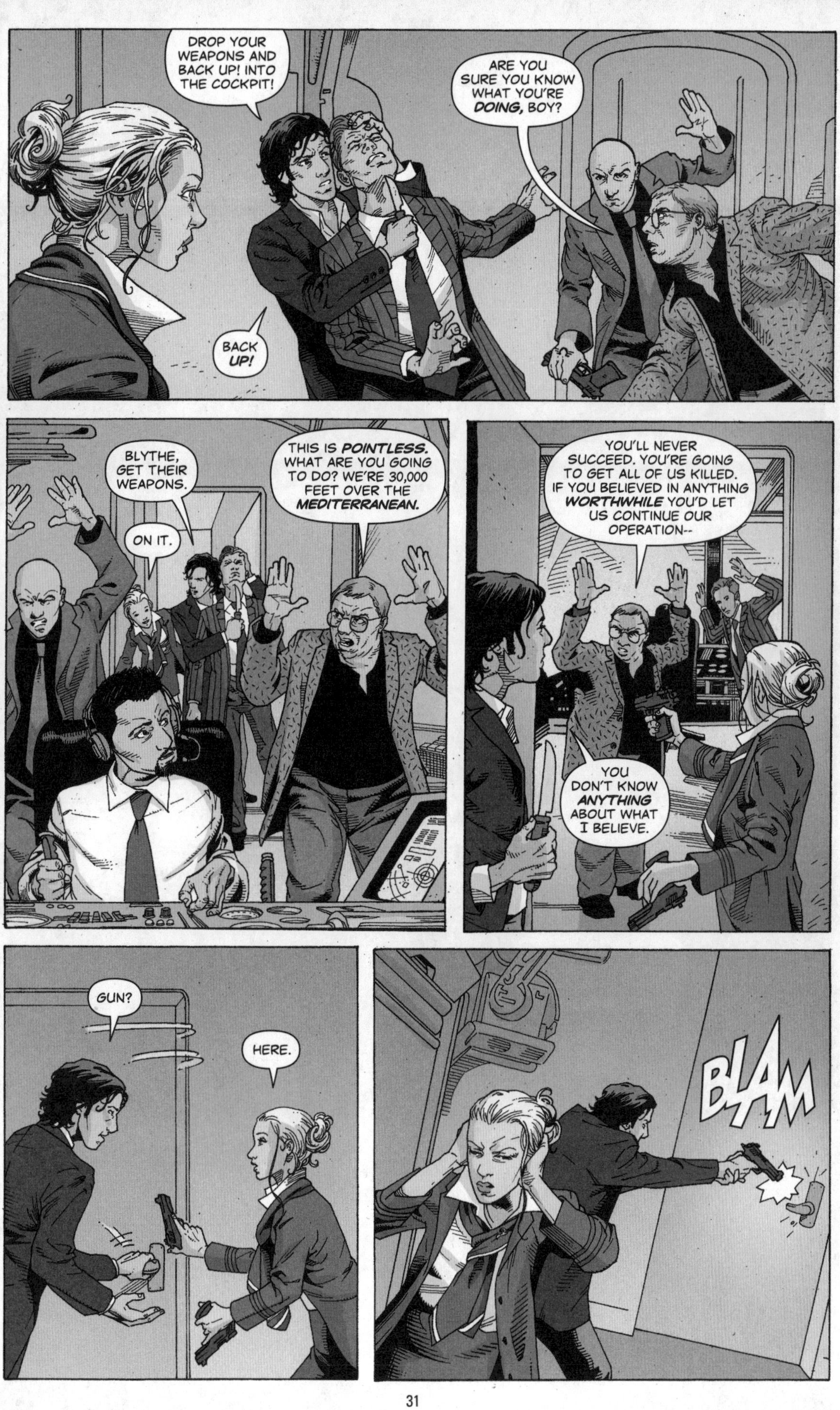

DROP YOUR WEAPONS AND BACK UP! INTO THE COCKPIT!
ARE YOU SURE YOU KNOW WHAT YOU'RE DOING, BOY?
BACK UP!
BLYTHE, GET THEIR WEAPONS.
ON IT.
THIS IS POINTLESS. WHAT ARE YOU GOING TO DO? WE'RE 30,000 FEET OVER THE MEDITERRANEAN.
YOU'LL NEVER SUCCEED. YOU'RE GOING TO GET ALL OF US KILLED. IF YOU BELIEVED IN ANYTHING WORTHWHILE YOU'D LET US CONTINUE OUR OPERATION--
YOU DON'T KNOW ANYTHING ABOUT WHAT I BELIEVE.
GUN?
HERE.
BLAM

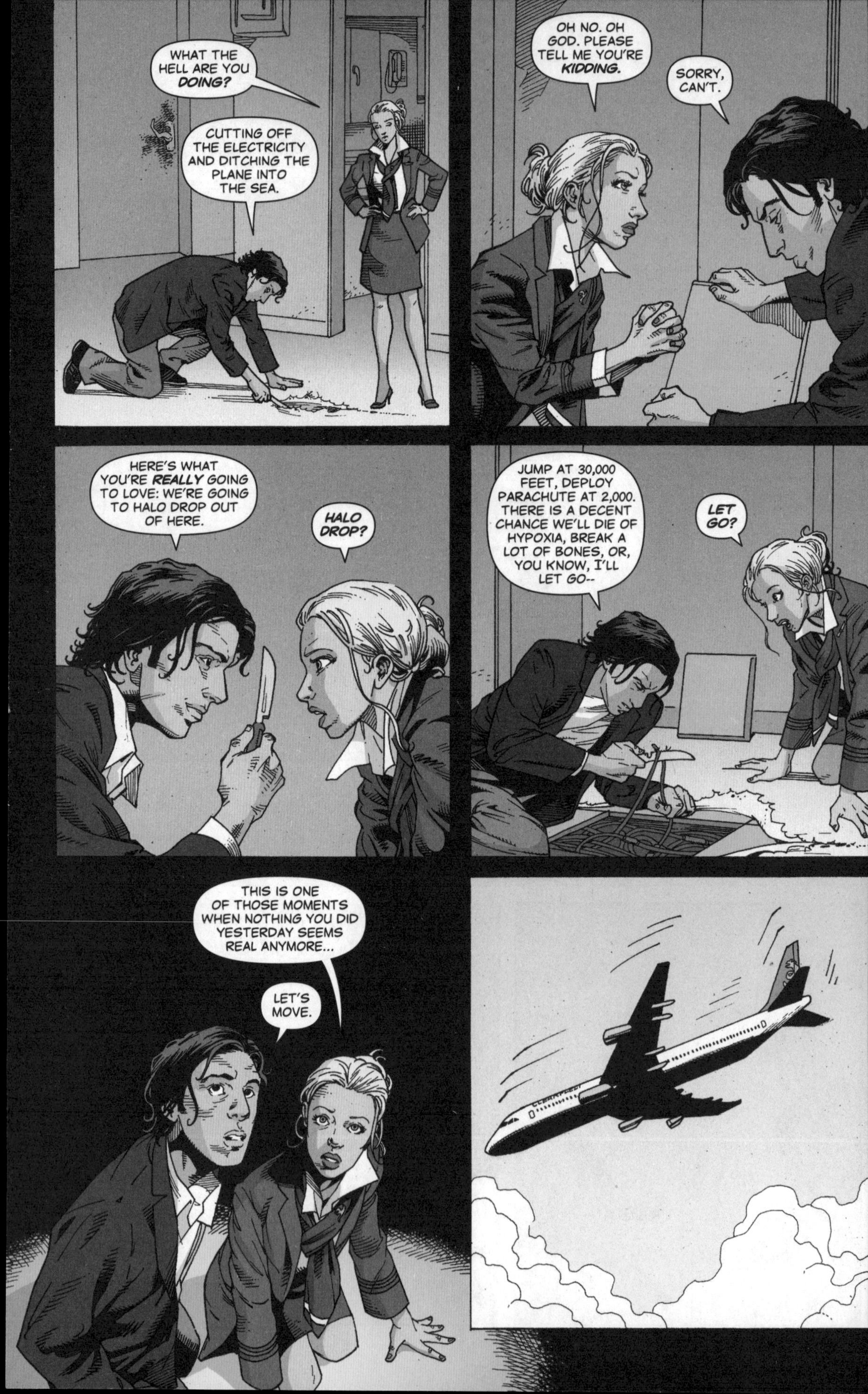
WHAT THE HELL ARE YOU DOING?
CUTTING OFF THE ELECTRICITY AND DITCHING THE PLANE INTO THE SEA.
OH NO. OH GOD. PLEASE TELL ME YOU'RE KIDDING.
SORRY, CAN'T.
HERE'S WHAT YOU'RE REALLY GOING TO LOVE: WE'RE GOING TO HALO DROP OUT OF HERE.
HALO DROP?
JUMP AT 30,000 FEET, DEPLOY PARACHUTE AT 2,000. THERE IS A DECENT CHANCE WE'LL DIE OF HYPOXIA, BREAK A LOT OF BONES, OR, YOU KNOW, I'LL LET GO--
LET GO?
THIS IS ONE OF THOSE MOMENTS WHEN NOTHING YOU DID YESTERDAY SEEMS REAL ANYMORE...
LET'S MOVE.

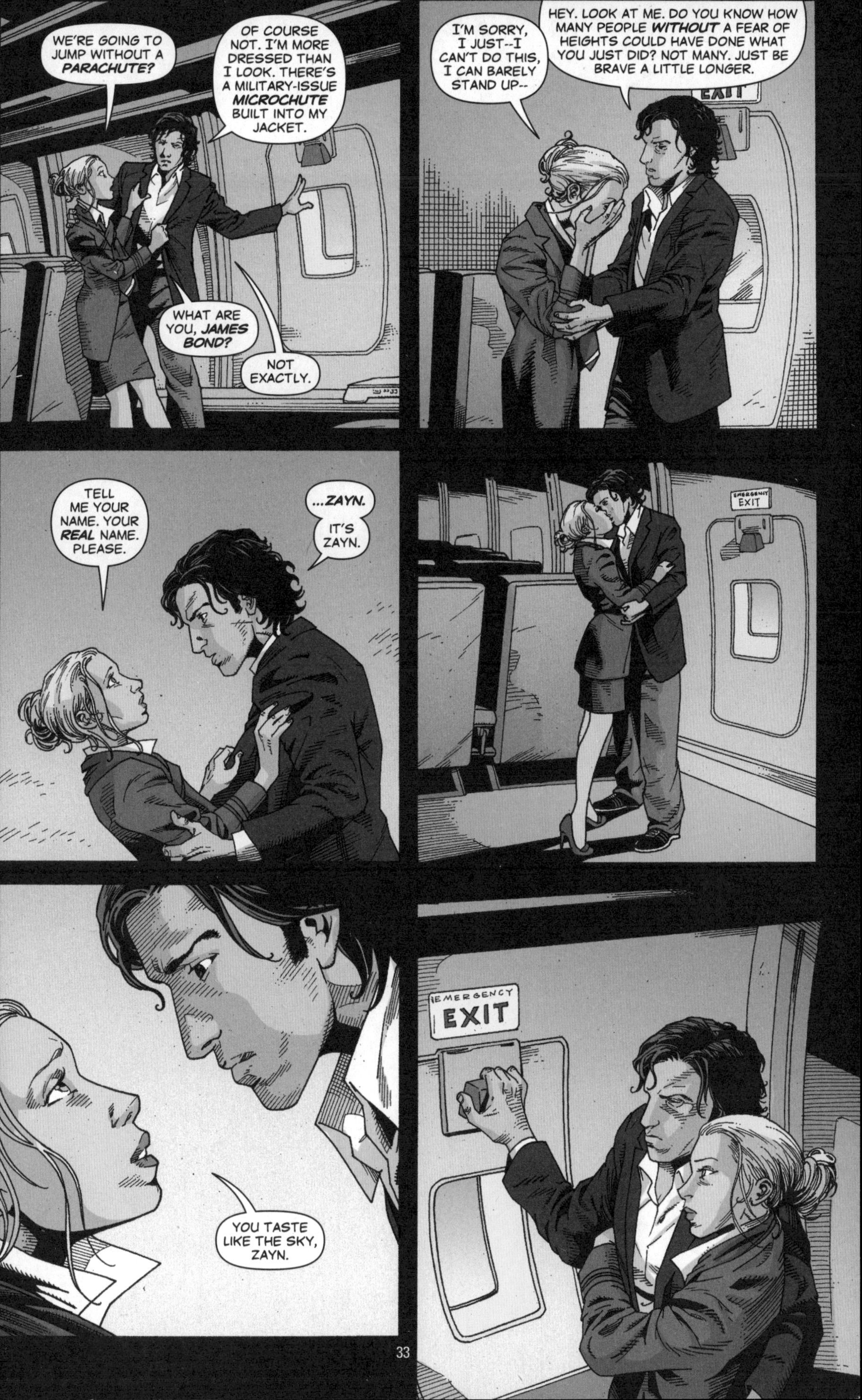
WE'RE GOING TO JUMP WITHOUT A *PARACHUTE?*
OF COURSE NOT. I'M MORE DRESSED THAN I LOOK. THERE'S A MILITARY-ISSUE *MICROCHUTE* BUILT INTO MY JACKET.
WHAT ARE YOU, *JAMES BOND?*
NOT EXACTLY.
I'M SORRY, I JUST--I CAN'T DO THIS, I CAN BARELY STAND UP--
HEY. LOOK AT ME. DO YOU KNOW HOW MANY PEOPLE *WITHOUT* A FEAR OF HEIGHTS COULD HAVE DONE WHAT YOU JUST DID? NOT MANY. JUST BE BRAVE A LITTLE LONGER.
EXIT
TELL ME YOUR NAME. YOUR *REAL* NAME. PLEASE.
...ZAYN.
IT'S ZAYN.
EMERGENCY
EXIT
YOU TASTE LIKE THE SKY, ZAYN.
EMERGENCY
EXIT

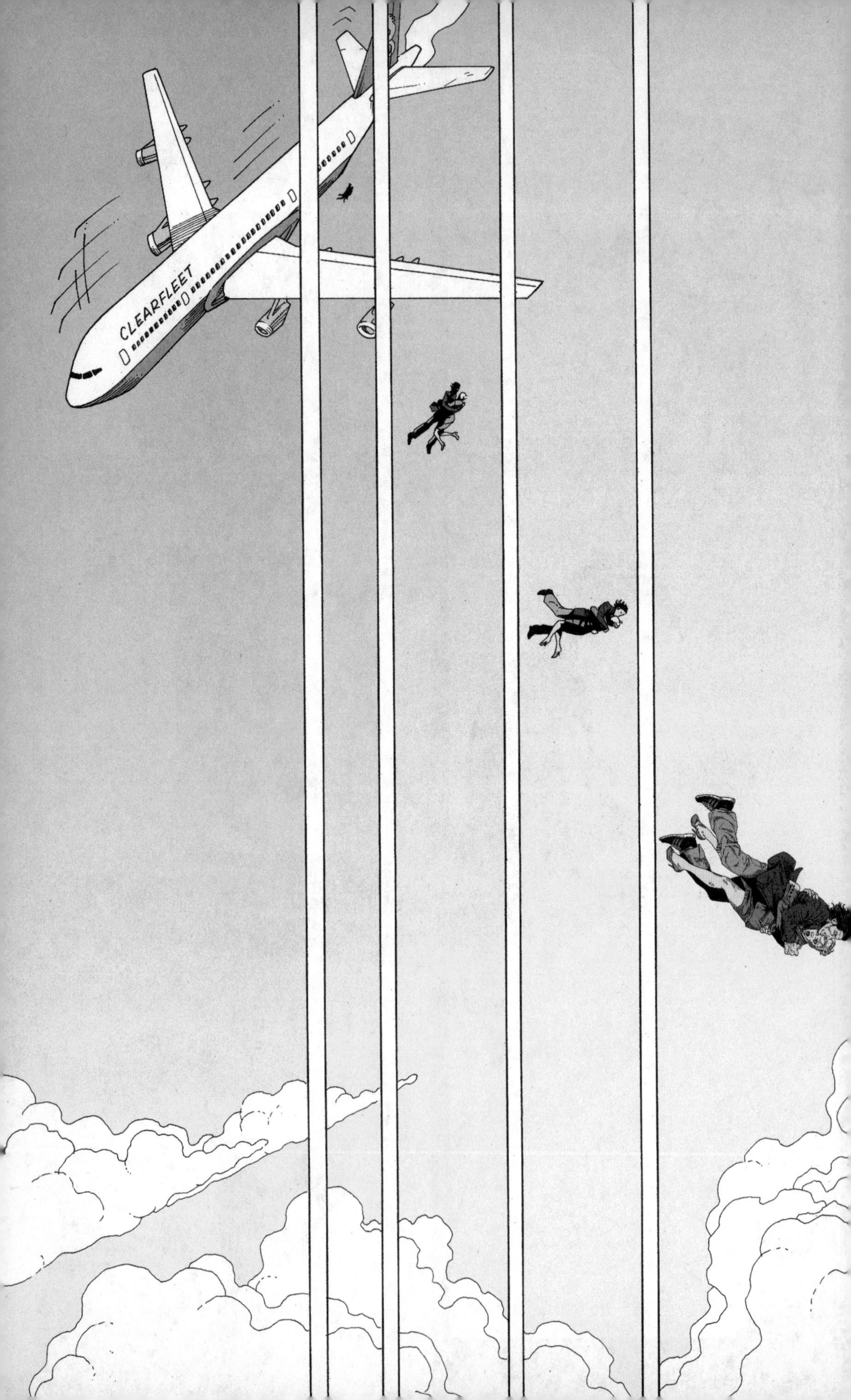
CLEARFLEET

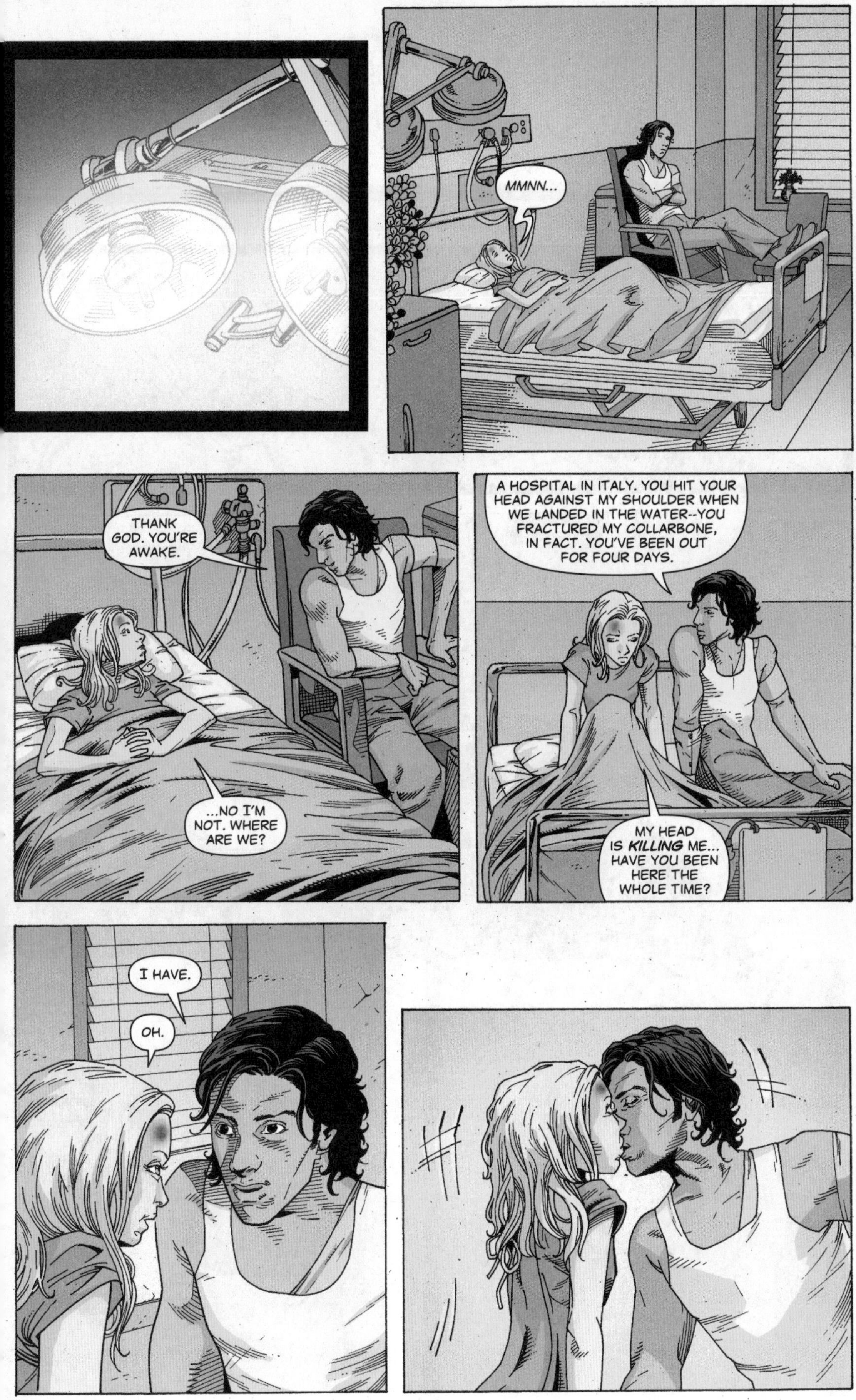

MMNN...
THANK GOD. YOU'RE AWAKE.
...NO I'M NOT. WHERE ARE WE?
A HOSPITAL IN ITALY. YOU HIT YOUR HEAD AGAINST MY SHOULDER WHEN WE LANDED IN THE WATER--YOU FRACTURED MY COLLARBONE, IN FACT. YOU'VE BEEN OUT FOR FOUR DAYS.
MY HEAD IS KILLING ME... HAVE YOU BEEN HERE THE WHOLE TIME?
I HAVE.
OH.

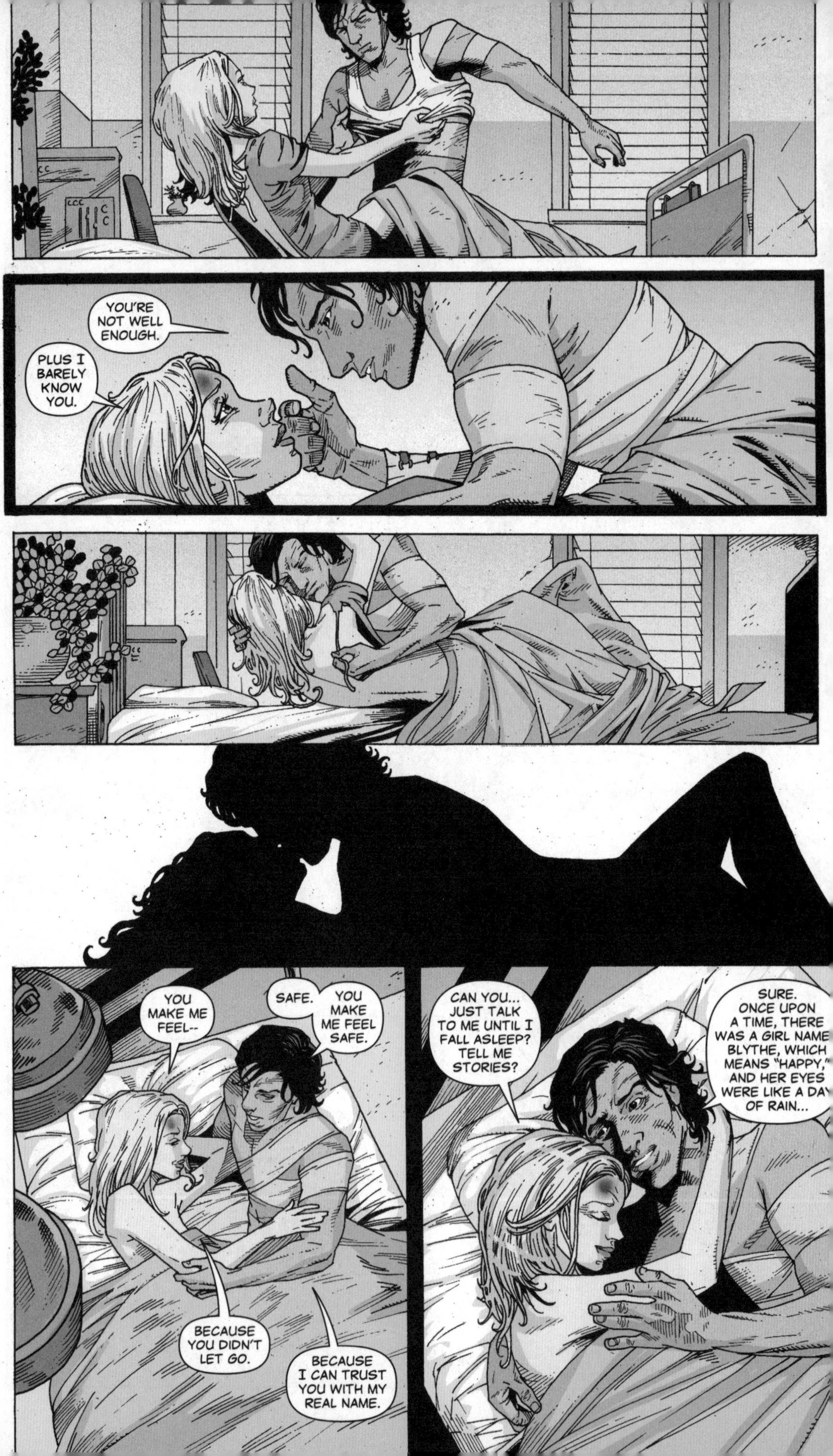
YOU'RE NOT WELL ENOUGH.
PLUS I BARELY KNOW YOU.
YOU MAKE ME FEEL--
SAFE.
YOU MAKE ME FEEL SAFE.
BECAUSE YOU DIDN'T LET GO.
BECAUSE I CAN TRUST YOU WITH MY REAL NAME.
CAN YOU... JUST TALK TO ME UNTIL I FALL ASLEEP? TELL ME STORIES?
SURE. ONCE UPON A TIME, THERE WAS A GIRL NAME BLYTHE, WHICH MEANS "HAPPY," AND HER EYES WERE LIKE A DA OF RAIN...

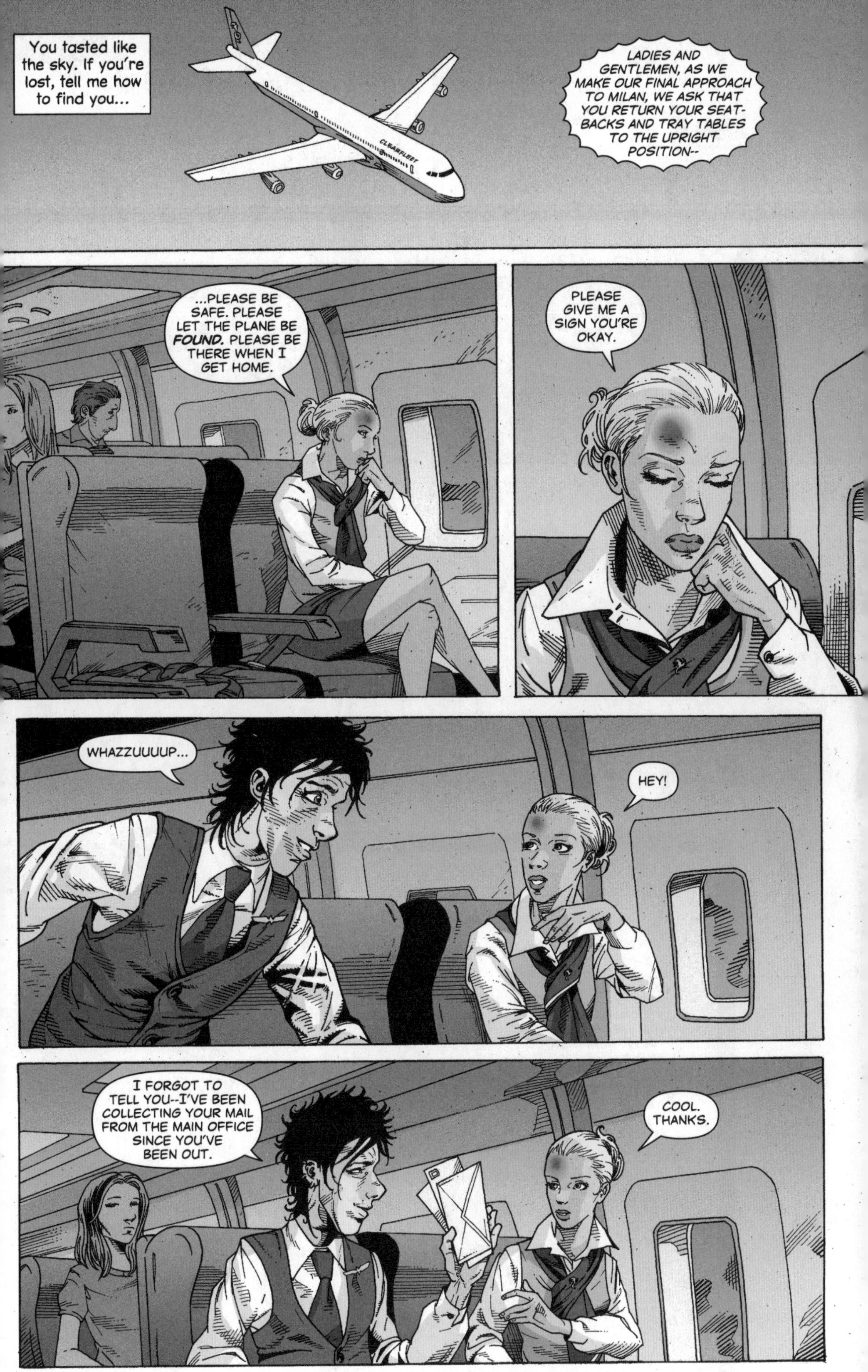
You tasted like the sky. If you're lost, tell me how to find you...
CLEARFLEET
LADIES AND GENTLEMEN, AS WE MAKE OUR FINAL APPROACH TO MILAN, WE ASK THAT YOU RETURN YOUR SEAT-BACKS AND TRAY TABLES TO THE UPRIGHT POSITION--
...PLEASE BE SAFE. PLEASE LET THE PLANE BE FOUND. PLEASE BE THERE WHEN I GET HOME.
PLEASE GIVE ME A SIGN YOU'RE OKAY.
WHAZZUUUUP...
HEY!
I FORGOT TO TELL YOU--I'VE BEEN COLLECTING YOUR MAIL FROM THE MAIN OFFICE SINCE YOU'VE BEEN OUT.
COOL. THANKS.

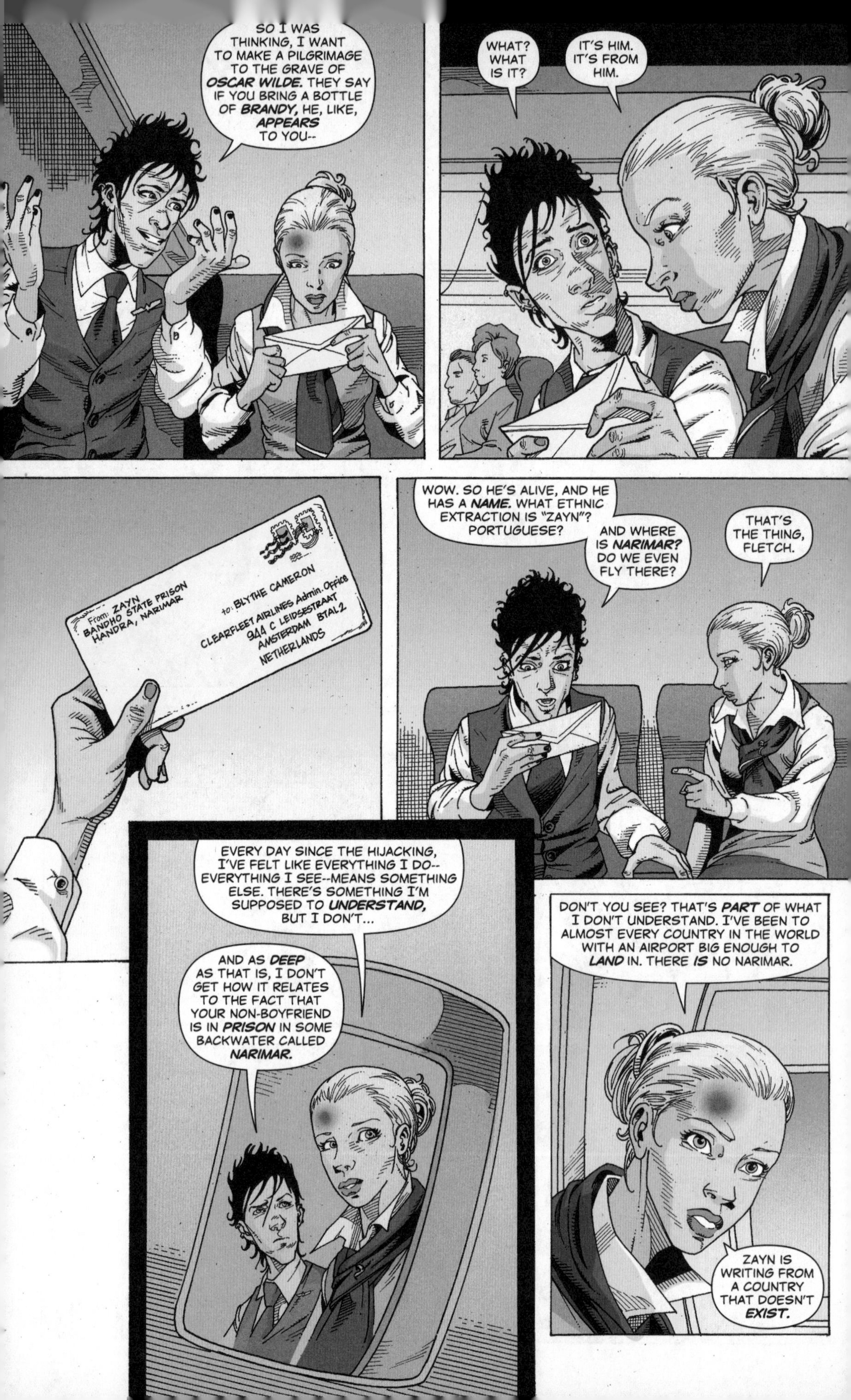
SO I WAS THINKING, I WANT TO MAKE A PILGRIMAGE TO THE GRAVE OF OSCAR WILDE. THEY SAY IF YOU BRING A BOTTLE OF BRANDY, HE, LIKE, APPEARS TO YOU--
WHAT? WHAT IS IT?
IT'S HIM. IT'S FROM HIM.
From: ZAYN
BANDHO STATE PRISON
HANDRA, NARIMAR
to: BLYTHE CAMERON
CLEARFLEET AIRLINES Admin. Office
944 C LEIDSESTRAAT
AMSTERDAM BTAL2
NETHERLANDS
WOW. SO HE'S ALIVE, AND HE HAS A NAME. WHAT ETHNIC EXTRACTION IS "ZAYN"? PORTUGUESE?
AND WHERE IS NARIMAR? DO WE EVEN FLY THERE?
THAT'S THE THING, FLETCH.
EVERY DAY SINCE THE HIJACKING, I'VE FELT LIKE EVERYTHING I DO--EVERYTHING I SEE--MEANS SOMETHING ELSE. THERE'S SOMETHING I'M SUPPOSED TO UNDERSTAND, BUT I DON'T...
AND AS DEEP AS THAT IS, I DON'T GET HOW IT RELATES TO THE FACT THAT YOUR NON-BOYFRIEND IS IN PRISON IN SOME BACKWATER CALLED NARIMAR.
DON'T YOU SEE? THAT'S PART OF WHAT I DON'T UNDERSTAND. I'VE BEEN TO ALMOST EVERY COUNTRY IN THE WORLD WITH AN AIRPORT BIG ENOUGH TO LAND IN. THERE IS NO NARIMAR.
ZAYN IS WRITING FROM A COUNTRY THAT DOESN'T EXIST.

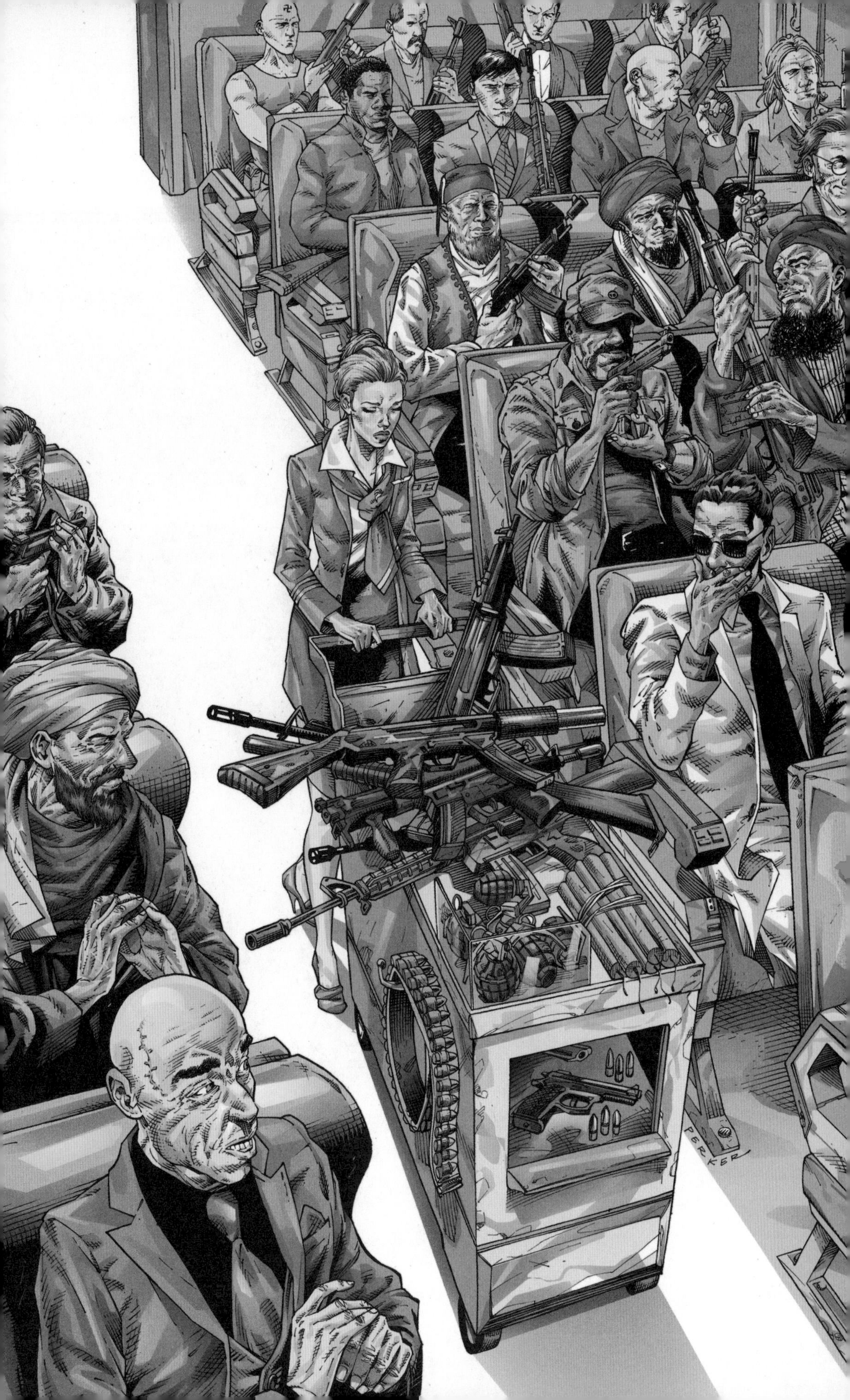
PERKER

CHAPTER 2

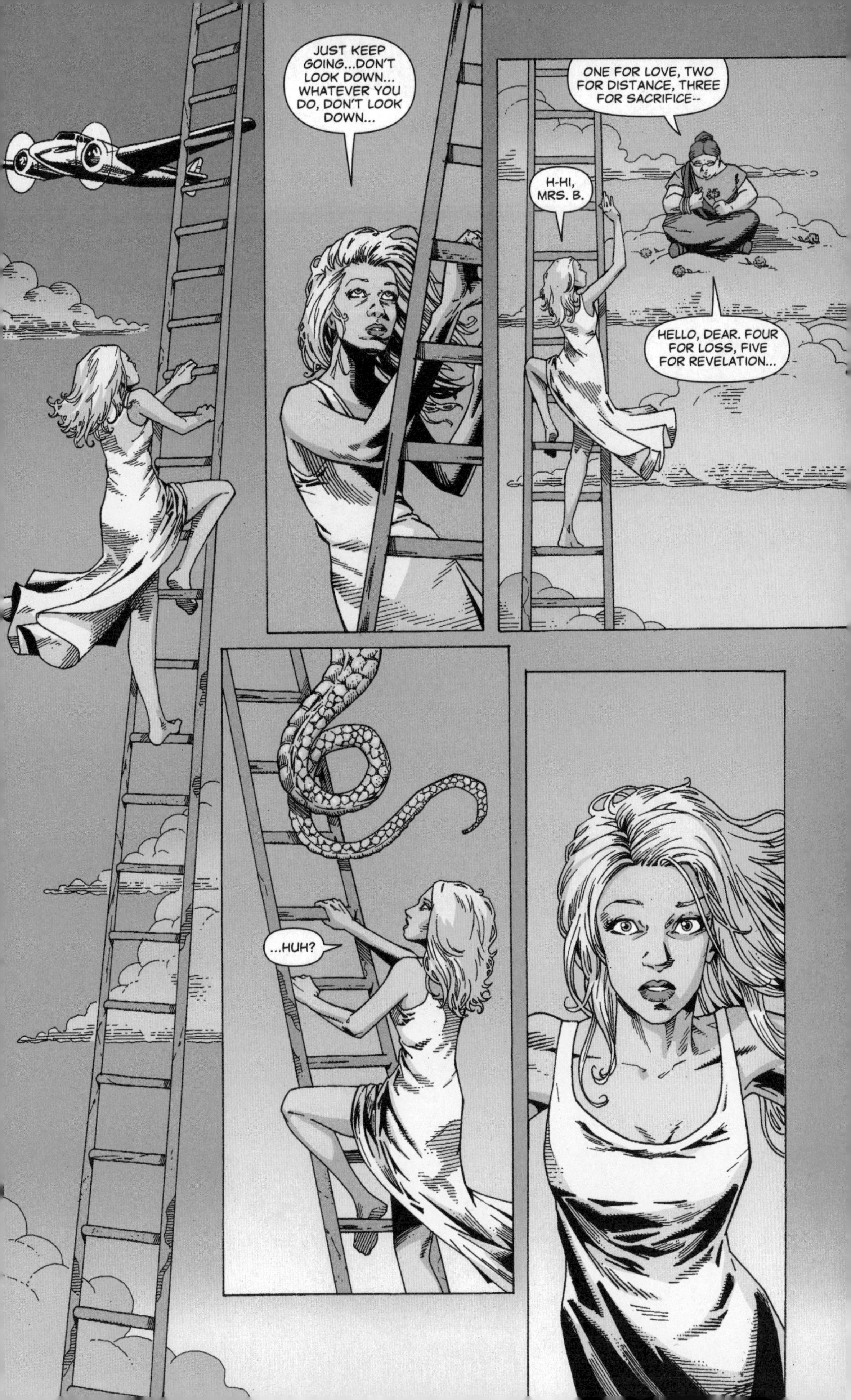
JUST KEEP GOING...DON'T LOOK DOWN... WHATEVER YOU DO, DON'T LOOK DOWN...
ONE FOR LOVE, TWO FOR DISTANCE, THREE FOR SACRIFICE--
H-HI, MRS. B.
HELLO, DEAR. FOUR FOR LOSS, FIVE FOR REVELATION...
...HUH?

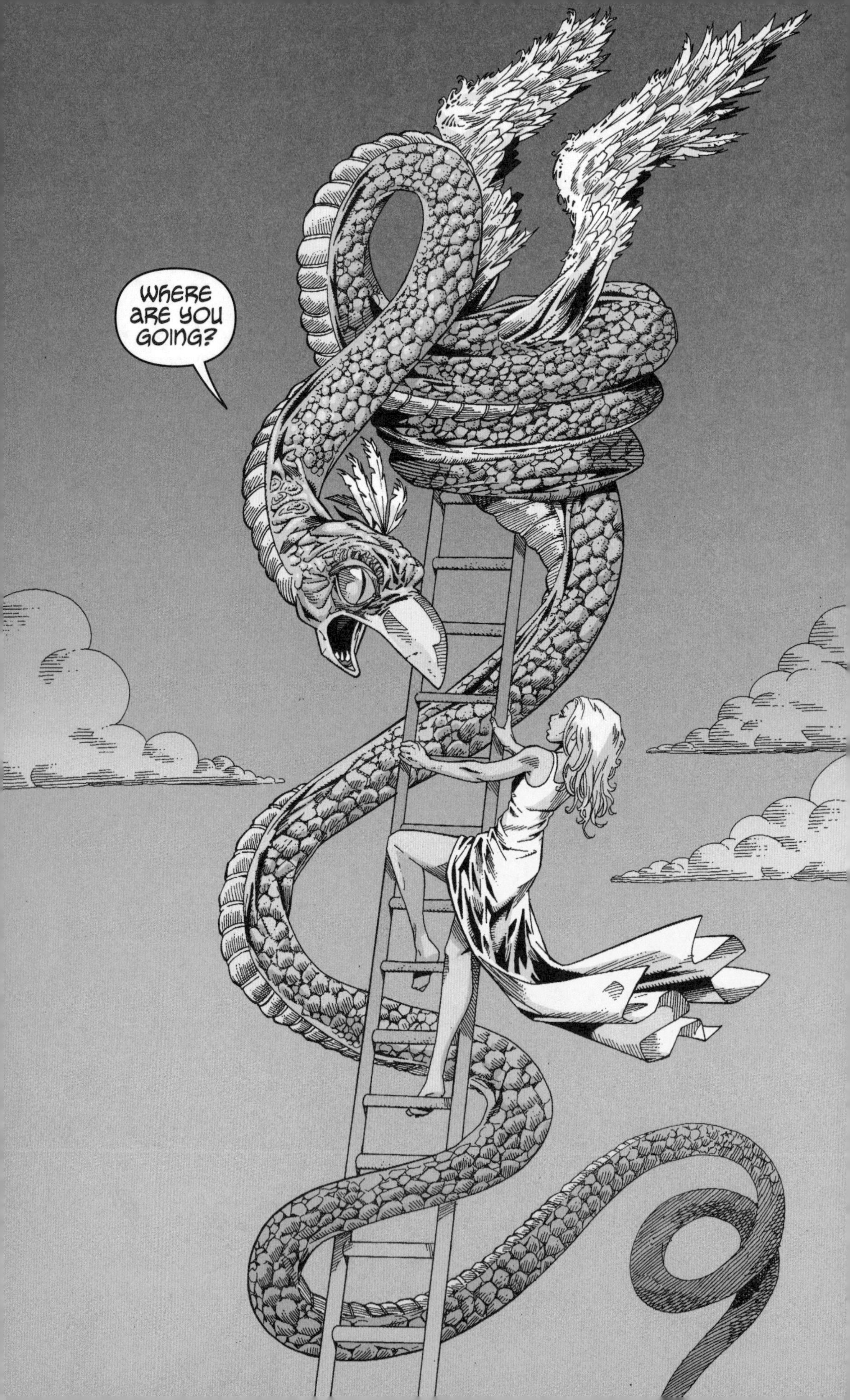
WHERE ARE YOU GOING?

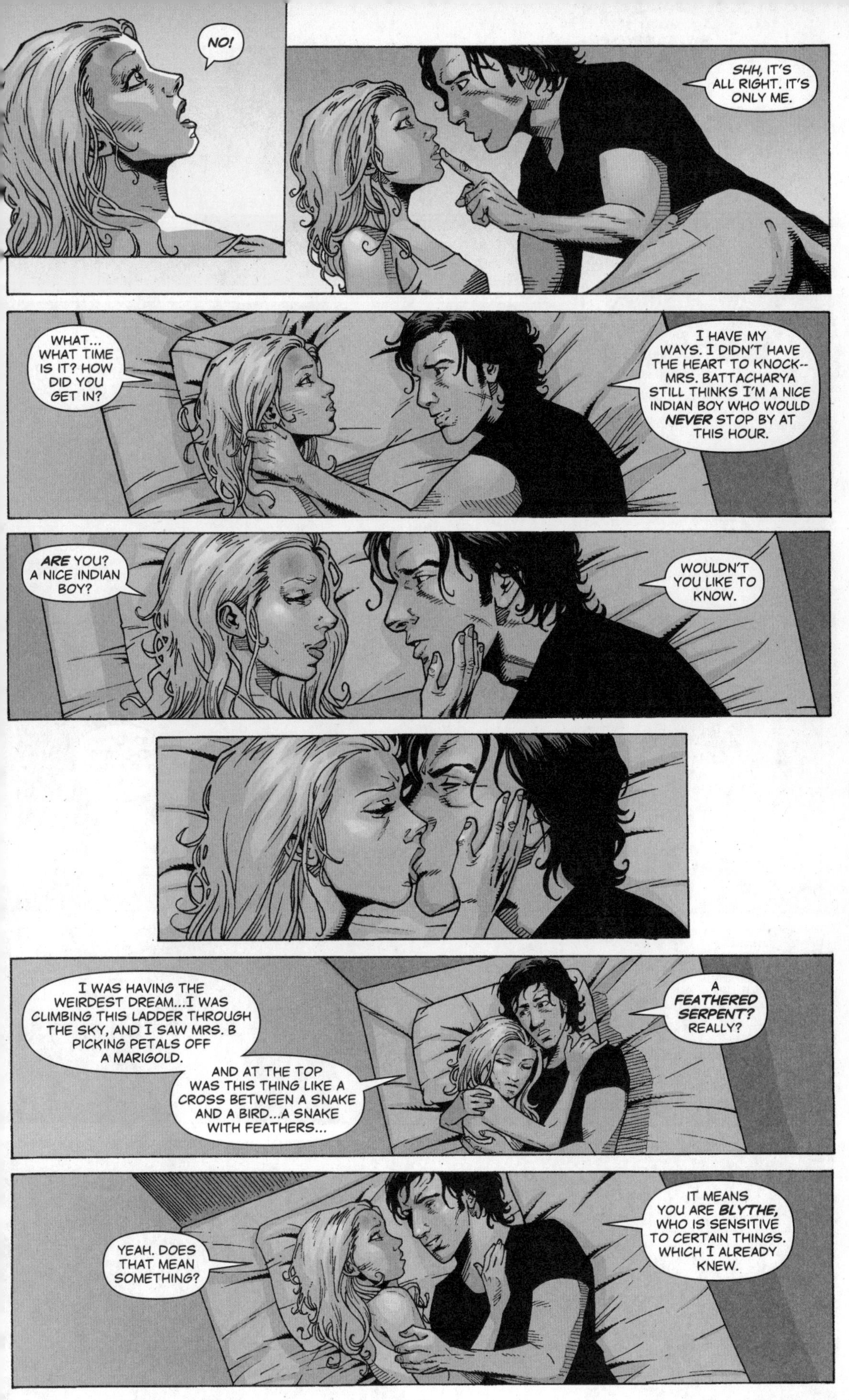
NO!
SHH, IT'S ALL RIGHT. IT'S ONLY ME.
WHAT... WHAT TIME IS IT? HOW DID YOU GET IN?
I HAVE MY WAYS. I DIDN'T HAVE THE HEART TO KNOCK-- MRS. BATTACHARYA STILL THINKS I'M A NICE INDIAN BOY WHO WOULD NEVER STOP BY AT THIS HOUR.
ARE YOU? A NICE INDIAN BOY?
WOULDN'T YOU LIKE TO KNOW.
I WAS HAVING THE WEIRDEST DREAM...I WAS CLIMBING THIS LADDER THROUGH THE SKY, AND I SAW MRS. B PICKING PETALS OFF A MARIGOLD.
AND AT THE TOP WAS THIS THING LIKE A CROSS BETWEEN A SNAKE AND A BIRD...A SNAKE WITH FEATHERS...
A FEATHERED SERPENT? REALLY?
YEAH. DOES THAT MEAN SOMETHING?
IT MEANS YOU ARE BLYTHE, WHO IS SENSITIVE TO CERTAIN THINGS. WHICH I ALREADY KNEW.

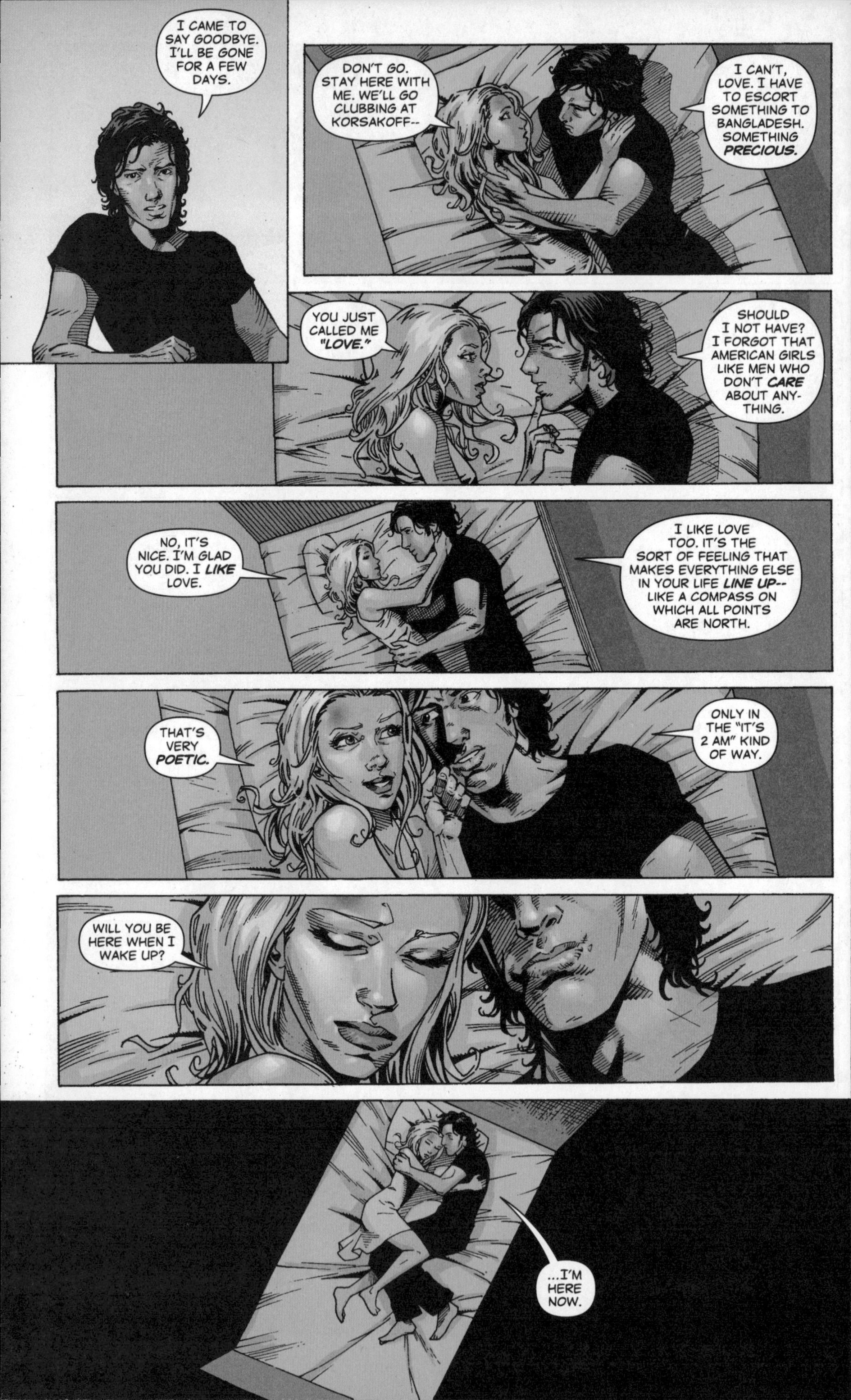
I CAME TO SAY GOODBYE. I'LL BE GONE FOR A FEW DAYS.
DON'T GO. STAY HERE WITH ME. WE'LL GO CLUBBING AT KORSAKOFF--
I CAN'T, LOVE. I HAVE TO ESCORT SOMETHING TO BANGLADESH. SOMETHING PRECIOUS.
YOU JUST CALLED ME "LOVE."
SHOULD I NOT HAVE? I FORGOT THAT AMERICAN GIRLS LIKE MEN WHO DON'T CARE ABOUT ANYTHING.
NO, IT'S NICE. I'M GLAD YOU DID. I LIKE LOVE.
I LIKE LOVE TOO. IT'S THE SORT OF FEELING THAT MAKES EVERYTHING ELSE IN YOUR LIFE LINE UP-- LIKE A COMPASS ON WHICH ALL POINTS ARE NORTH.
THAT'S VERY POETIC.
ONLY IN THE "IT'S 2 AM" KIND OF WAY.
WILL YOU BE HERE WHEN I WAKE UP?
...I'M HERE NOW.

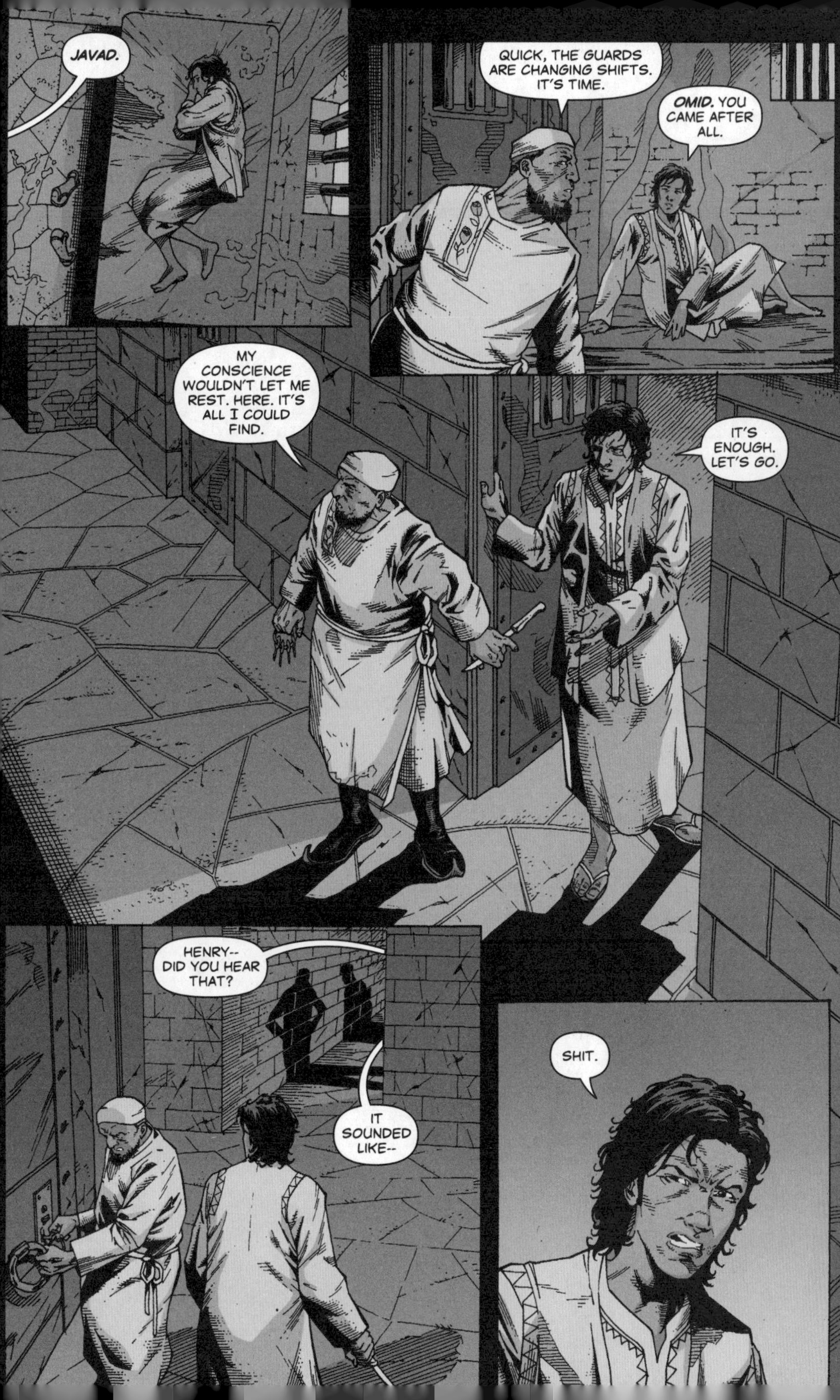
JAVAD.
QUICK, THE GUARDS ARE CHANGING SHIFTS. IT'S TIME.
OMID. YOU CAME AFTER ALL.
MY CONSCIENCE WOULDN'T LET ME REST. HERE. IT'S ALL I COULD FIND.
IT'S ENOUGH. LET'S GO.
HENRY-- DID YOU HEAR THAT?
IT SOUNDED LIKE--
SHIT.

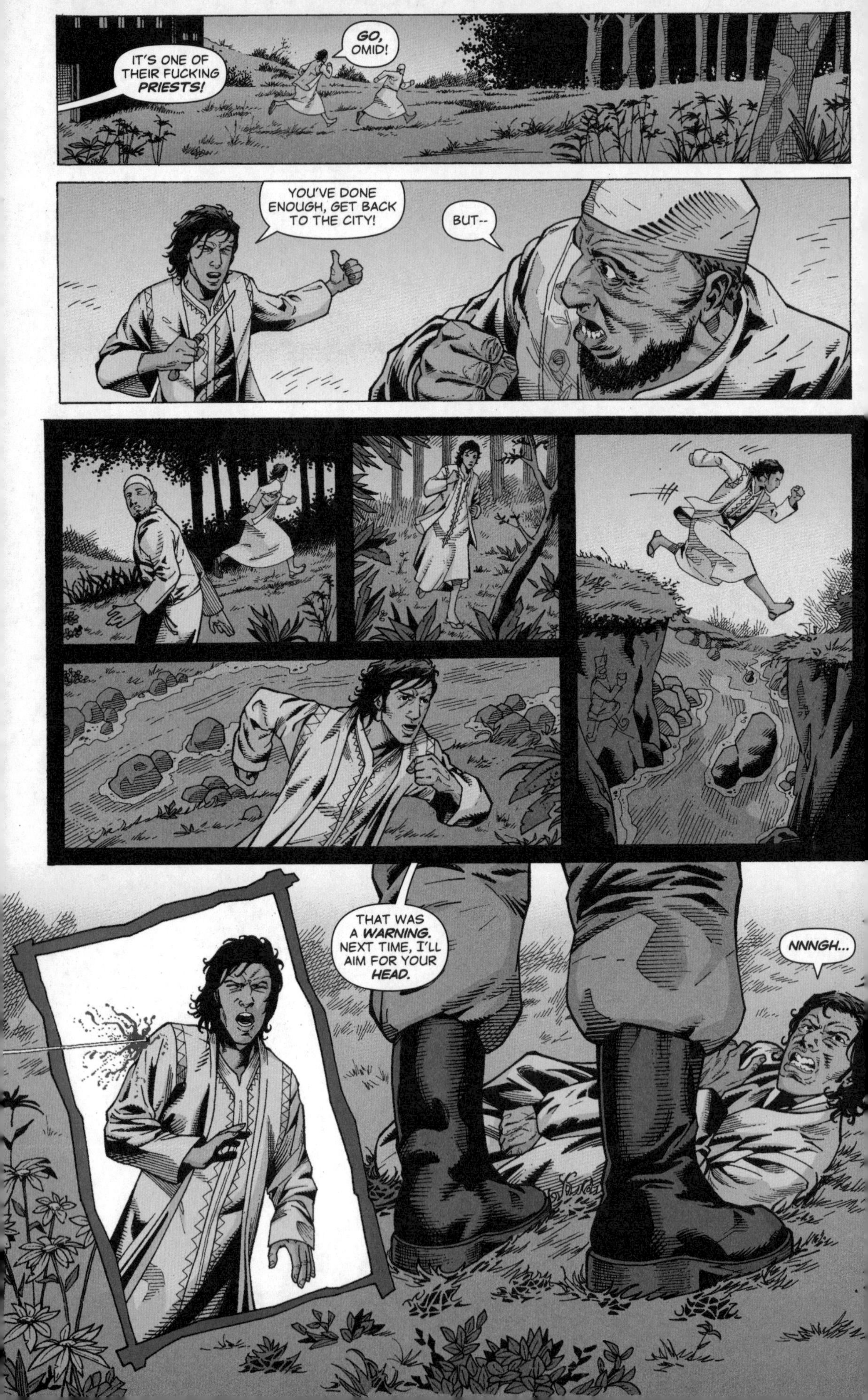

GO, OMID!
IT'S ONE OF THEIR FUCKING PRIESTS!
YOU'VE DONE ENOUGH, GET BACK TO THE CITY!
BUT--
THAT WAS A WARNING. NEXT TIME, I'LL AIM FOR YOUR HEAD.
NNNGH...

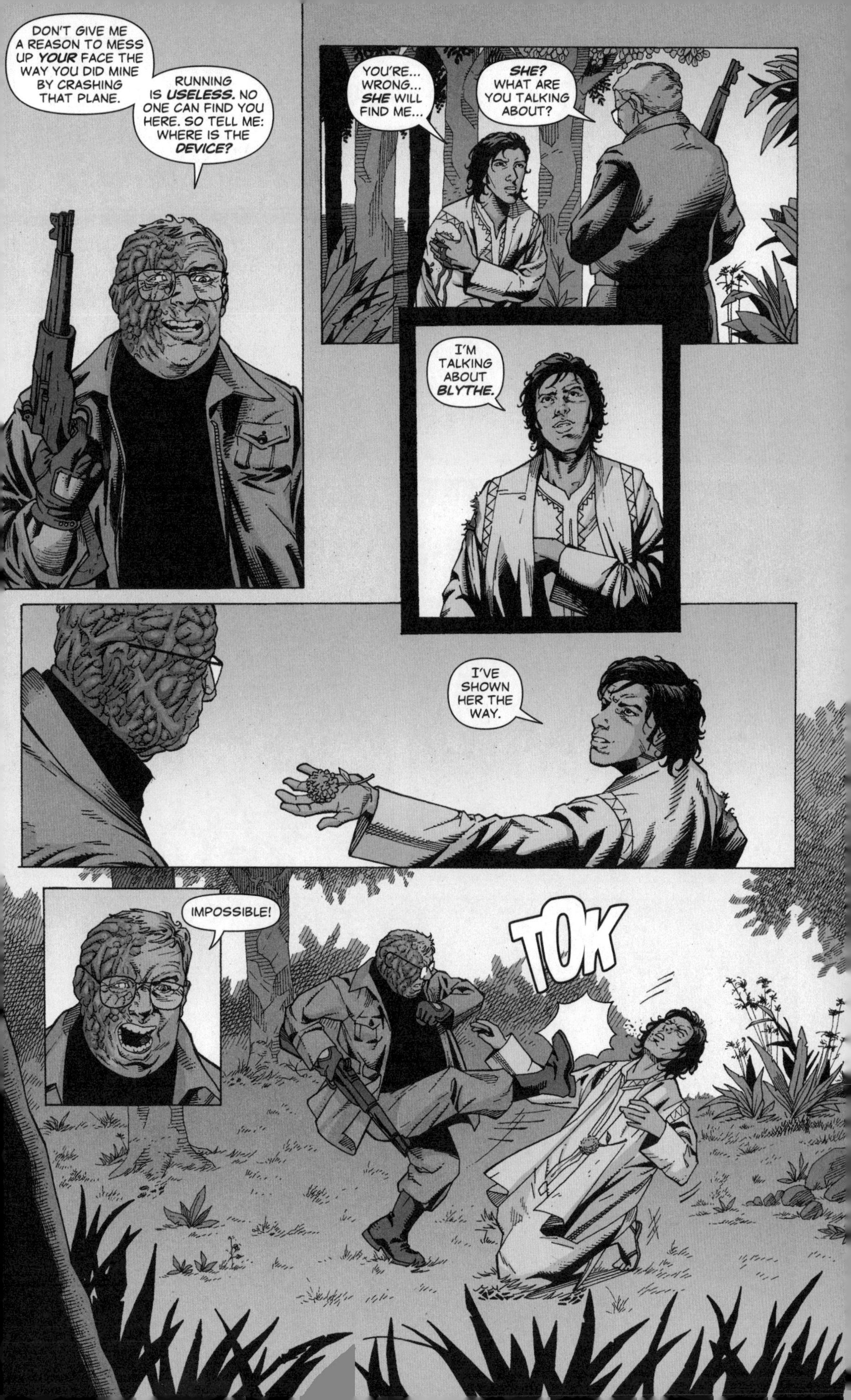
DON'T GIVE ME A REASON TO MESS UP YOUR FACE THE WAY YOU DID MINE BY CRASHING THAT PLANE.
RUNNING IS USELESS. NO ONE CAN FIND YOU HERE. SO TELL ME: WHERE IS THE DEVICE?
YOU'RE... WRONG... SHE WILL FIND ME...
SHE? WHAT ARE YOU TALKING ABOUT?
I'M TALKING ABOUT BLYTHE.
I'VE SHOWN HER THE WAY.
IMPOSSIBLE!
TOK

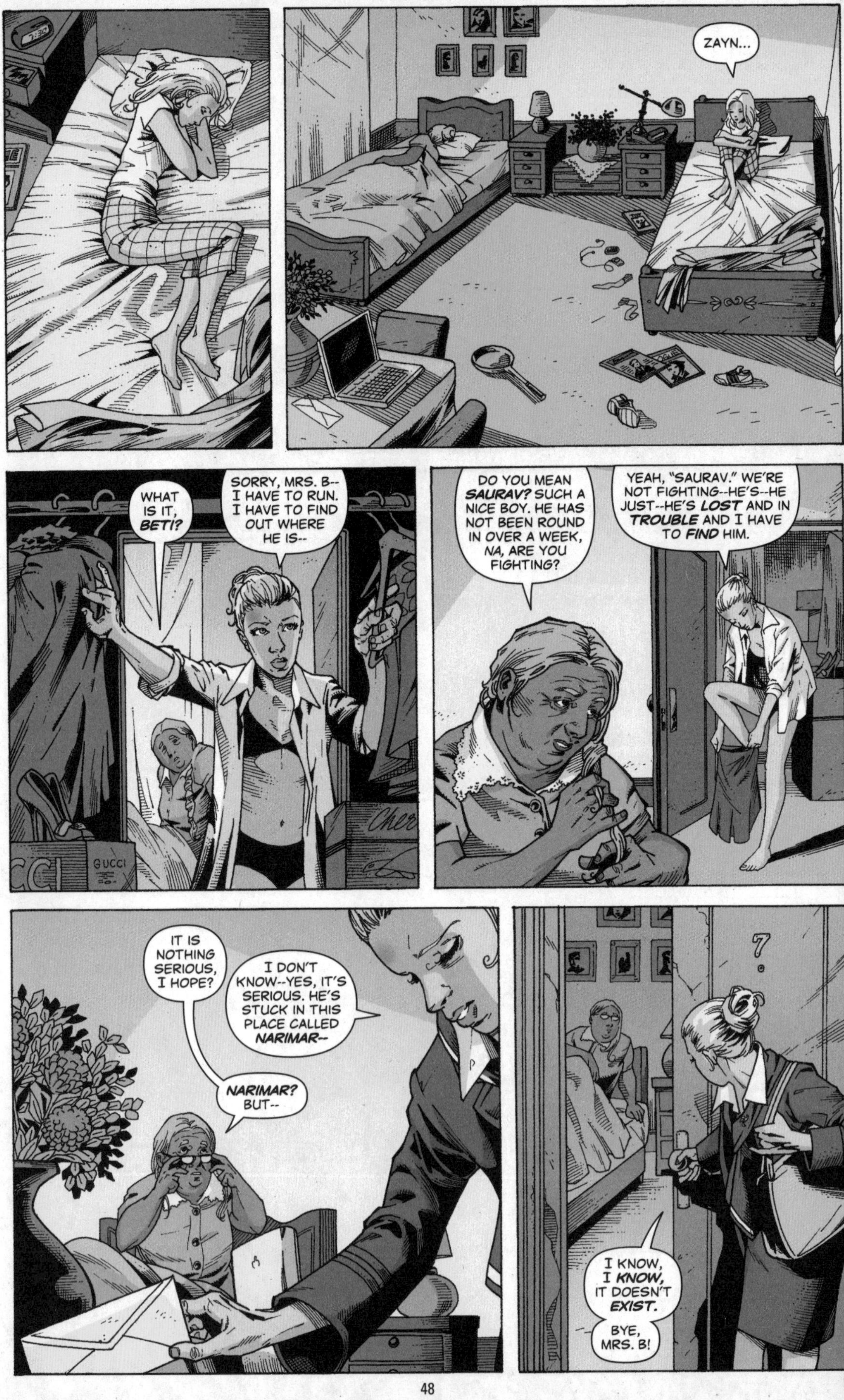
ZAYN...
WHAT IS IT, BETI?
SORRY, MRS. B-- I HAVE TO RUN. I HAVE TO FIND OUT WHERE HE IS--
DO YOU MEAN SAURAV? SUCH A NICE BOY. HE HAS NOT BEEN ROUND IN OVER A WEEK, NA, ARE YOU FIGHTING?
YEAH, "SAURAV." WE'RE NOT FIGHTING--HE'S--HE JUST--HE'S LOST AND IN TROUBLE AND I HAVE TO FIND HIM.
IT IS NOTHING SERIOUS, I HOPE?
I DON'T KNOW--YES, IT'S SERIOUS. HE'S STUCK IN THIS PLACE CALLED NARIMAR--
NARIMAR? BUT--
I KNOW, I KNOW, IT DOESN'T EXIST.
BYE, MRS. B!

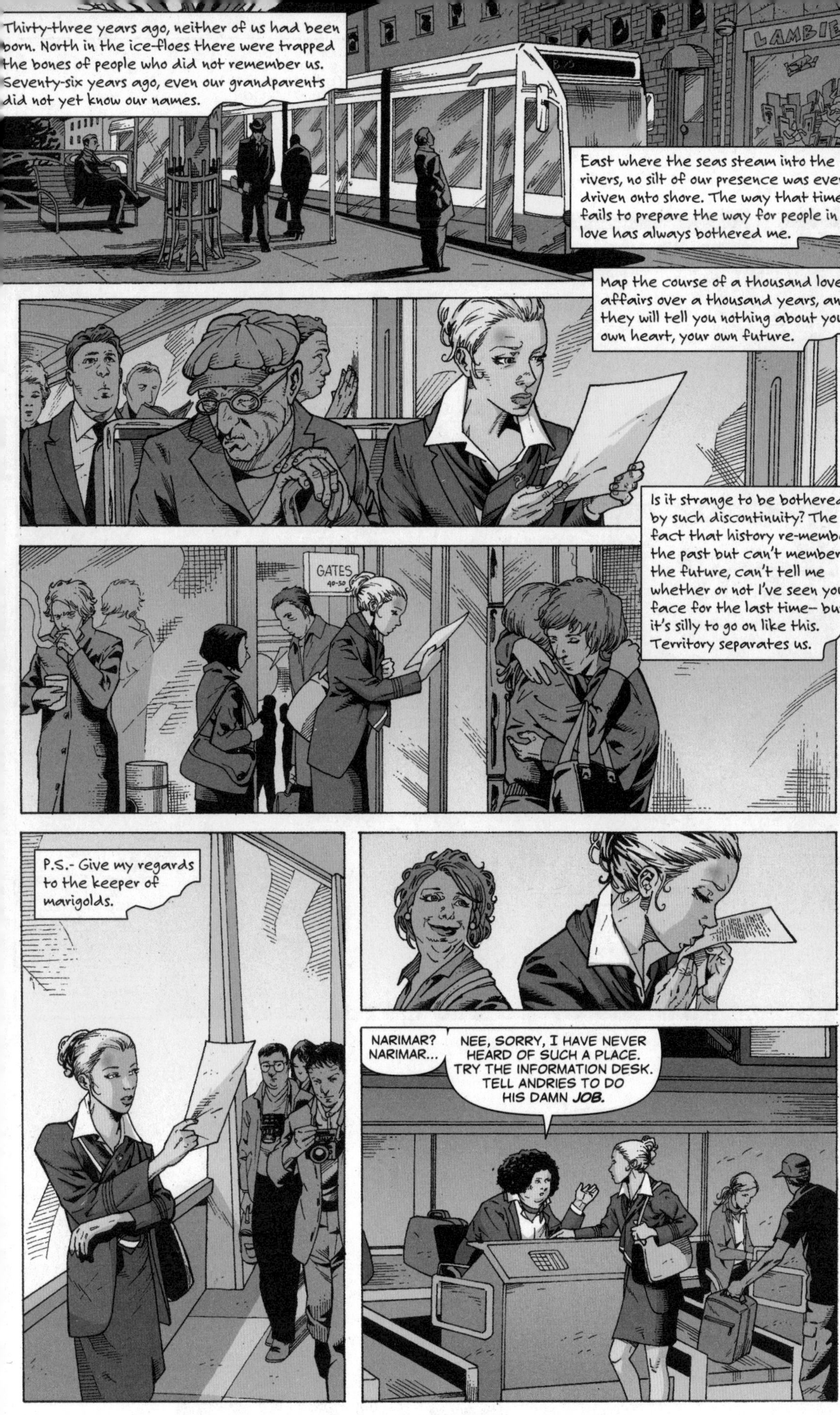
Thirty-three years ago, neither of us had been born. North in the ice-floes there were trapped the bones of people who did not remember us. Seventy-six years ago, even our grandparents did not yet know our names.
LAMBIEK
East where the seas steam into the rivers, no silt of our presence was ever driven onto shore. The way that time fails to prepare the way for people in love has always bothered me.
Map the course of a thousand love affairs over a thousand years, and they will tell you nothing about your own heart, your own future.
Is it strange to be bothered by such discontinuity? The fact that history re-members the past but can't member the future, can't tell me whether or not I've seen your face for the last time-- but it's silly to go on like this. Territory separates us.
GATES
40-50
P.S.- Give my regards to the keeper of marigolds.
NARIMAR? NARIMAR...
NEE, SORRY, I HAVE NEVER HEARD OF SUCH A PLACE. TRY THE INFORMATION DESK. TELL ANDRIES TO DO HIS DAMN JOB.

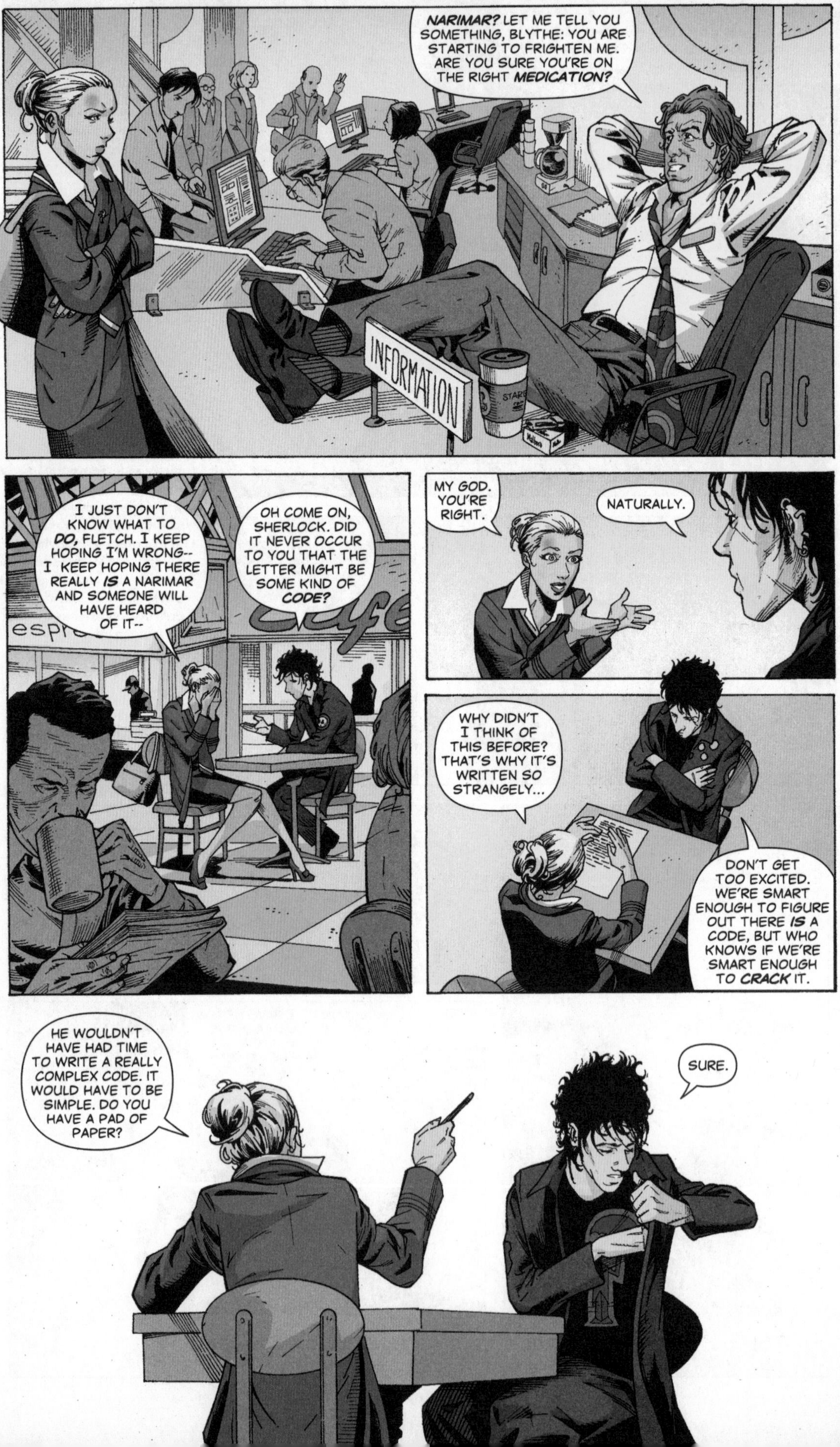
NARIMAR? LET ME TELL YOU SOMETHING, BLYTHE: YOU ARE STARTING TO FRIGHTEN ME. ARE YOU SURE YOU'RE ON THE RIGHT MEDICATION?
INFORMATION
I JUST DON'T KNOW WHAT TO DO, FLETCH. I KEEP HOPING I'M WRONG-- I KEEP HOPING THERE REALLY IS A NARIMAR AND SOMEONE WILL HAVE HEARD OF IT--
OH COME ON, SHERLOCK. DID IT NEVER OCCUR TO YOU THAT THE LETTER MIGHT BE SOME KIND OF CODE?
MY GOD. YOU'RE RIGHT.
NATURALLY.
WHY DIDN'T I THINK OF THIS BEFORE? THAT'S WHY IT'S WRITTEN SO STRANGELY...
DON'T GET TOO EXCITED. WE'RE SMART ENOUGH TO FIGURE OUT THERE IS A CODE, BUT WHO KNOWS IF WE'RE SMART ENOUGH TO CRACK IT.
HE WOULDN'T HAVE HAD TIME TO WRITE A REALLY COMPLEX CODE. IT WOULD HAVE TO BE SIMPLE. DO YOU HAVE A PAD OF PAPER?
SURE.

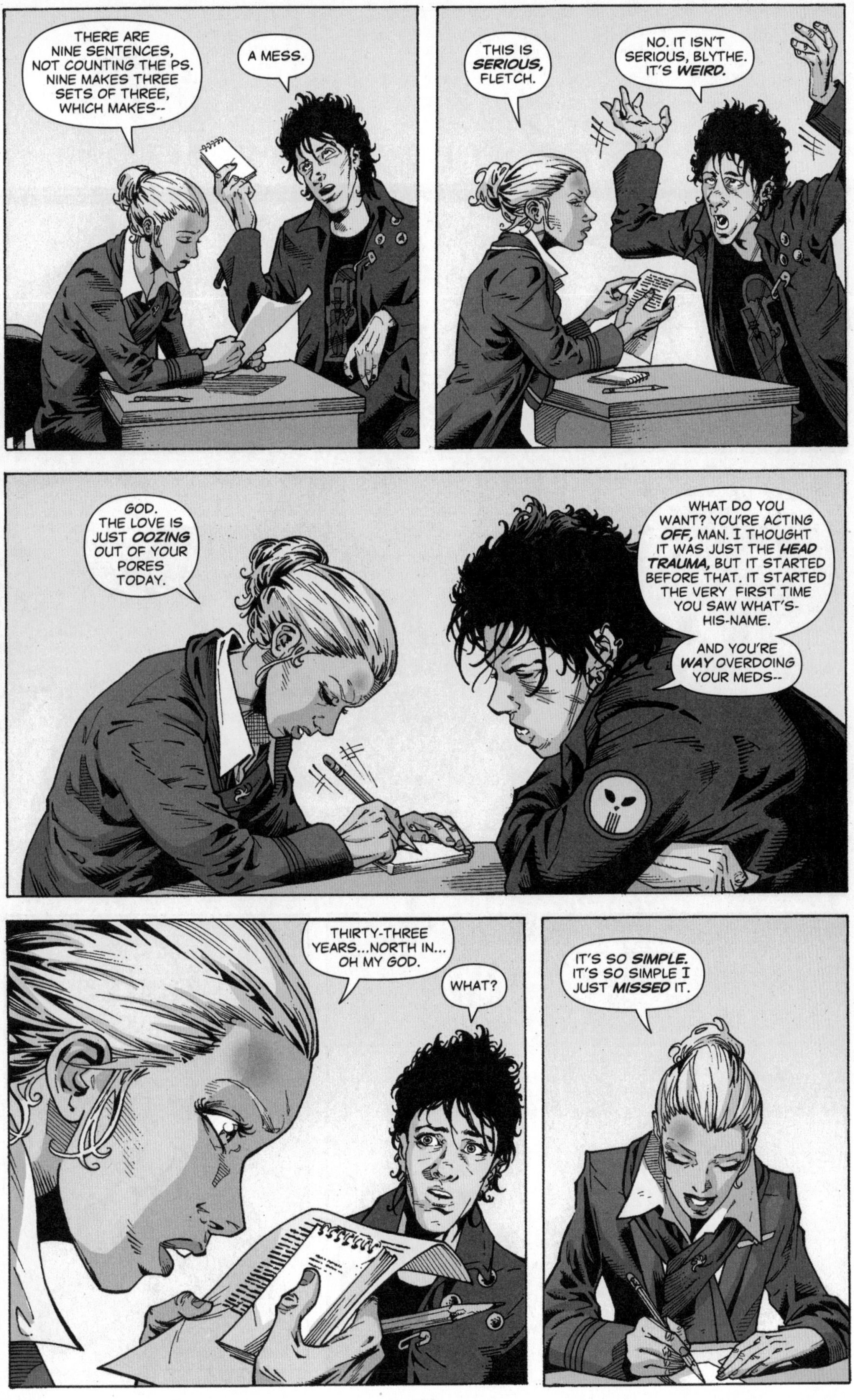
THERE ARE NINE SENTENCES, NOT COUNTING THE PS. NINE MAKES THREE SETS OF THREE, WHICH MAKES--
A MESS.
THIS IS SERIOUS, FLETCH.
NO. IT ISN'T SERIOUS, BLYTHE. IT'S WEIRD.
GOD. THE LOVE IS JUST OOZING OUT OF YOUR PORES TODAY.
WHAT DO YOU WANT? YOU'RE ACTING OFF, MAN. I THOUGHT IT WAS JUST THE HEAD TRAUMA, BUT IT STARTED BEFORE THAT. IT STARTED THE VERY FIRST TIME YOU SAW WHAT'S-HIS-NAME.
AND YOU'RE WAY OVERDOING YOUR MEDS--
THIRTY-THREE YEARS...NORTH IN... OH MY GOD.
WHAT?
IT'S SO SIMPLE. IT'S SO SIMPLE I JUST MISSED IT.

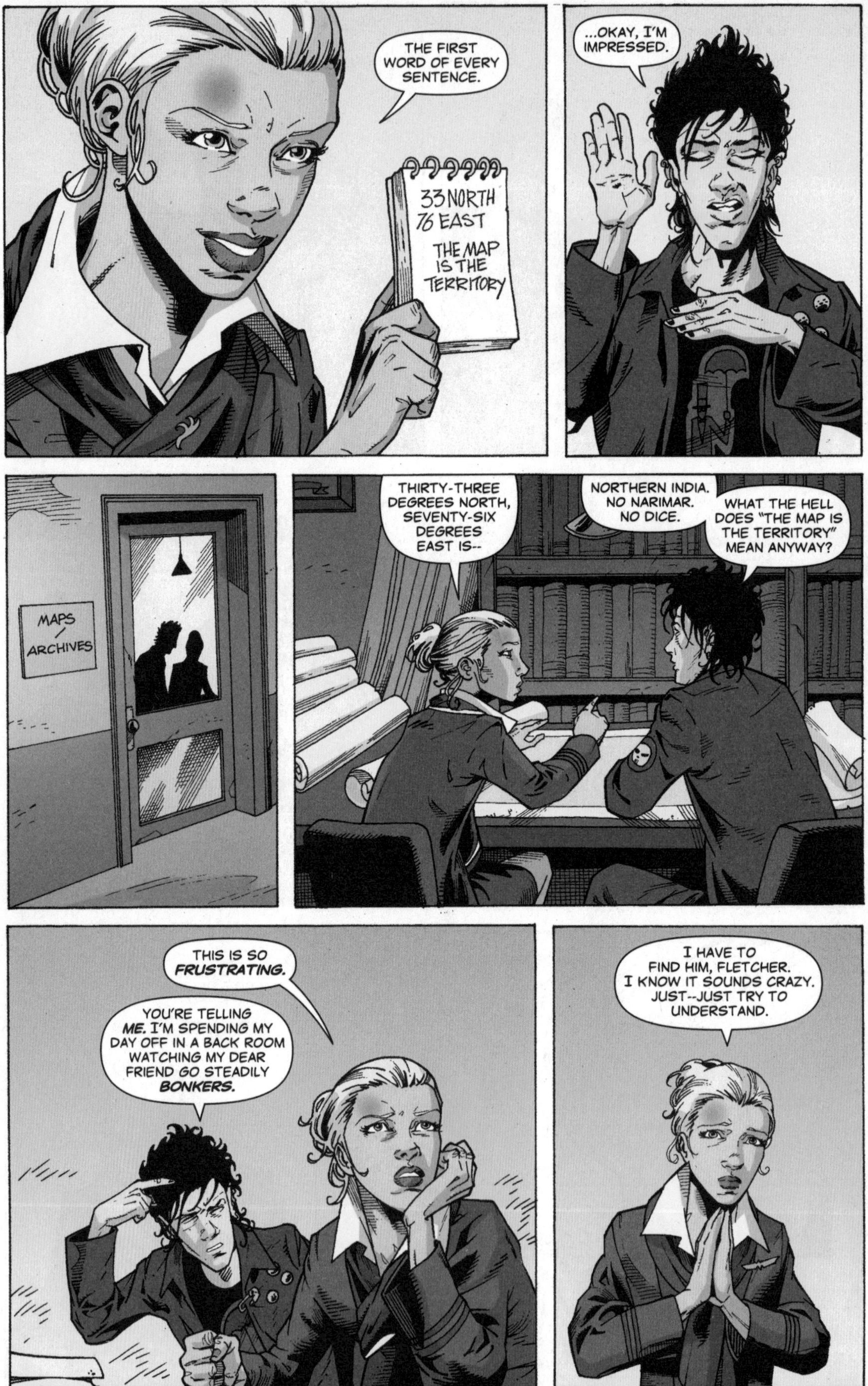
THE FIRST WORD OF EVERY SENTENCE.
33 NORTH
76 EAST
THE MAP IS THE TERRITORY
...OKAY, I'M IMPRESSED.
MAPS / ARCHIVES
THIRTY-THREE DEGREES NORTH, SEVENTY-SIX DEGREES EAST IS--
NORTHERN INDIA. NO NARIMAR. NO DICE.
WHAT THE HELL DOES "THE MAP IS THE TERRITORY" MEAN ANYWAY?
THIS IS SO **FRUSTRATING.**
YOU'RE TELLING **ME.** I'M SPENDING MY DAY OFF IN A BACK ROOM WATCHING MY DEAR FRIEND GO STEADILY **BONKERS.**
I HAVE TO FIND HIM, FLETCHER. I KNOW IT SOUNDS CRAZY. JUST--JUST TRY TO UNDERSTAND.

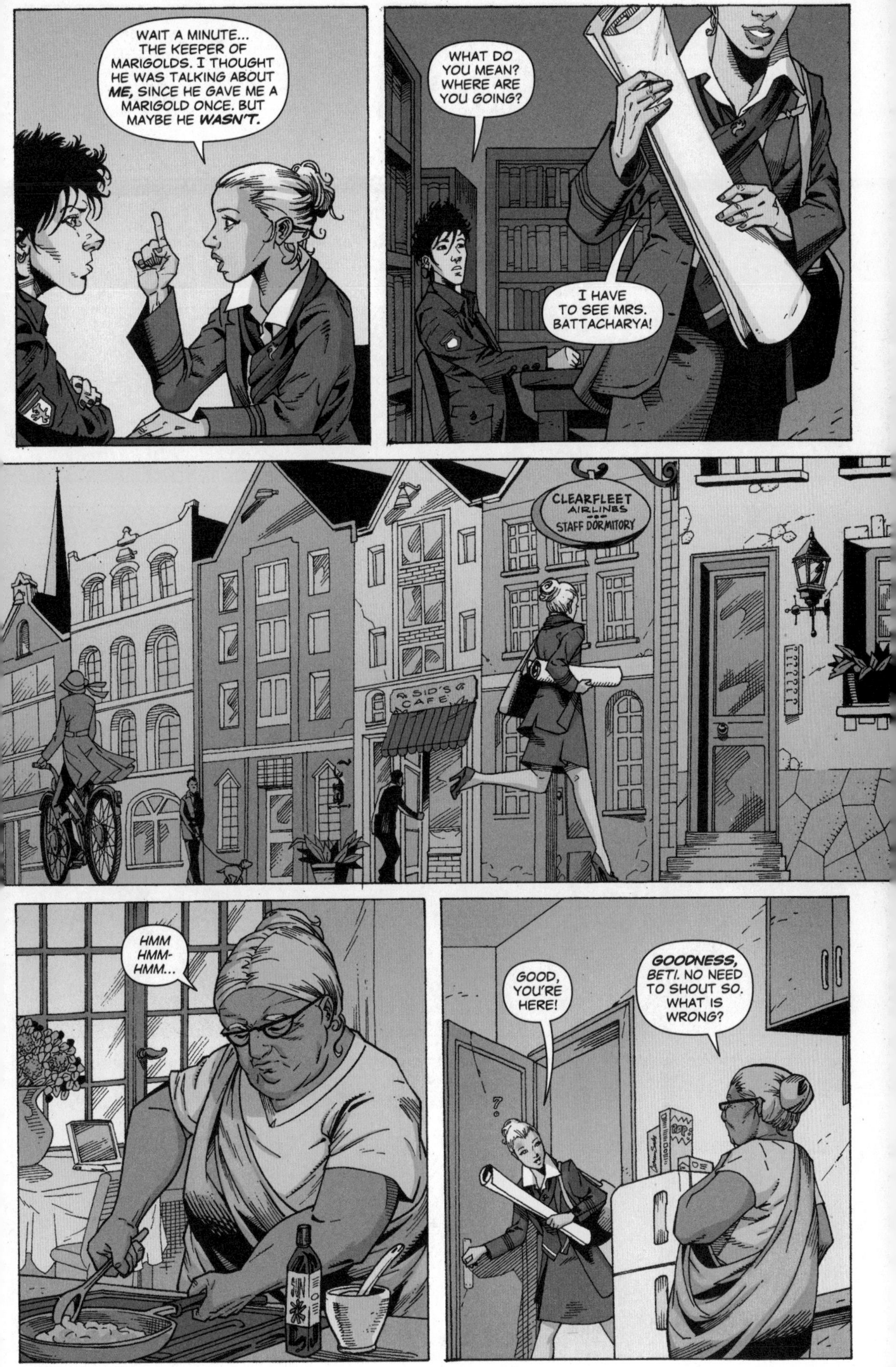

WAIT A MINUTE... THE KEEPER OF MARIGOLDS. I THOUGHT HE WAS TALKING ABOUT *ME,* SINCE HE GAVE ME A MARIGOLD ONCE. BUT MAYBE HE *WASN'T.*
WHAT DO YOU MEAN? WHERE ARE YOU GOING?
I HAVE TO SEE MRS. BATTACHARYA!
CLEARFLEET AIRLINES STAFF DORMITORY
SID'S CAFE
HMM HMM-HMM...
SUN
GOOD, YOU'RE HERE!
?
GOODNESS, BETI. NO NEED TO SHOUT SO. WHAT IS WRONG?

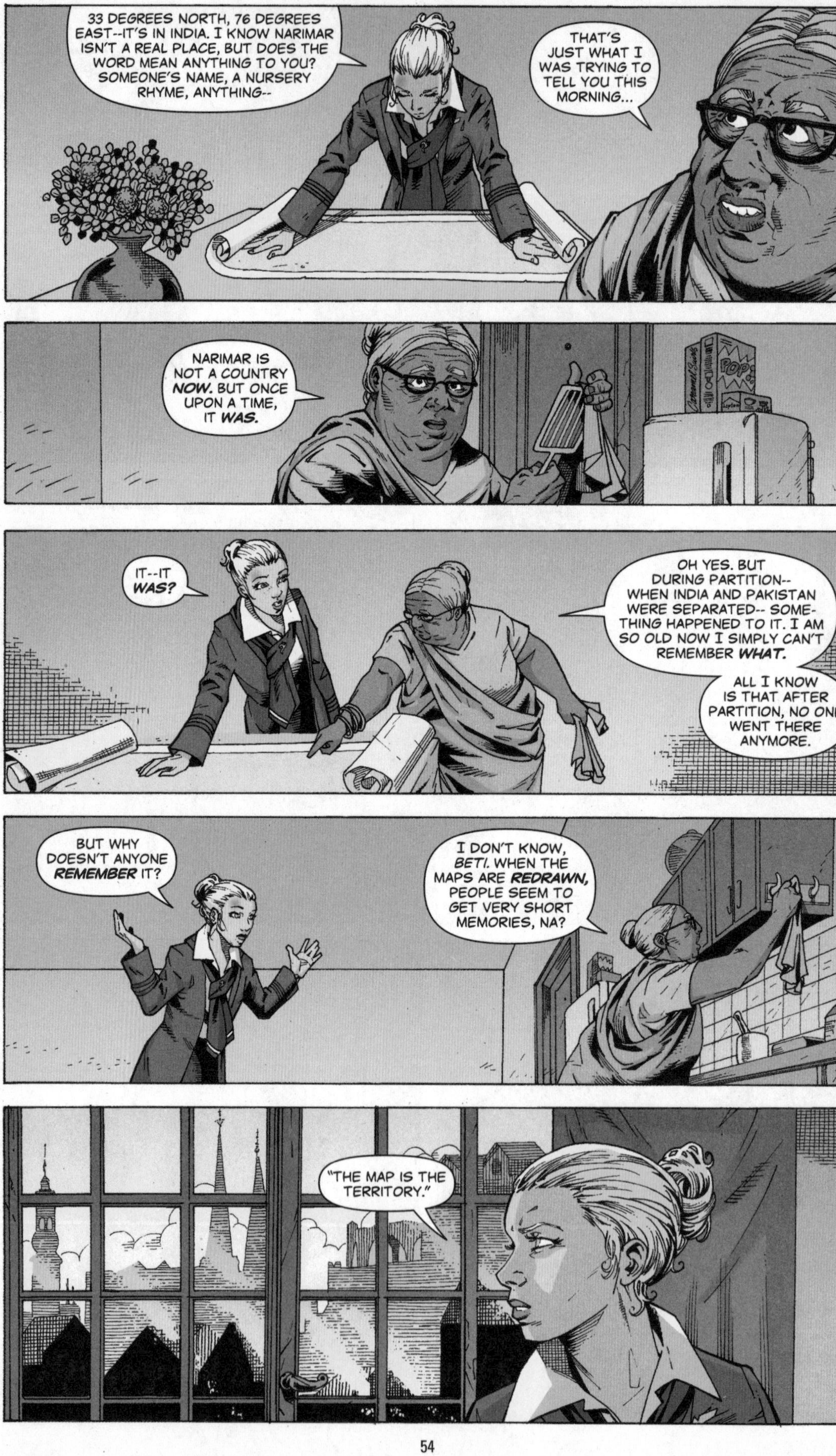
33 DEGREES NORTH, 76 DEGREES EAST--IT'S IN INDIA. I KNOW NARIMAR ISN'T A REAL PLACE, BUT DOES THE WORD MEAN ANYTHING TO YOU? SOMEONE'S NAME, A NURSERY RHYME, ANYTHING--
THAT'S JUST WHAT I WAS TRYING TO TELL YOU THIS MORNING...
NARIMAR IS NOT A COUNTRY NOW. BUT ONCE UPON A TIME, IT WAS.
IT--IT WAS?
OH YES. BUT DURING PARTITION-- WHEN INDIA AND PAKISTAN WERE SEPARATED-- SOMETHING HAPPENED TO IT. I AM SO OLD NOW I SIMPLY CAN'T REMEMBER WHAT.
ALL I KNOW IS THAT AFTER PARTITION, NO ONE WENT THERE ANYMORE.
BUT WHY DOESN'T ANYONE REMEMBER IT?
I DON'T KNOW, BETI. WHEN THE MAPS ARE REDRAWN, PEOPLE SEEM TO GET VERY SHORT MEMORIES, NA?
"THE MAP IS THE TERRITORY."

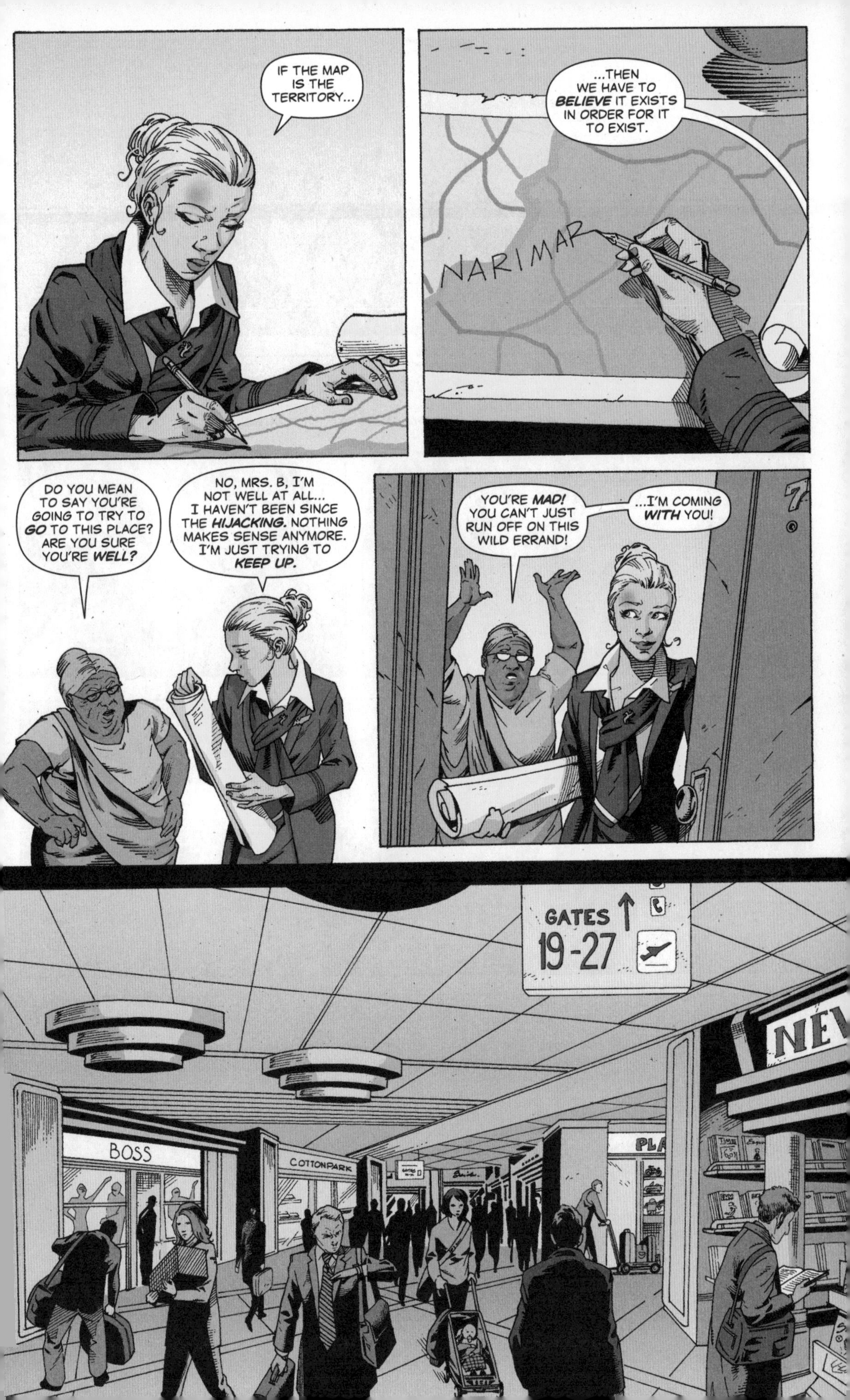
IF THE MAP IS THE TERRITORY...
...THEN WE HAVE TO BELIEVE IT EXISTS IN ORDER FOR IT TO EXIST.
NARIMAR
DO YOU MEAN TO SAY YOU'RE GOING TO TRY TO GO TO THIS PLACE? ARE YOU SURE YOU'RE WELL?
NO, MRS. B, I'M NOT WELL AT ALL... I HAVEN'T BEEN SINCE THE HIJACKING. NOTHING MAKES SENSE ANYMORE. I'M JUST TRYING TO KEEP UP.
YOU'RE MAD! YOU CAN'T JUST RUN OFF ON THIS WILD ERRAND!
...I'M COMING WITH YOU!
GATES
19-27
BOSS
COTTONPARK
NEV
PLA
TIME

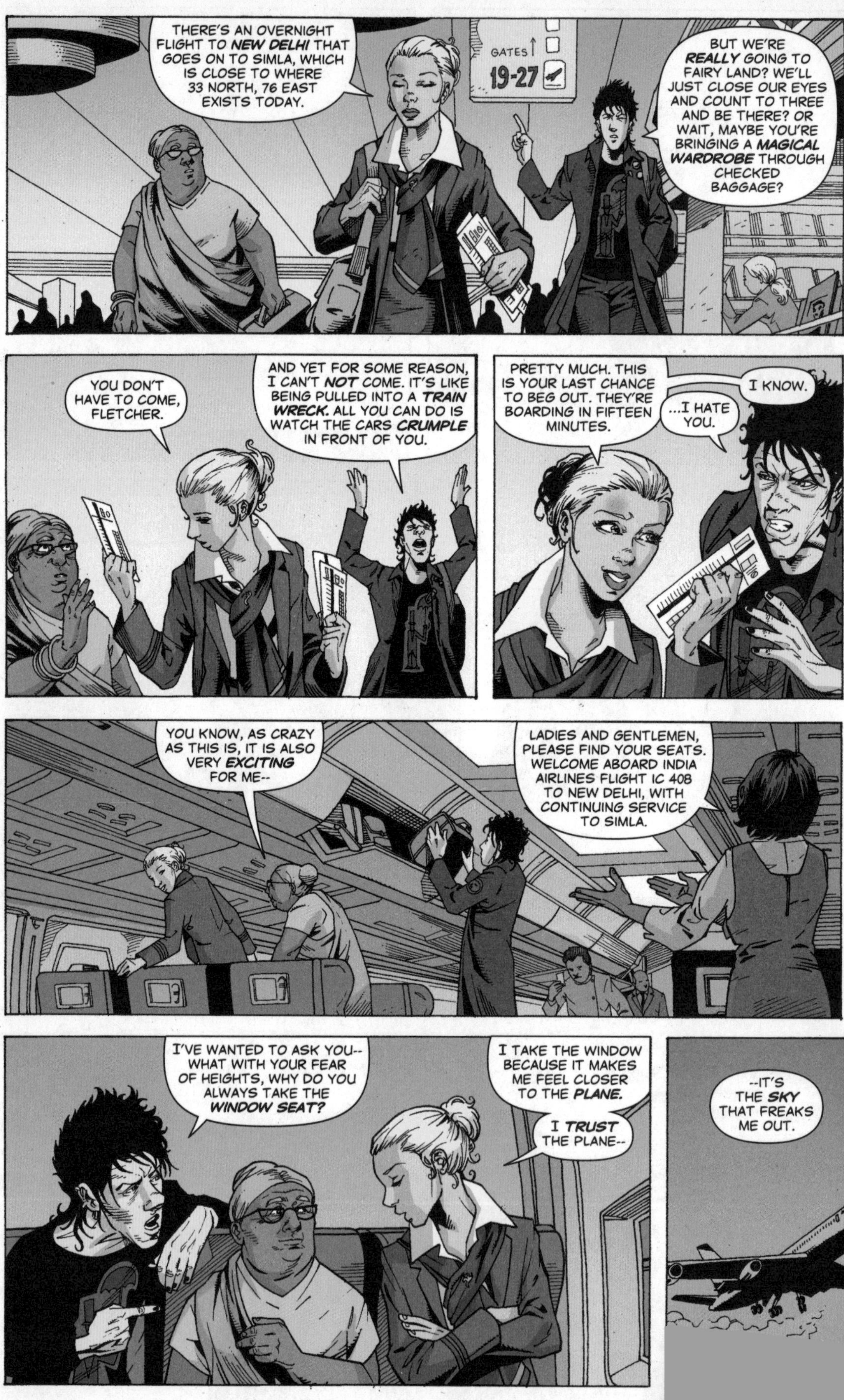
THERE'S AN OVERNIGHT FLIGHT TO NEW DELHI THAT GOES ON TO SIMLA, WHICH IS CLOSE TO WHERE 33 NORTH, 76 EAST EXISTS TODAY.
GATES 19-27
BUT WE'RE REALLY GOING TO FAIRY LAND? WE'LL JUST CLOSE OUR EYES AND COUNT TO THREE AND BE THERE? OR WAIT, MAYBE YOU'RE BRINGING A MAGICAL WARDROBE THROUGH CHECKED BAGGAGE?
YOU DON'T HAVE TO COME, FLETCHER.
AND YET FOR SOME REASON, I CAN'T NOT COME. IT'S LIKE BEING PULLED INTO A TRAIN WRECK. ALL YOU CAN DO IS WATCH THE CARS CRUMPLE IN FRONT OF YOU.
PRETTY MUCH. THIS IS YOUR LAST CHANCE TO BEG OUT. THEY'RE BOARDING IN FIFTEEN MINUTES.
...I HATE YOU.
I KNOW.
YOU KNOW, AS CRAZY AS THIS IS, IT IS ALSO VERY EXCITING FOR ME--
LADIES AND GENTLEMEN, PLEASE FIND YOUR SEATS. WELCOME ABOARD INDIA AIRLINES FLIGHT IC 408 TO NEW DELHI, WITH CONTINUING SERVICE TO SIMLA.
I'VE WANTED TO ASK YOU--WHAT WITH YOUR FEAR OF HEIGHTS, WHY DO YOU ALWAYS TAKE THE WINDOW SEAT?
I TAKE THE WINDOW BECAUSE IT MAKES ME FEEL CLOSER TO THE PLANE.
I TRUST THE PLANE--
--IT'S THE SKY THAT FREAKS ME OUT.

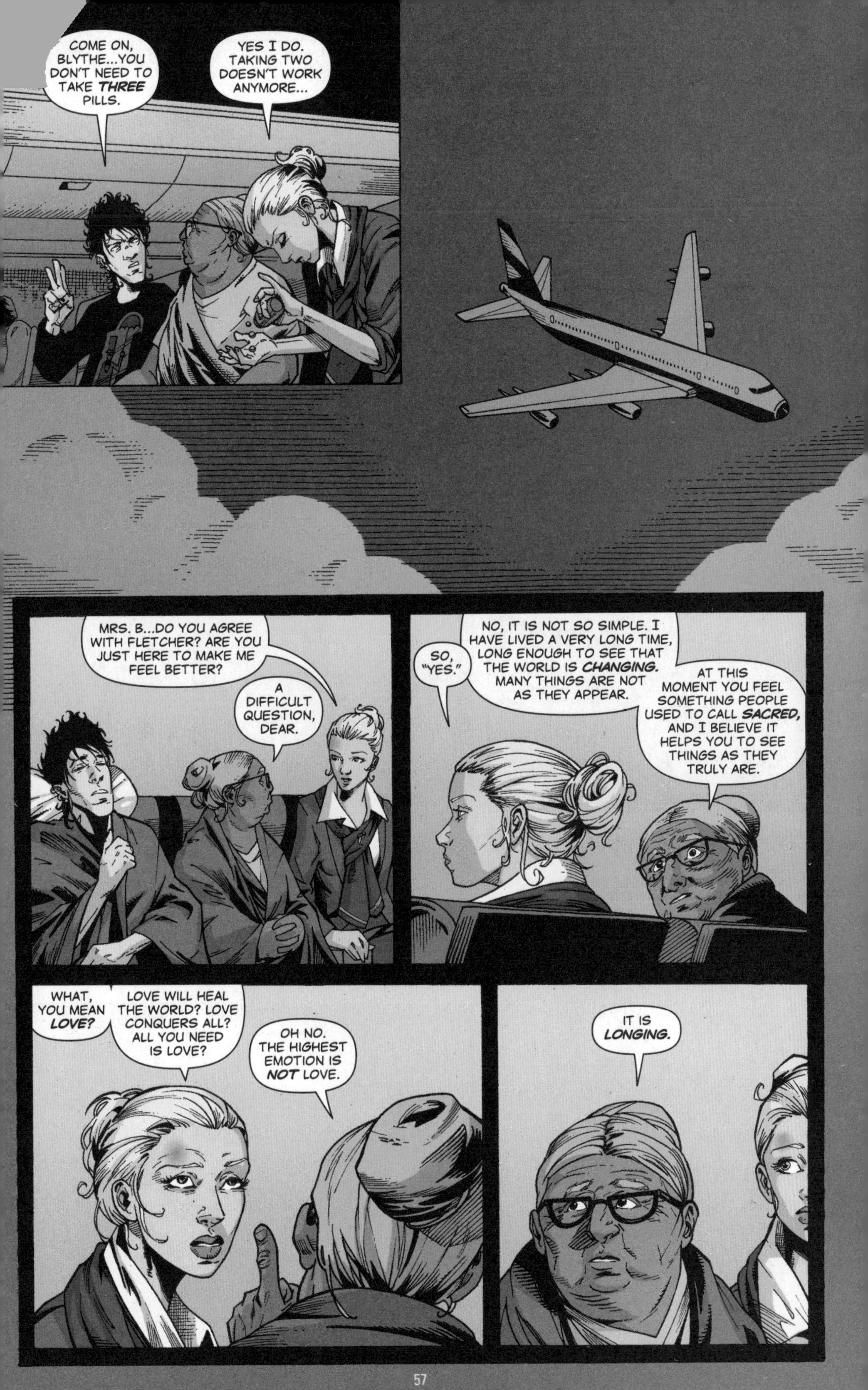
COME ON, BLYTHE...YOU DON'T NEED TO TAKE ***THREE*** PILLS.
YES I DO. TAKING TWO DOESN'T WORK ANYMORE...
MRS. B...DO YOU AGREE WITH FLETCHER? ARE YOU JUST HERE TO MAKE ME FEEL BETTER?
A DIFFICULT QUESTION, DEAR.
SO, "YES."
NO, IT IS NOT SO SIMPLE. I HAVE LIVED A VERY LONG TIME, LONG ENOUGH TO SEE THAT THE WORLD IS ***CHANGING.*** MANY THINGS ARE NOT AS THEY APPEAR.
AT THIS MOMENT YOU FEEL SOMETHING PEOPLE USED TO CALL ***SACRED,*** AND I BELIEVE IT HELPS YOU TO SEE THINGS AS THEY TRULY ARE.
WHAT, YOU MEAN ***LOVE?***
LOVE WILL HEAL THE WORLD? LOVE CONQUERS ALL? ALL YOU NEED IS LOVE?
OH NO. THE HIGHEST EMOTION IS ***NOT*** LOVE.
IT IS ***LONGING.***

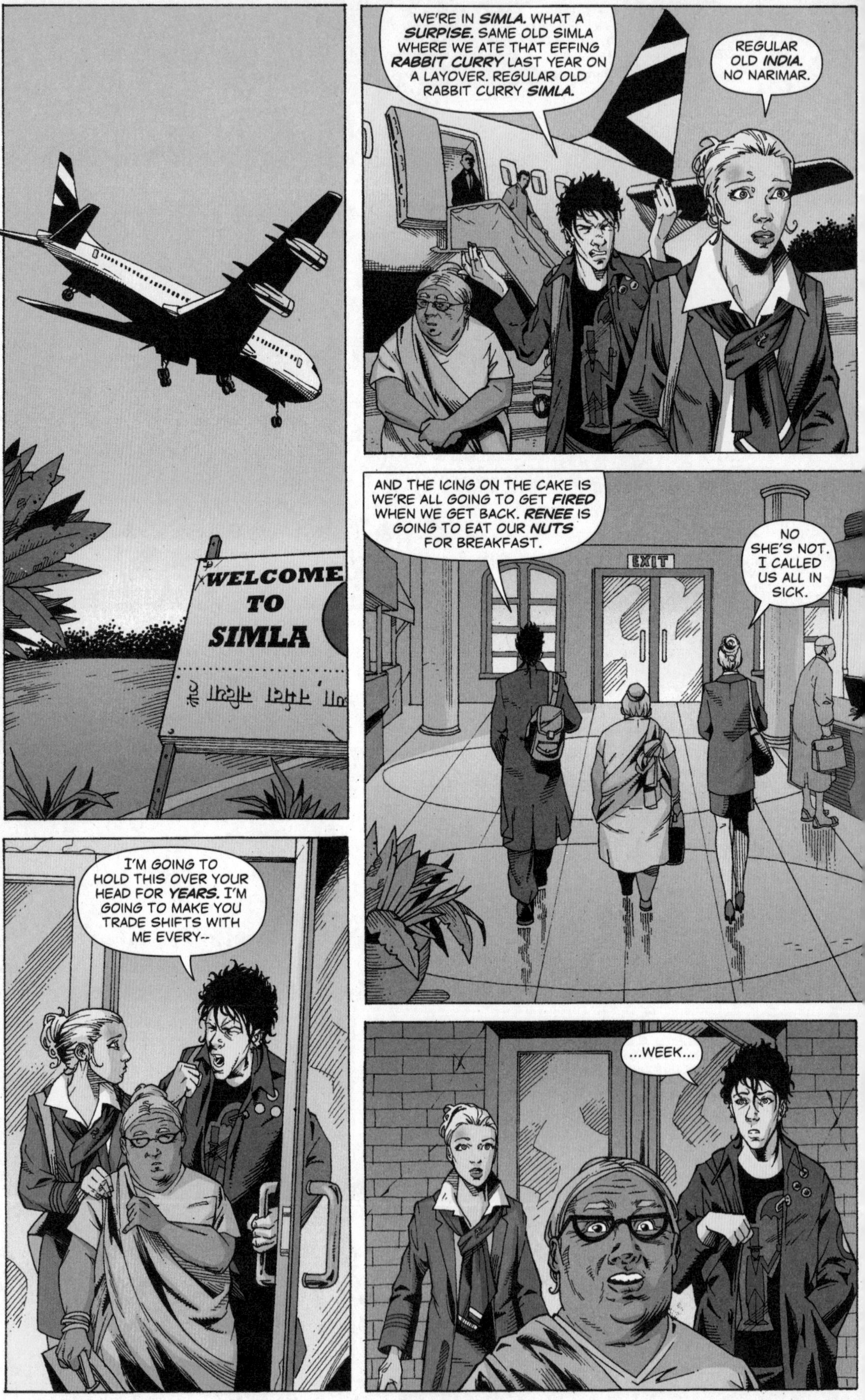
WELCOME TO SIMLA
WE'RE IN SIMLA. WHAT A SURPISE. SAME OLD SIMLA WHERE WE ATE THAT EFFING RABBIT CURRY LAST YEAR ON A LAYOVER. REGULAR OLD RABBIT CURRY SIMLA.
REGULAR OLD INDIA. NO NARIMAR.
AND THE ICING ON THE CAKE IS WE'RE ALL GOING TO GET FIRED WHEN WE GET BACK. RENEE IS GOING TO EAT OUR NUTS FOR BREAKFAST.
EXIT
NO SHE'S NOT. I CALLED US ALL IN SICK.
I'M GOING TO HOLD THIS OVER YOUR HEAD FOR YEARS. I'M GOING TO MAKE YOU TRADE SHIFTS WITH ME EVERY--
...WEEK...

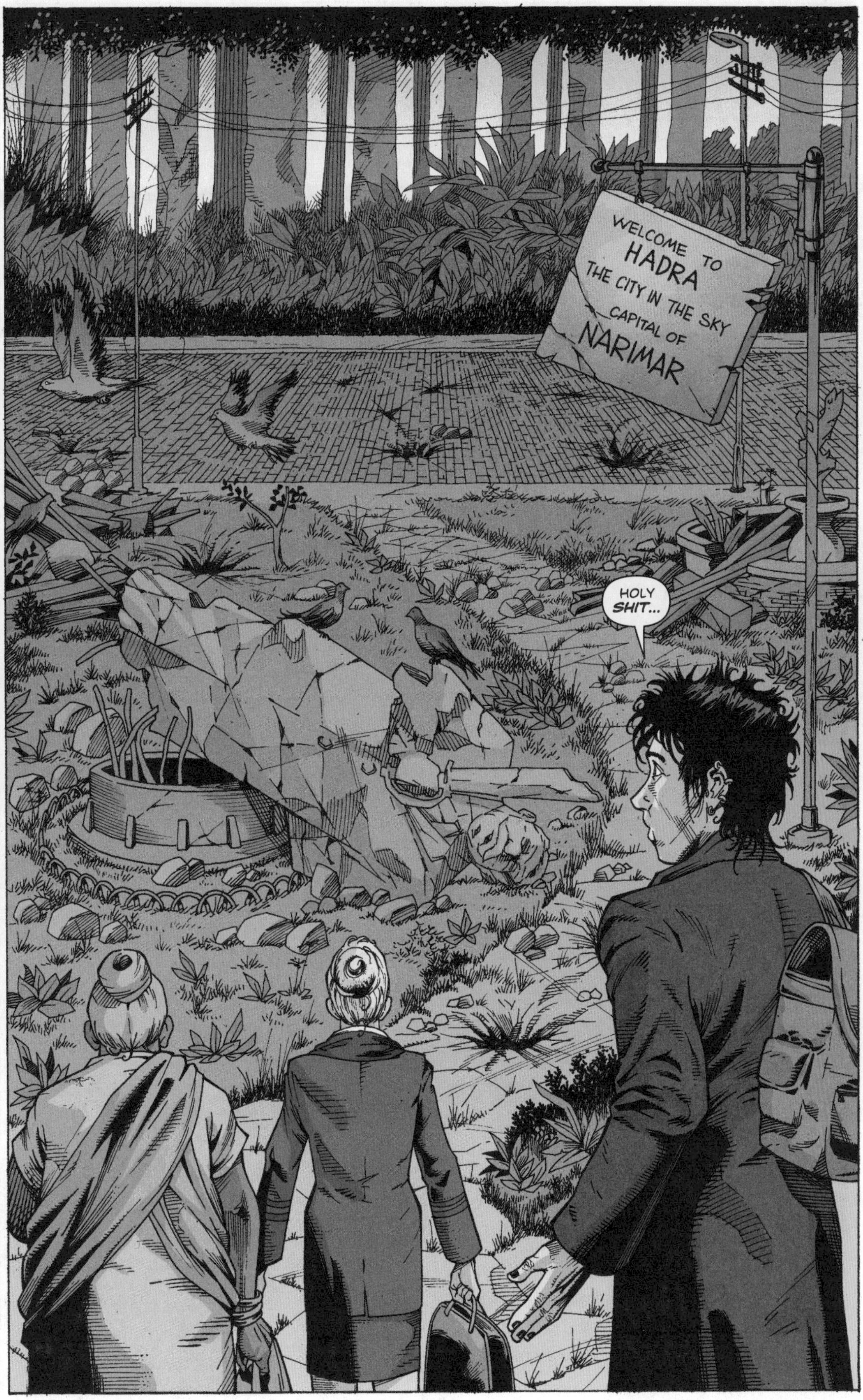
WELCOME TO
HADRA
THE CITY IN THE SKY
CAPITAL OF
NARIMAR
HOLY SHIT...

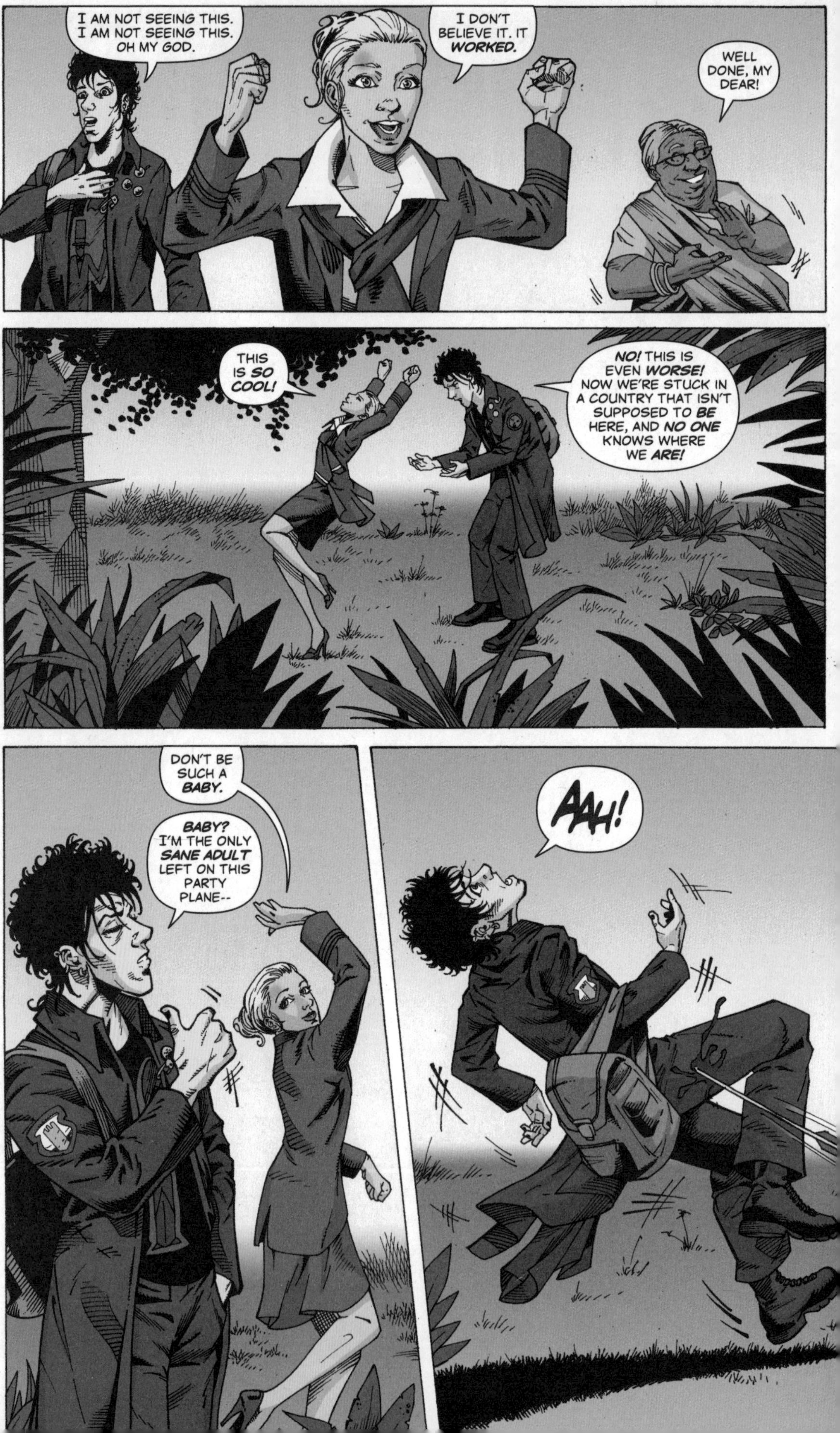
I AM NOT SEEING THIS. I AM NOT SEEING THIS. OH MY GOD.
I DON'T BELIEVE IT. IT WORKED.
WELL DONE, MY DEAR!
THIS IS SO COOL!
NO! THIS IS EVEN WORSE! NOW WE'RE STUCK IN A COUNTRY THAT ISN'T SUPPOSED TO BE HERE, AND NO ONE KNOWS WHERE WE ARE!
DON'T BE SUCH A BABY.
BABY? I'M THE ONLY SANE ADULT LEFT ON THIS PARTY PLANE--
AAH!

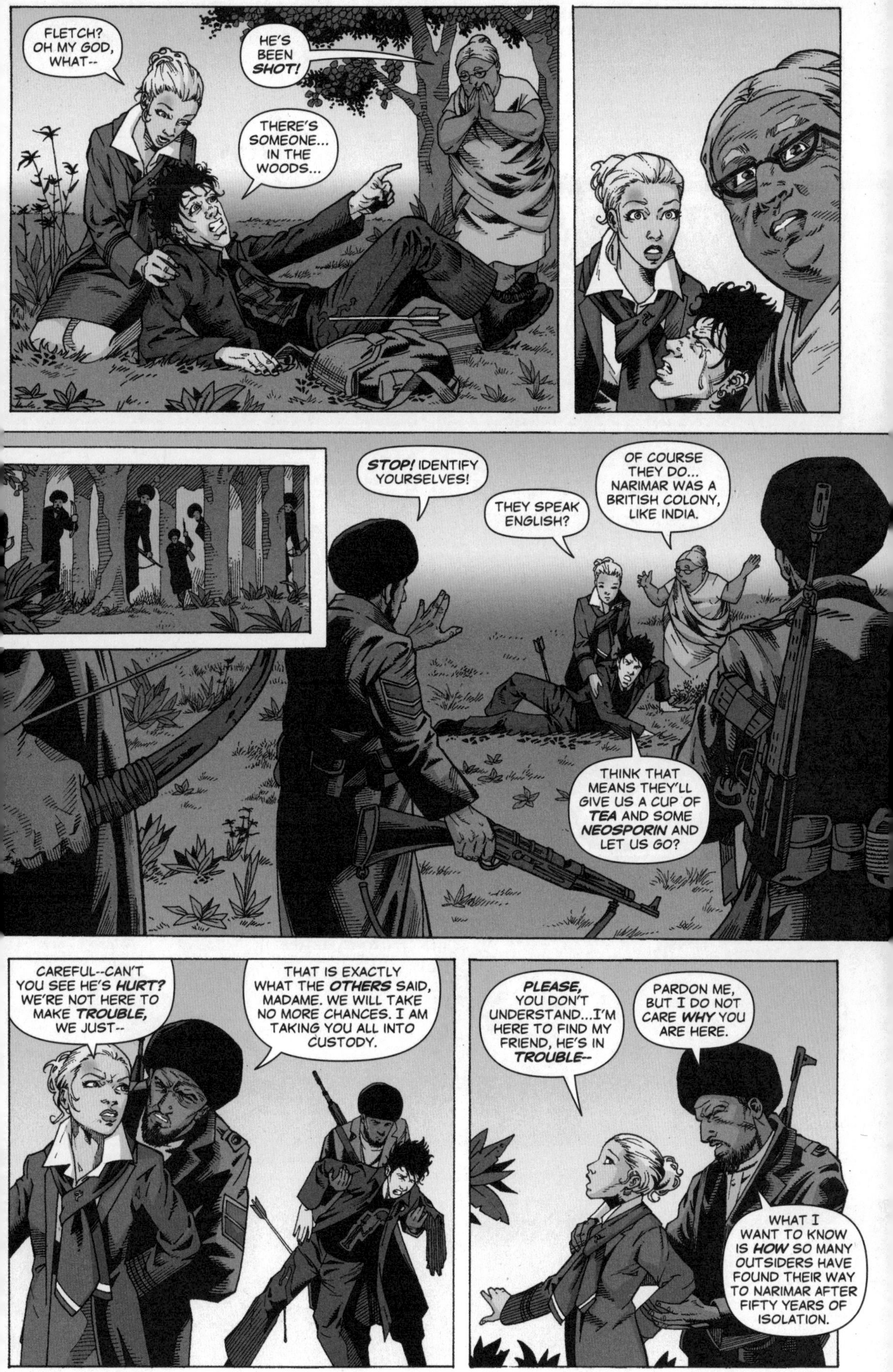
FLETCH? OH MY GOD, WHAT--
HE'S BEEN SHOT!
THERE'S SOMEONE... IN THE WOODS...
STOP! IDENTIFY YOURSELVES!
THEY SPEAK ENGLISH?
OF COURSE THEY DO... NARIMAR WAS A BRITISH COLONY, LIKE INDIA.
THINK THAT MEANS THEY'LL GIVE US A CUP OF TEA AND SOME NEOSPORIN AND LET US GO?
CAREFUL--CAN'T YOU SEE HE'S HURT? WE'RE NOT HERE TO MAKE TROUBLE, WE JUST--
THAT IS EXACTLY WHAT THE OTHERS SAID, MADAME. WE WILL TAKE NO MORE CHANCES. I AM TAKING YOU ALL INTO CUSTODY.
PLEASE, YOU DON'T UNDERSTAND...I'M HERE TO FIND MY FRIEND, HE'S IN TROUBLE--
PARDON ME, BUT I DO NOT CARE WHY YOU ARE HERE.
WHAT I WANT TO KNOW IS HOW SO MANY OUTSIDERS HAVE FOUND THEIR WAY TO NARIMAR AFTER FIFTY YEARS OF ISOLATION.

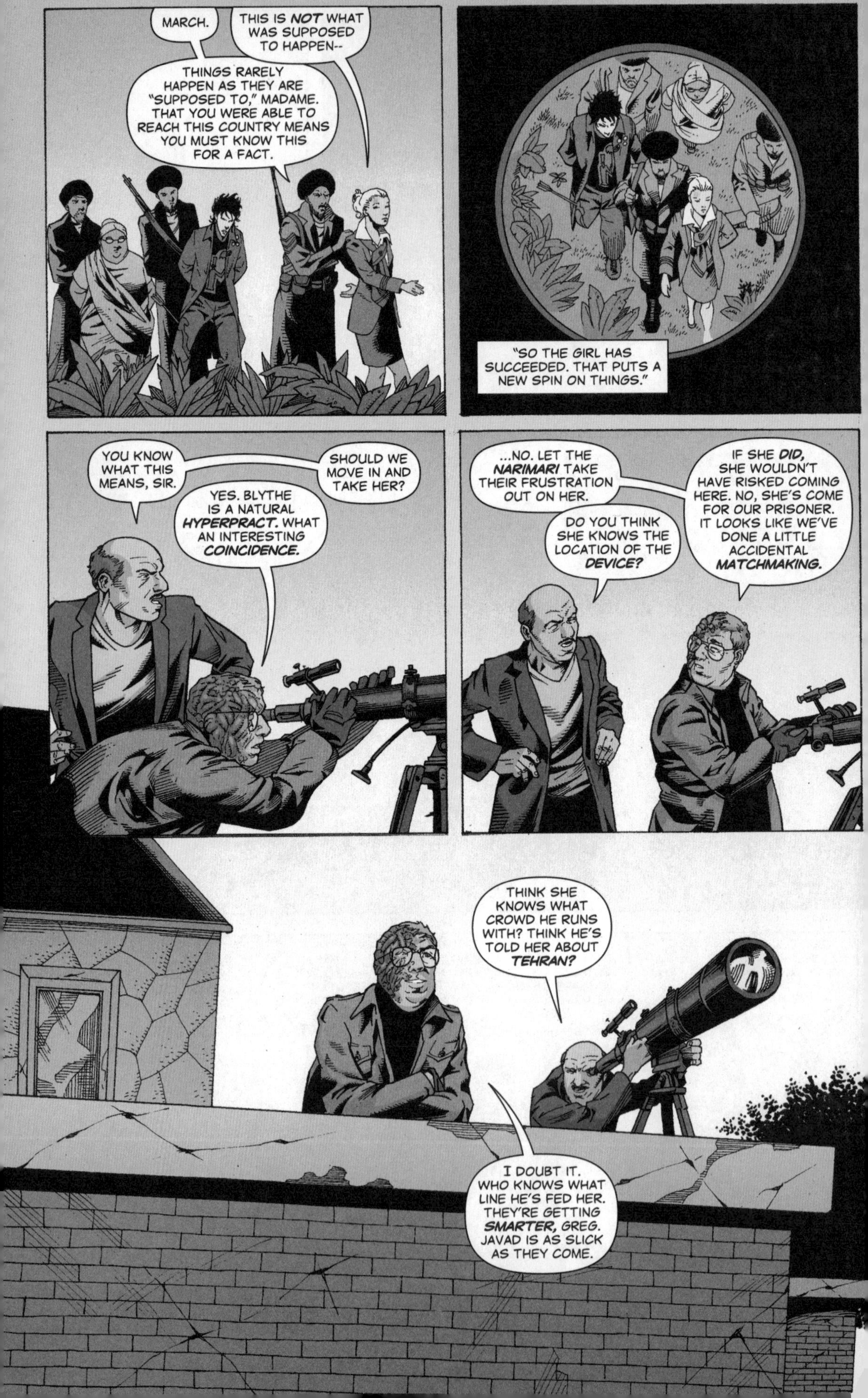
MARCH.
THIS IS NOT WHAT WAS SUPPOSED TO HAPPEN--
THINGS RARELY HAPPEN AS THEY ARE "SUPPOSED TO," MADAME. THAT YOU WERE ABLE TO REACH THIS COUNTRY MEANS YOU MUST KNOW THIS FOR A FACT.
"SO THE GIRL HAS SUCCEEDED. THAT PUTS A NEW SPIN ON THINGS."
YOU KNOW WHAT THIS MEANS, SIR.
SHOULD WE MOVE IN AND TAKE HER?
YES. BLYTHE IS A NATURAL HYPERPRACT. WHAT AN INTERESTING COINCIDENCE.
...NO. LET THE NARIMARI TAKE THEIR FRUSTRATION OUT ON HER.
DO YOU THINK SHE KNOWS THE LOCATION OF THE DEVICE?
IF SHE DID, SHE WOULDN'T HAVE RISKED COMING HERE. NO, SHE'S COME FOR OUR PRISONER. IT LOOKS LIKE WE'VE DONE A LITTLE ACCIDENTAL MATCHMAKING.
THINK SHE KNOWS WHAT CROWD HE RUNS WITH? THINK HE'S TOLD HER ABOUT TEHRAN?
I DOUBT IT. WHO KNOWS WHAT LINE HE'S FED HER. THEY'RE GETTING SMARTER, GREG. JAVAD IS AS SLICK AS THEY COME.

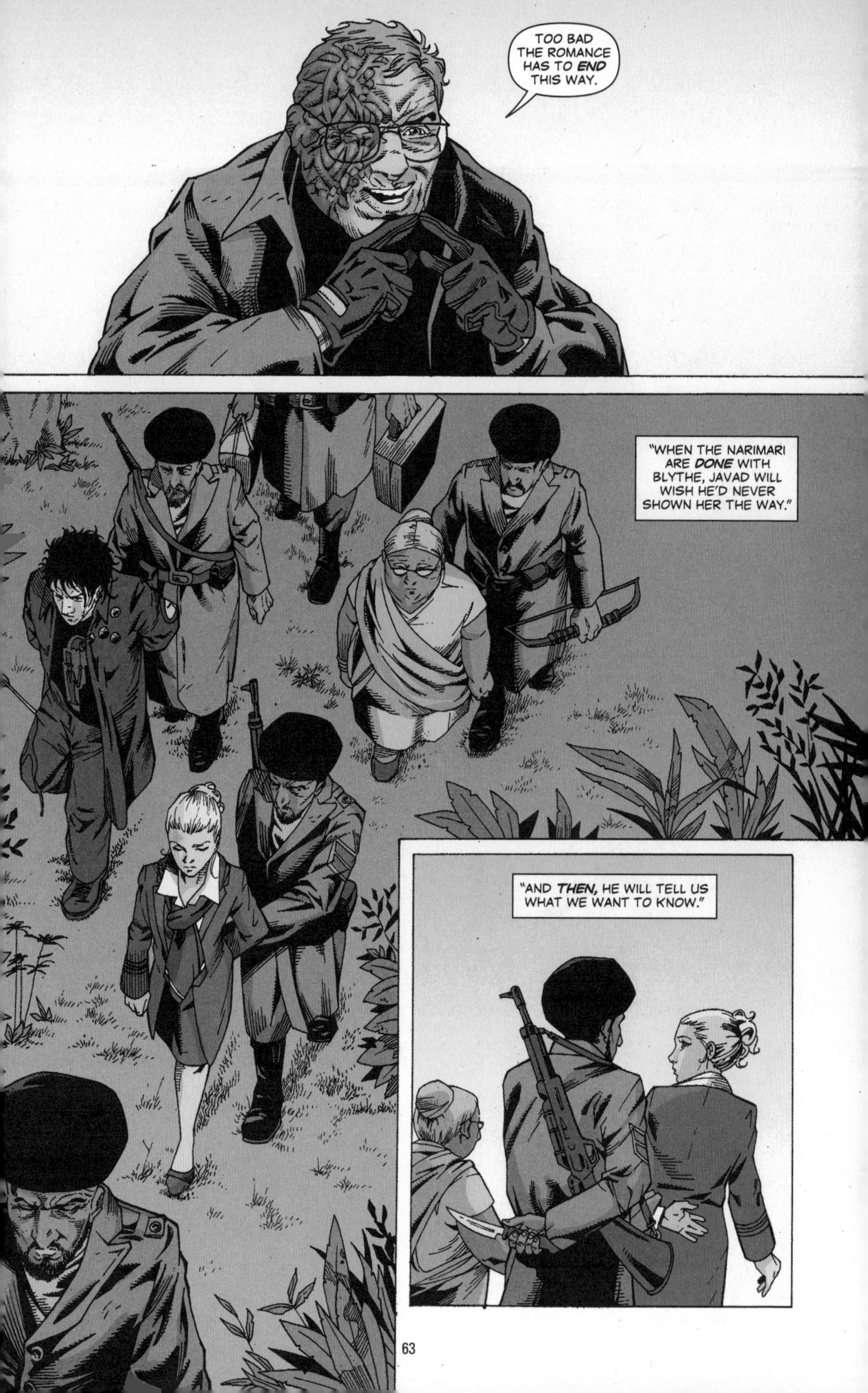
TOO BAD THE ROMANCE HAS TO END THIS WAY.
"WHEN THE NARIMARI ARE DONE WITH BLYTHE, JAVAD WILL WISH HE'D NEVER SHOWN HER THE WAY."
"AND THEN, HE WILL TELL US WHAT WE WANT TO KNOW."

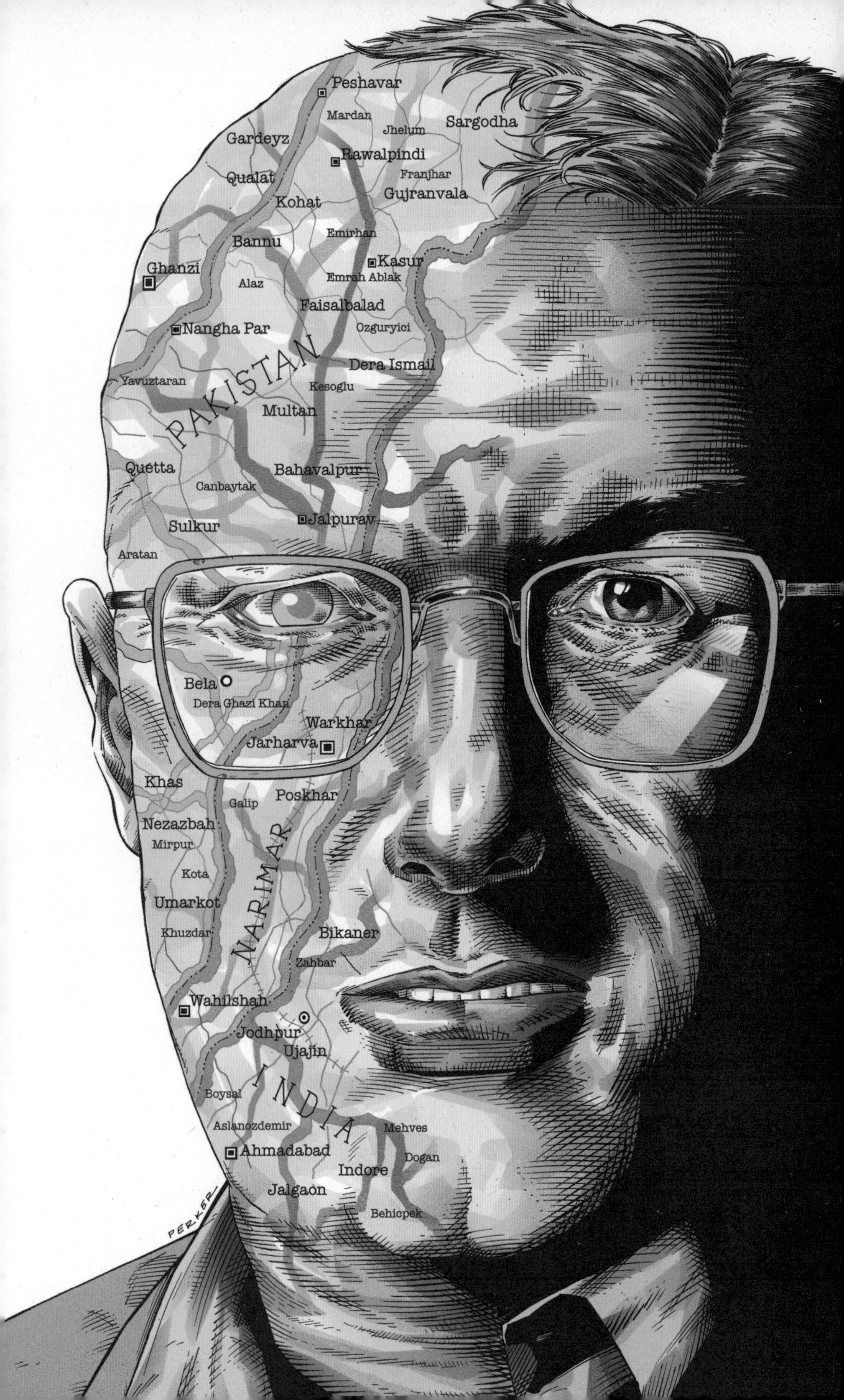
Peshavar
Mardan
Jhelum
Sargodha
Gardeyz
Rawalpindi
Franjhar
Qualat
Gujranvala
Kohat
Emirhan
Bannu
Kasur
Ghanzi
Emrah Ablak
Alaz
Faisalbalad
Nangha Par
Ozguryici
PAKISTAN
Dera Ismail
Yavuztaran
Kesoglu
Multan
Quetta
Bahavalpur
Canbaytak
Jalpurav
Sulkur
Aratan
Bela
Dera Ghazi Khan
Warkhar
Jarharva
Khas
Poskhar
Galip
Nezazbah
Mirpur
NARIMAR
Kota
Umarkot
Khuzdar
Bikaner
Zahbar
Wahilshah
Jodhpur
Ujajin
INDIA
Boysal
Aslanozdemir
Mehves
Ahmadabad
Dogan
Indore
Jalgaon
Behicpek
PERKER

CHAPTER 3

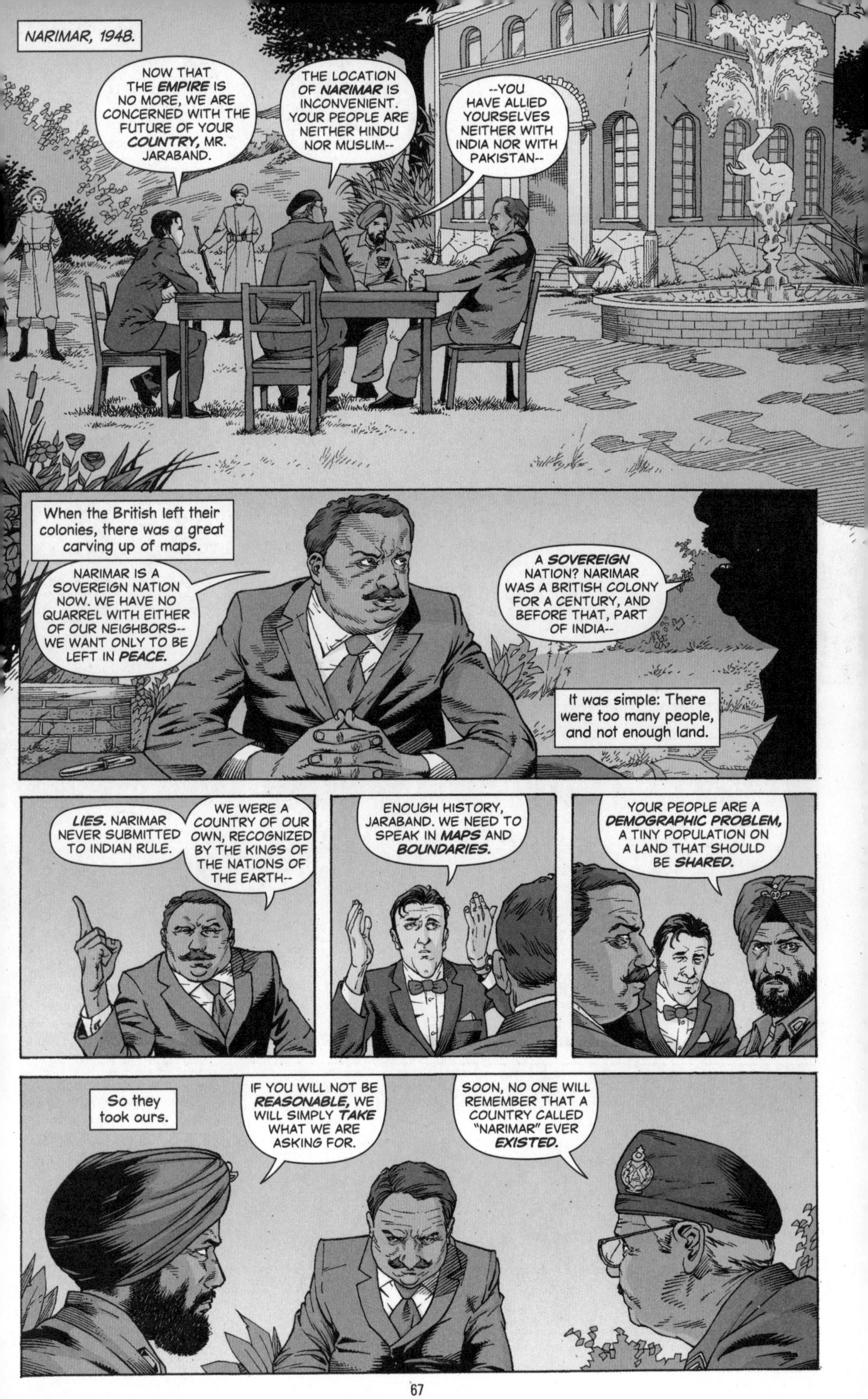
NARIMAR, 1948.
NOW THAT THE EMPIRE IS NO MORE, WE ARE CONCERNED WITH THE FUTURE OF YOUR COUNTRY, MR. JARABAND.
THE LOCATION OF NARIMAR IS INCONVENIENT. YOUR PEOPLE ARE NEITHER HINDU NOR MUSLIM--
--YOU HAVE ALLIED YOURSELVES NEITHER WITH INDIA NOR WITH PAKISTAN--
When the British left their colonies, there was a great carving up of maps.
NARIMAR IS A SOVEREIGN NATION NOW. WE HAVE NO QUARREL WITH EITHER OF OUR NEIGHBORS-- WE WANT ONLY TO BE LEFT IN PEACE.
A SOVEREIGN NATION? NARIMAR WAS A BRITISH COLONY FOR A CENTURY, AND BEFORE THAT, PART OF INDIA--
It was simple: There were too many people, and not enough land.
LIES. NARIMAR NEVER SUBMITTED TO INDIAN RULE.
WE WERE A COUNTRY OF OUR OWN, RECOGNIZED BY THE KINGS OF THE NATIONS OF THE EARTH--
ENOUGH HISTORY, JARABAND. WE NEED TO SPEAK IN MAPS AND BOUNDARIES.
YOUR PEOPLE ARE A DEMOGRAPHIC PROBLEM, A TINY POPULATION ON A LAND THAT SHOULD BE SHARED.
So they took ours.
IF YOU WILL NOT BE REASONABLE, WE WILL SIMPLY TAKE WHAT WE ARE ASKING FOR.
SOON, NO ONE WILL REMEMBER THAT A COUNTRY CALLED "NARIMAR" EVER EXISTED.

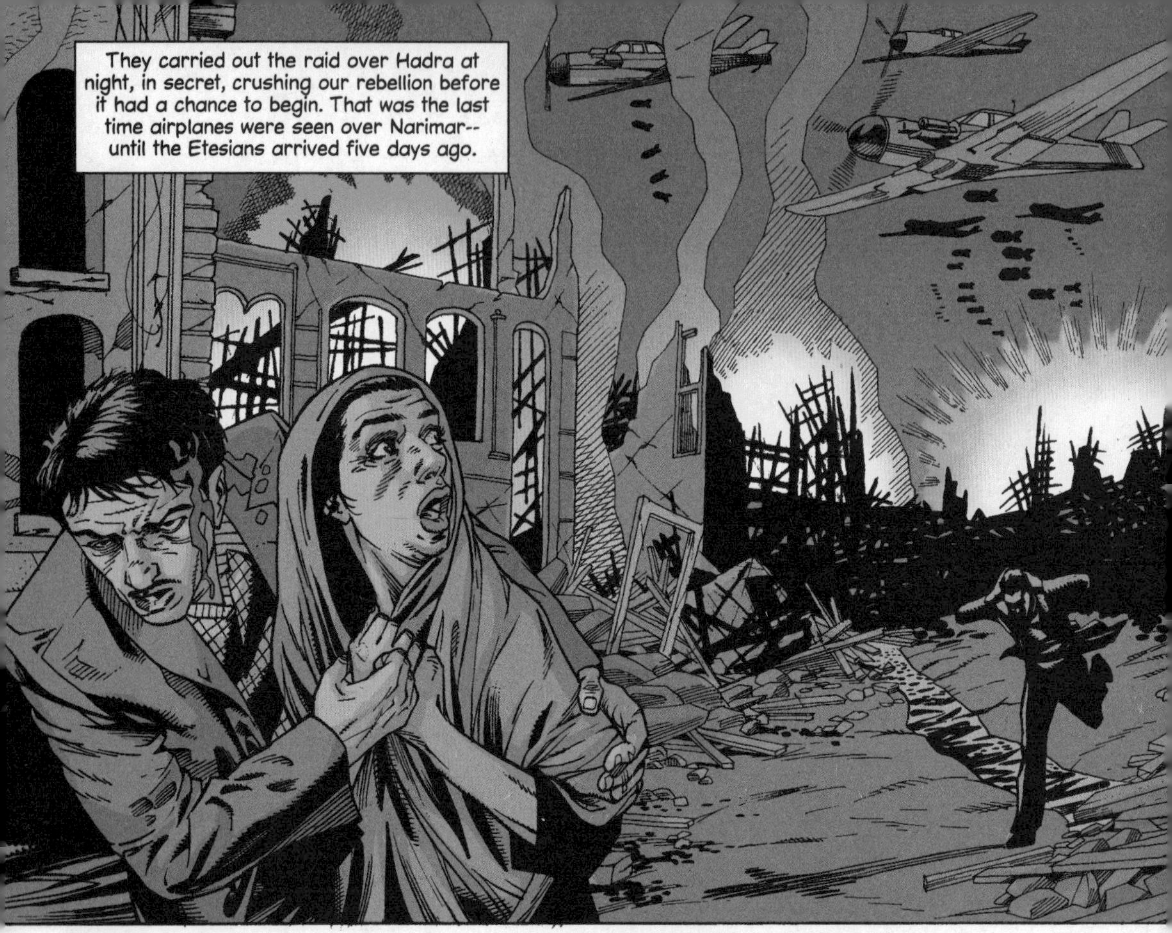
They carried out the raid over Hadra at night, in secret, crushing our rebellion before it had a chance to begin. That was the last time airplanes were seen over Narimar-- until the Etesians arrived five days ago.

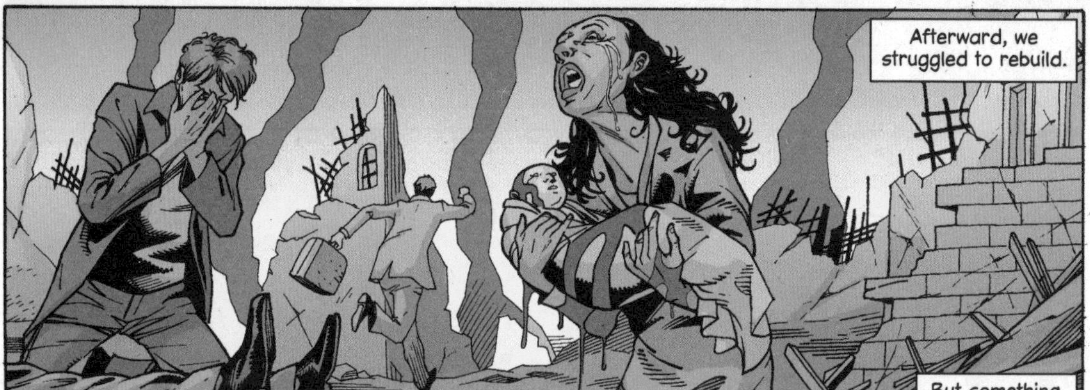
Afterward, we struggled to rebuild.
But something had *changed.*

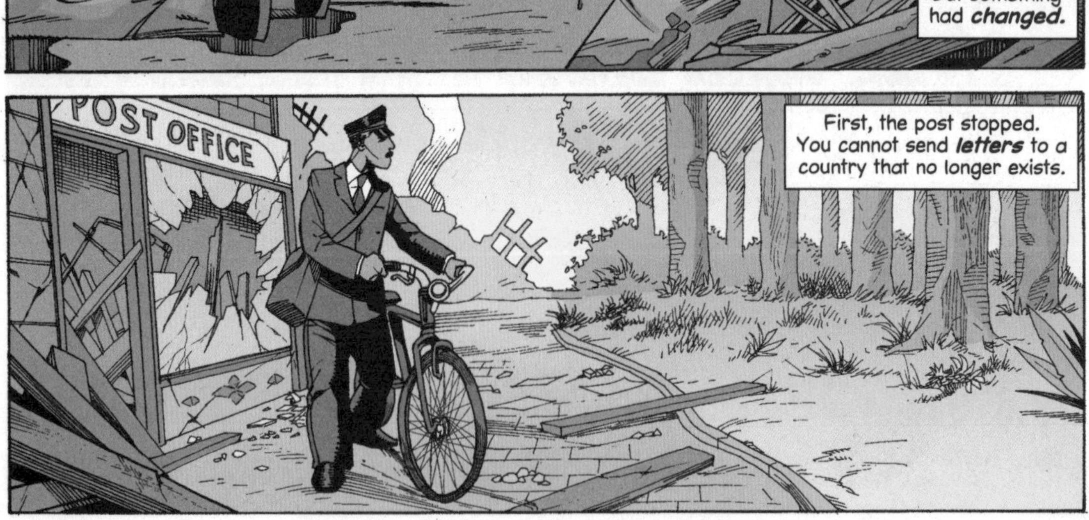
POST OFFICE
First, the post stopped. You cannot send *letters* to a country that no longer exists.

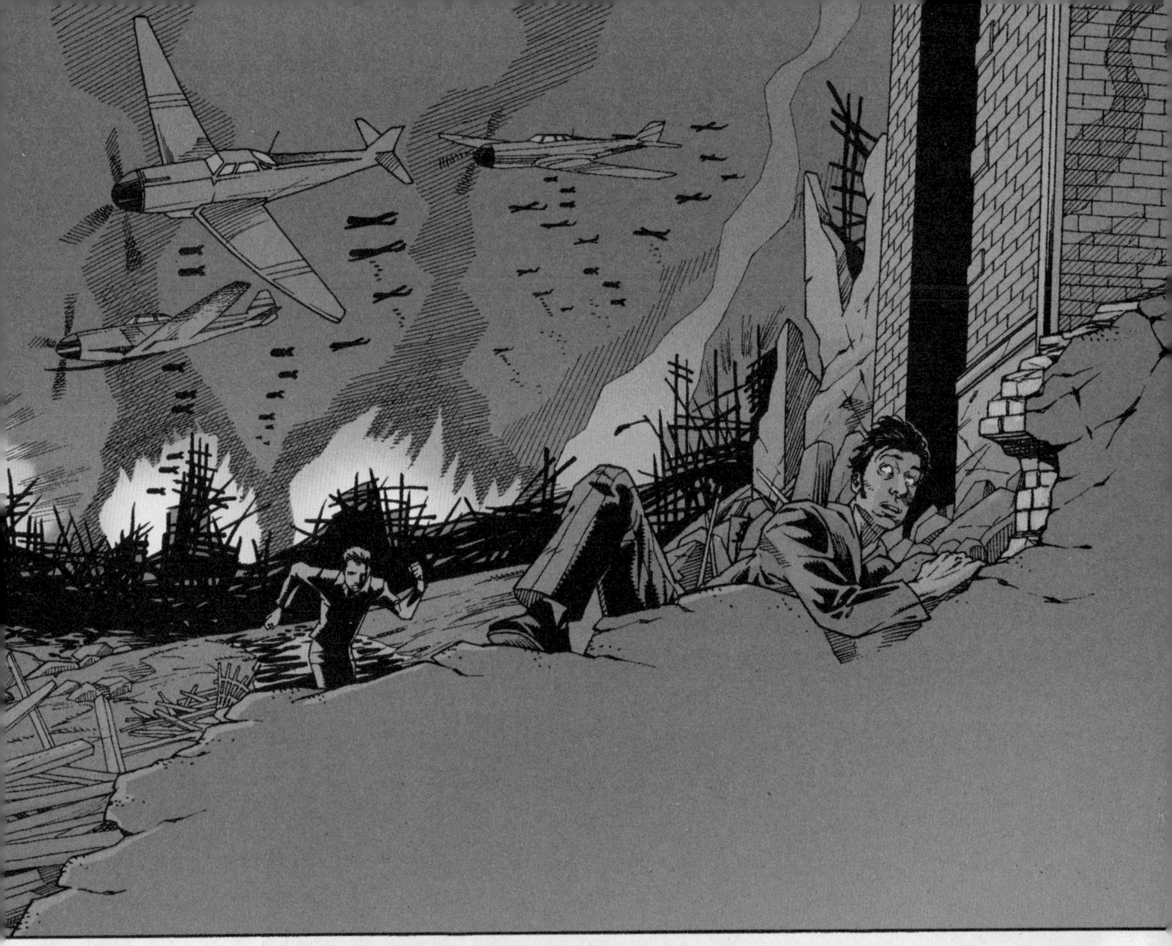

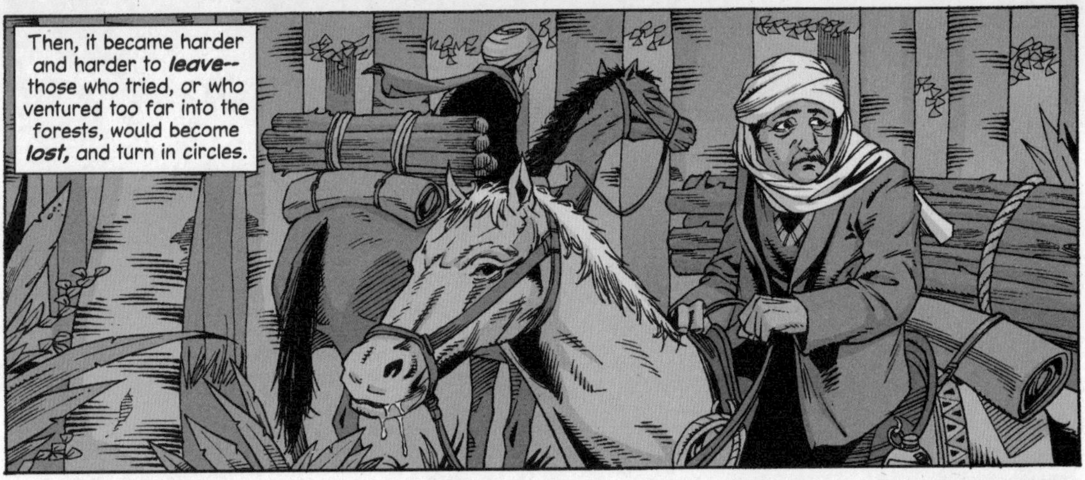
Then, it became harder and harder to *leave*--those who tried, or who ventured too far into the forests, would become *lost*, and turn in circles.

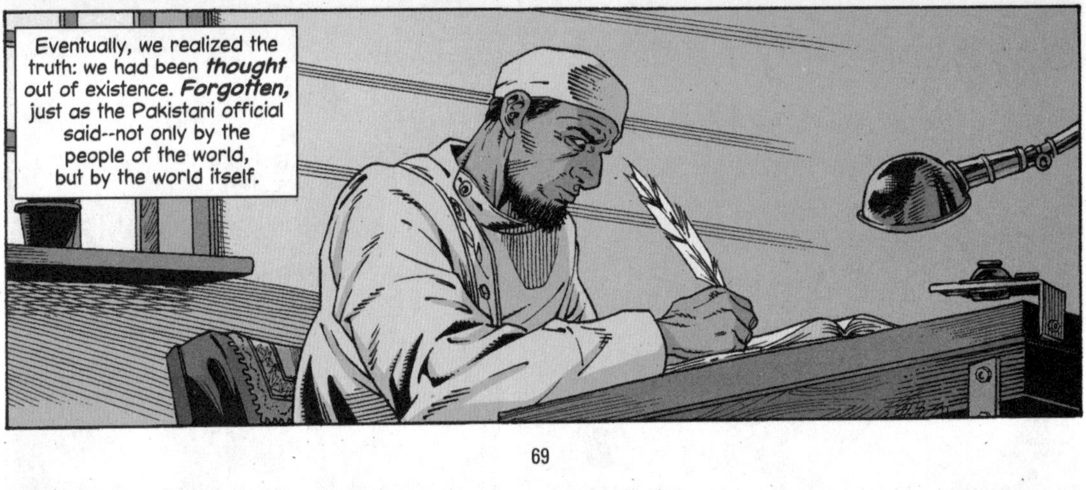
Eventually, we realized the truth: we had been *thought* out of existence. *Forgotten*, just as the Pakistani official said--not only by the people of the world, but by the world itself.

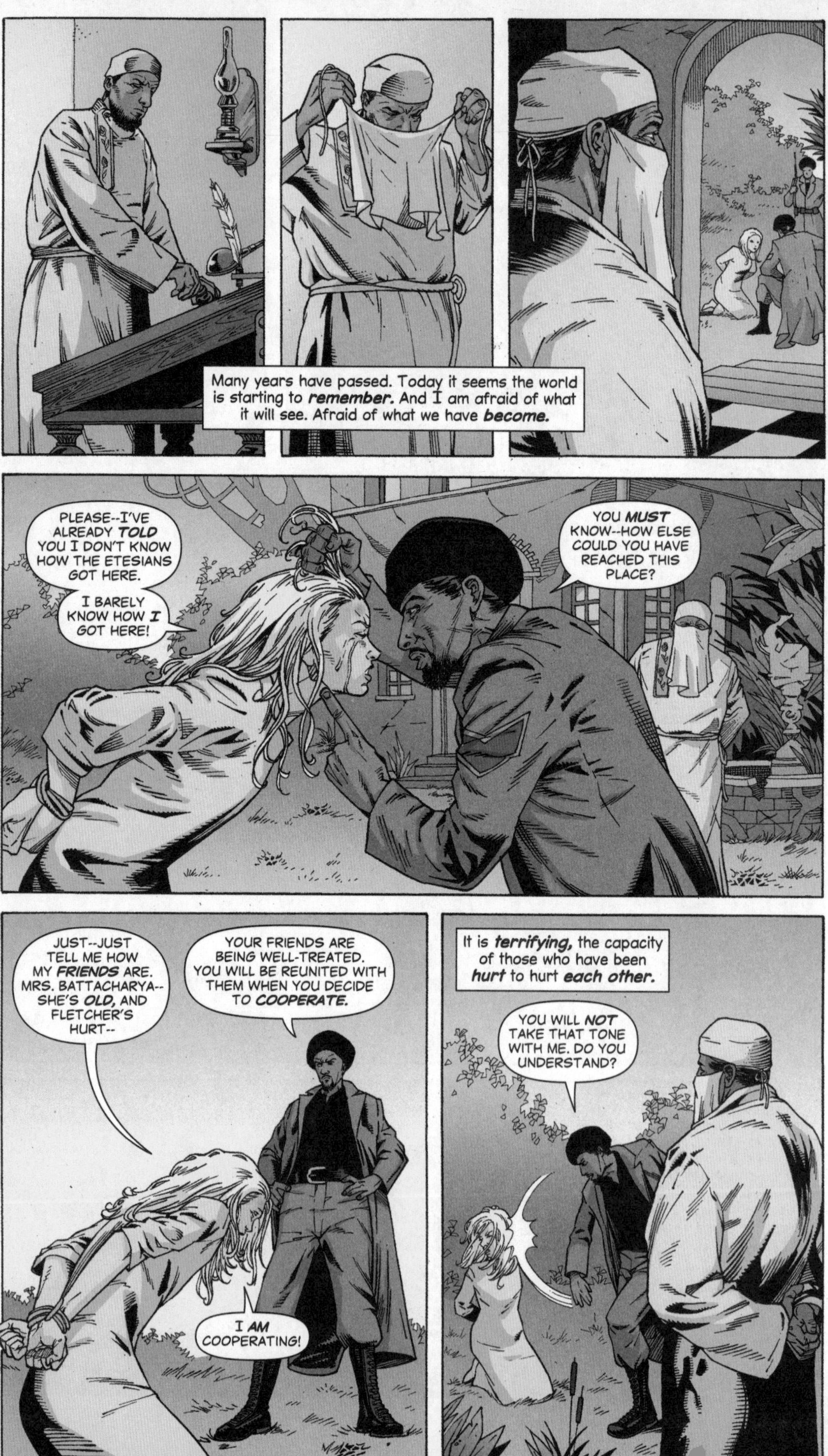

Many years have passed. Today it seems the world is starting to *remember.* And I am afraid of what it will see. Afraid of what we have *become.*
PLEASE--I'VE ALREADY *TOLD* YOU I DON'T KNOW HOW THE ETESIANS GOT HERE.
I BARELY KNOW HOW *I* GOT HERE!
YOU *MUST* KNOW--HOW ELSE COULD YOU HAVE REACHED THIS PLACE?
JUST--JUST TELL ME HOW MY *FRIENDS* ARE. MRS. BATTACHARYA--SHE'S *OLD,* AND FLETCHER'S HURT--
YOUR FRIENDS ARE BEING WELL-TREATED. YOU WILL BE REUNITED WITH THEM WHEN YOU DECIDE TO *COOPERATE.*
I *AM* COOPERATING!
It is *terrifying,* the capacity of those who have been *hurt* to hurt *each other.*
YOU WILL *NOT* TAKE THAT TONE WITH ME. DO YOU UNDERSTAND?

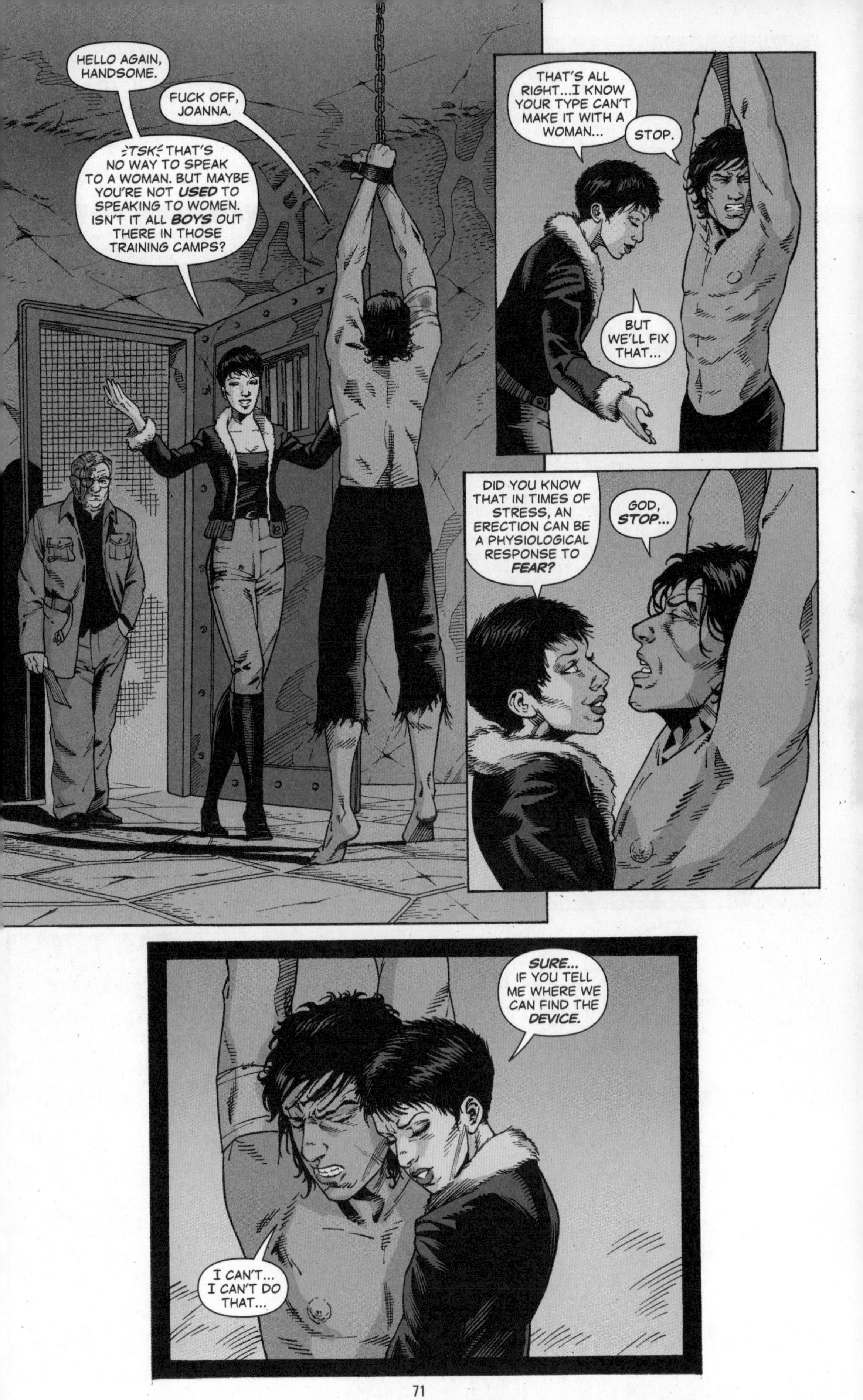
HELLO AGAIN, HANDSOME.
FUCK OFF, JOANNA.
TSK THAT'S NO WAY TO SPEAK TO A WOMAN. BUT MAYBE YOU'RE NOT USED TO SPEAKING TO WOMEN. ISN'T IT ALL BOYS OUT THERE IN THOSE TRAINING CAMPS?
THAT'S ALL RIGHT...I KNOW YOUR TYPE CAN'T MAKE IT WITH A WOMAN...
STOP.
BUT WE'LL FIX THAT...
DID YOU KNOW THAT IN TIMES OF STRESS, AN ERECTION CAN BE A PHYSIOLOGICAL RESPONSE TO FEAR?
GOD, STOP...
SURE... IF YOU TELL ME WHERE WE CAN FIND THE DEVICE.
I CAN'T... I CAN'T DO THAT...

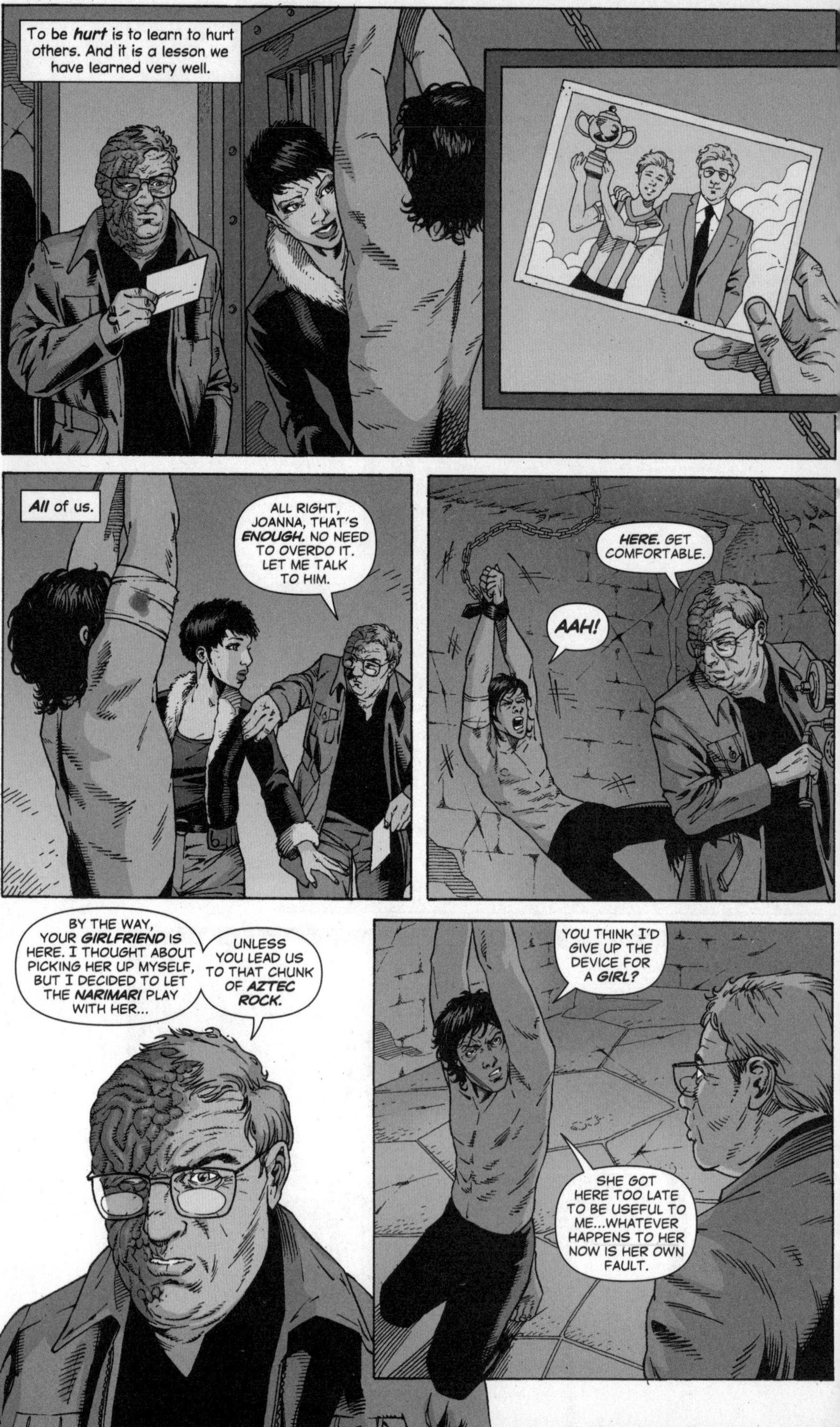
To be **hurt** is to learn to hurt others. And it is a lesson we have learned very well.
All of us.
ALL RIGHT, JOANNA, THAT'S **ENOUGH.** NO NEED TO OVERDO IT. LET ME TALK TO HIM.
HERE. GET COMFORTABLE.
AAH!
BY THE WAY, YOUR **GIRLFRIEND** IS HERE. I THOUGHT ABOUT PICKING HER UP MYSELF, BUT I DECIDED TO LET THE **NARIMARI** PLAY WITH HER...
UNLESS YOU LEAD US TO THAT CHUNK OF **AZTEC ROCK.**
YOU THINK I'D GIVE UP THE DEVICE FOR A **GIRL?**
SHE GOT HERE TOO LATE TO BE USEFUL TO ME...WHATEVER HAPPENS TO HER NOW IS HER OWN FAULT.

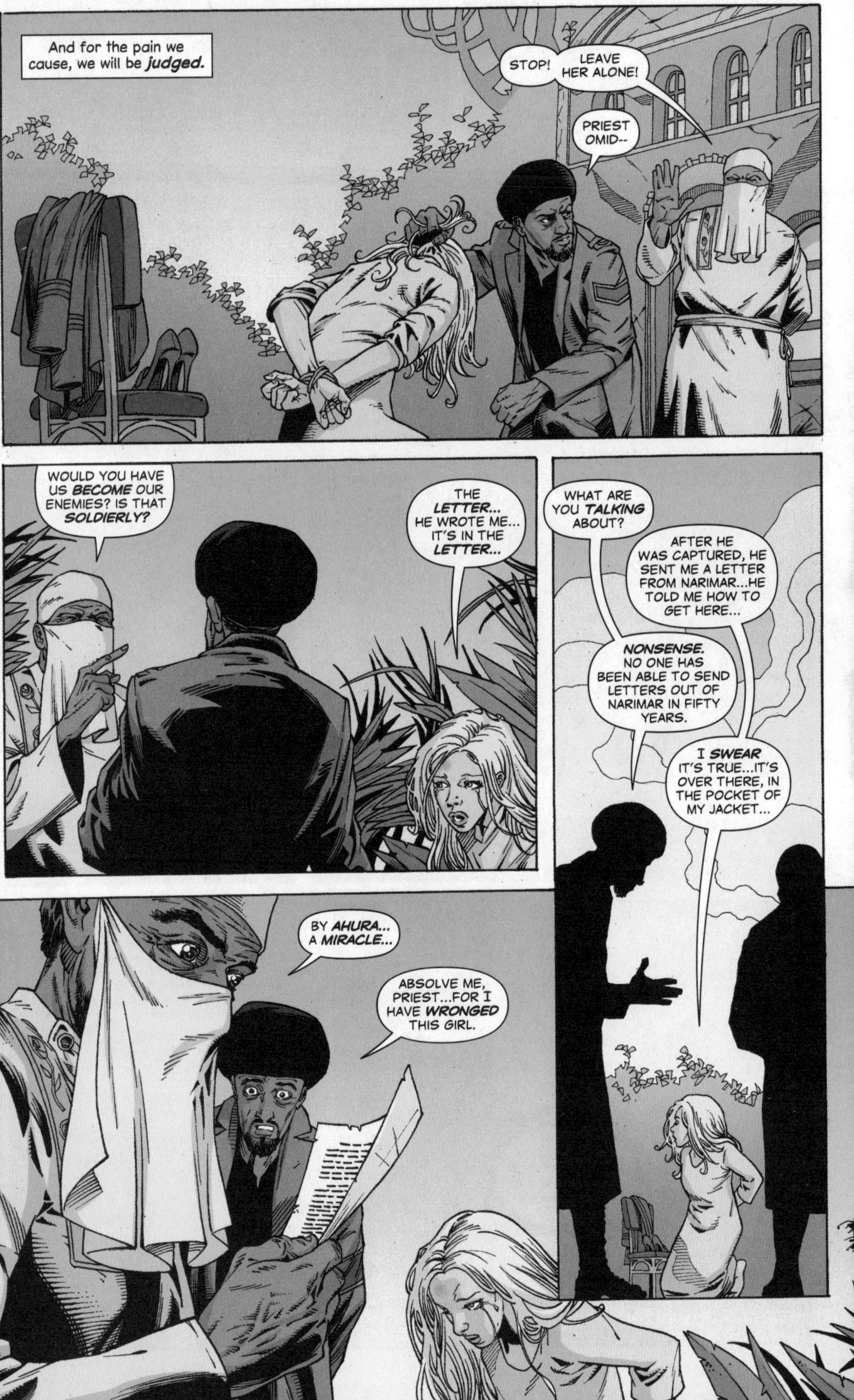
And for the pain we cause, we will be ***judged.***
STOP!
LEAVE HER ALONE!
PRIEST OMID--
WOULD YOU HAVE US ***BECOME*** OUR ENEMIES? IS THAT ***SOLDIERLY?***
THE ***LETTER...*** HE WROTE ME... IT'S IN THE ***LETTER...***
WHAT ARE YOU ***TALKING*** ABOUT?
AFTER HE WAS CAPTURED, HE SENT ME A LETTER FROM NARIMAR...HE TOLD ME HOW TO GET HERE...
NONSENSE. NO ONE HAS BEEN ABLE TO SEND LETTERS OUT OF NARIMAR IN FIFTY YEARS.
I ***SWEAR*** IT'S TRUE...IT'S OVER THERE, IN THE POCKET OF MY JACKET...
BY ***AHURA...*** A ***MIRACLE...***
ABSOLVE ME, PRIEST...FOR I HAVE ***WRONGED*** THIS GIRL.

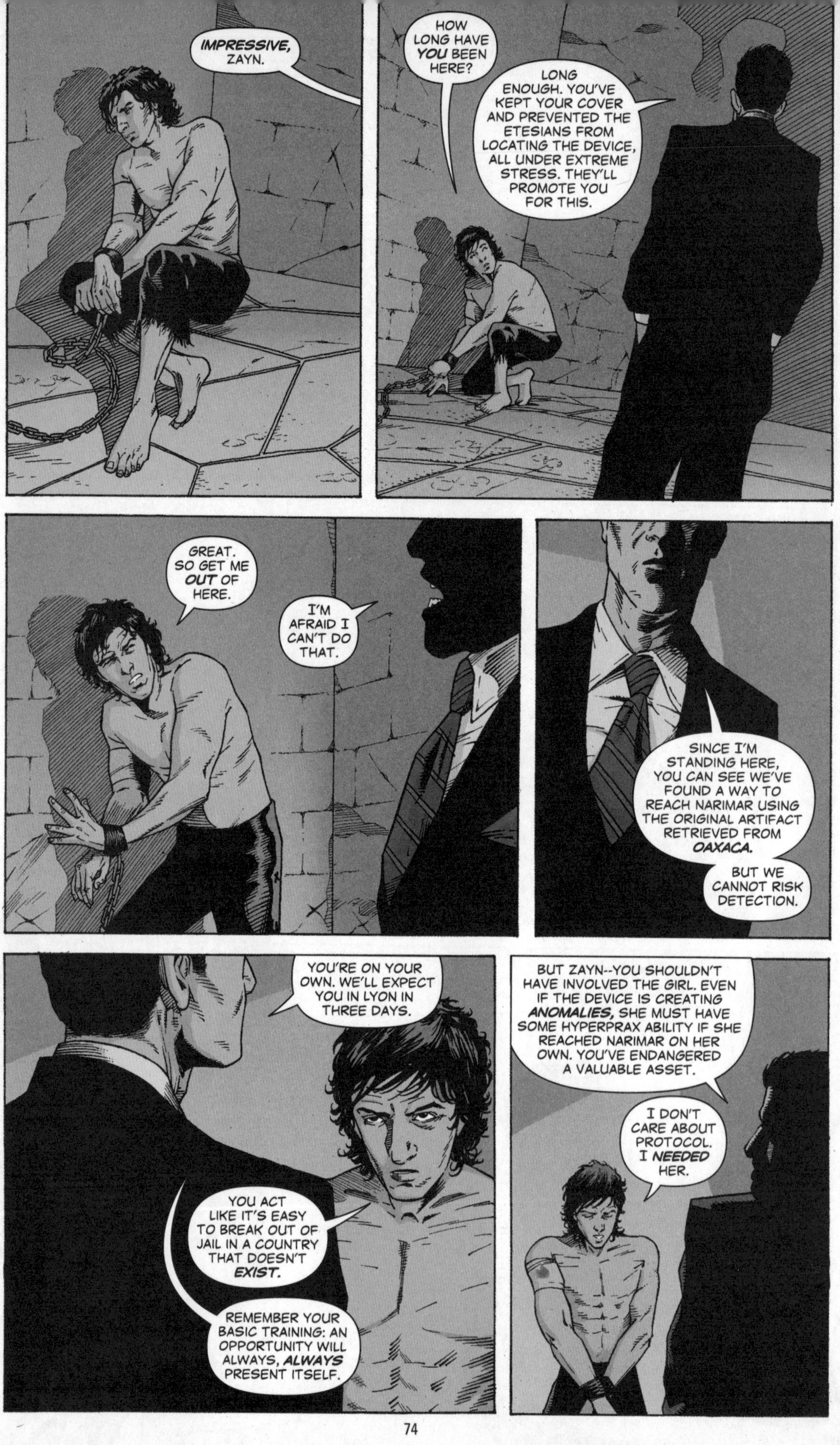
IMPRESSIVE, ZAYN.
HOW LONG HAVE YOU BEEN HERE?
LONG ENOUGH. YOU'VE KEPT YOUR COVER AND PREVENTED THE ETESIANS FROM LOCATING THE DEVICE, ALL UNDER EXTREME STRESS. THEY'LL PROMOTE YOU FOR THIS.
GREAT. SO GET ME OUT OF HERE.
I'M AFRAID I CAN'T DO THAT.
SINCE I'M STANDING HERE, YOU CAN SEE WE'VE FOUND A WAY TO REACH NARIMAR USING THE ORIGINAL ARTIFACT RETRIEVED FROM OAXACA.
BUT WE CANNOT RISK DETECTION.
YOU'RE ON YOUR OWN. WE'LL EXPECT YOU IN LYON IN THREE DAYS.
YOU ACT LIKE IT'S EASY TO BREAK OUT OF JAIL IN A COUNTRY THAT DOESN'T EXIST.
REMEMBER YOUR BASIC TRAINING: AN OPPORTUNITY WILL ALWAYS, ALWAYS PRESENT ITSELF.
BUT ZAYN--YOU SHOULDN'T HAVE INVOLVED THE GIRL. EVEN IF THE DEVICE IS CREATING ANOMALIES, SHE MUST HAVE SOME HYPERPRAX ABILITY IF SHE REACHED NARIMAR ON HER OWN. YOU'VE ENDANGERED A VALUABLE ASSET.
I DON'T CARE ABOUT PROTOCOL. I NEEDED HER.

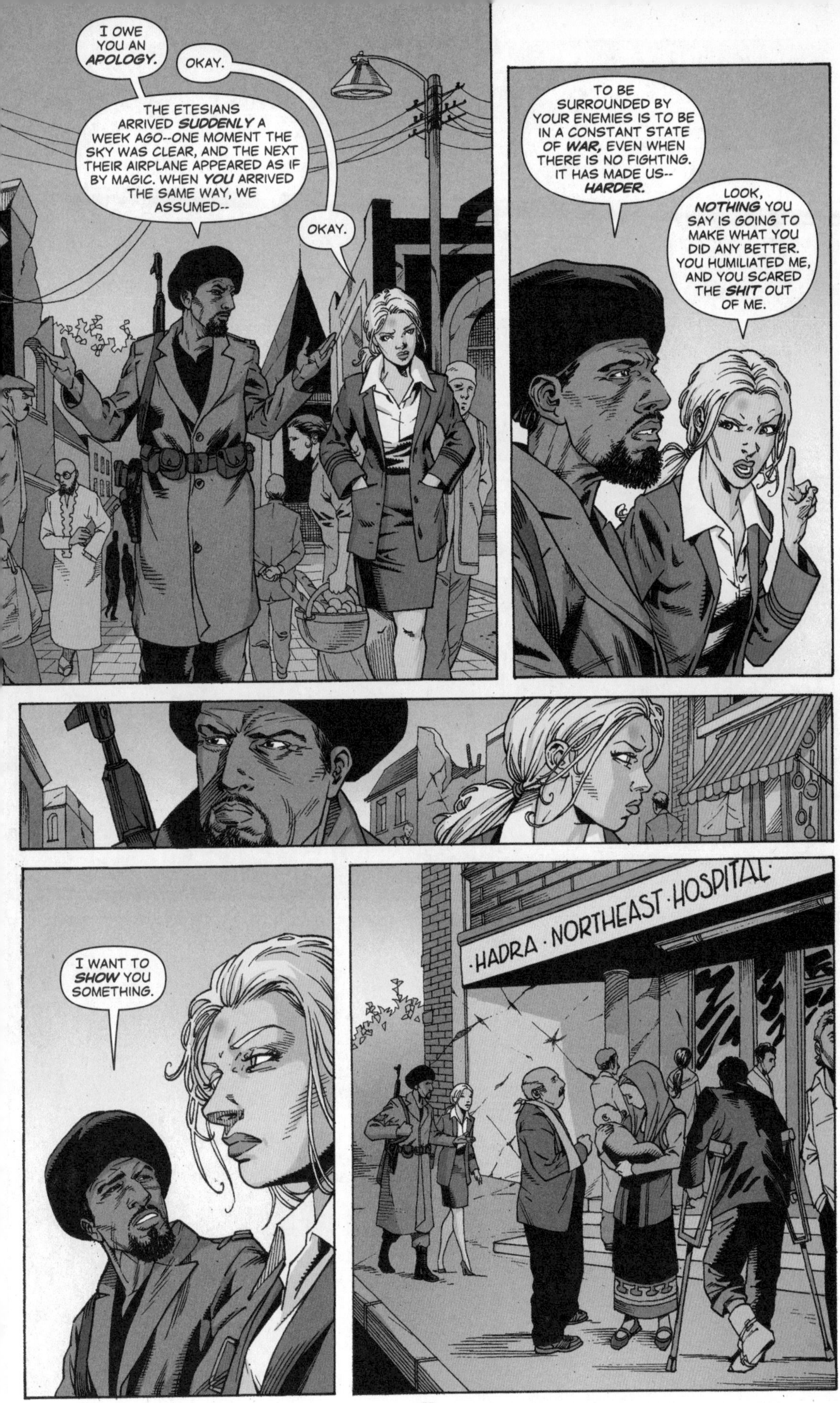
I OWE YOU AN APOLOGY.
OKAY.
THE ETESIANS ARRIVED SUDDENLY A WEEK AGO--ONE MOMENT THE SKY WAS CLEAR, AND THE NEXT THEIR AIRPLANE APPEARED AS IF BY MAGIC. WHEN YOU ARRIVED THE SAME WAY, WE ASSUMED--
OKAY.
TO BE SURROUNDED BY YOUR ENEMIES IS TO BE IN A CONSTANT STATE OF WAR, EVEN WHEN THERE IS NO FIGHTING. IT HAS MADE US-- HARDER.
LOOK, NOTHING YOU SAY IS GOING TO MAKE WHAT YOU DID ANY BETTER. YOU HUMILIATED ME, AND YOU SCARED THE SHIT OUT OF ME.
I WANT TO SHOW YOU SOMETHING.
·HADRA · NORTHEAST · HOSPITAL·

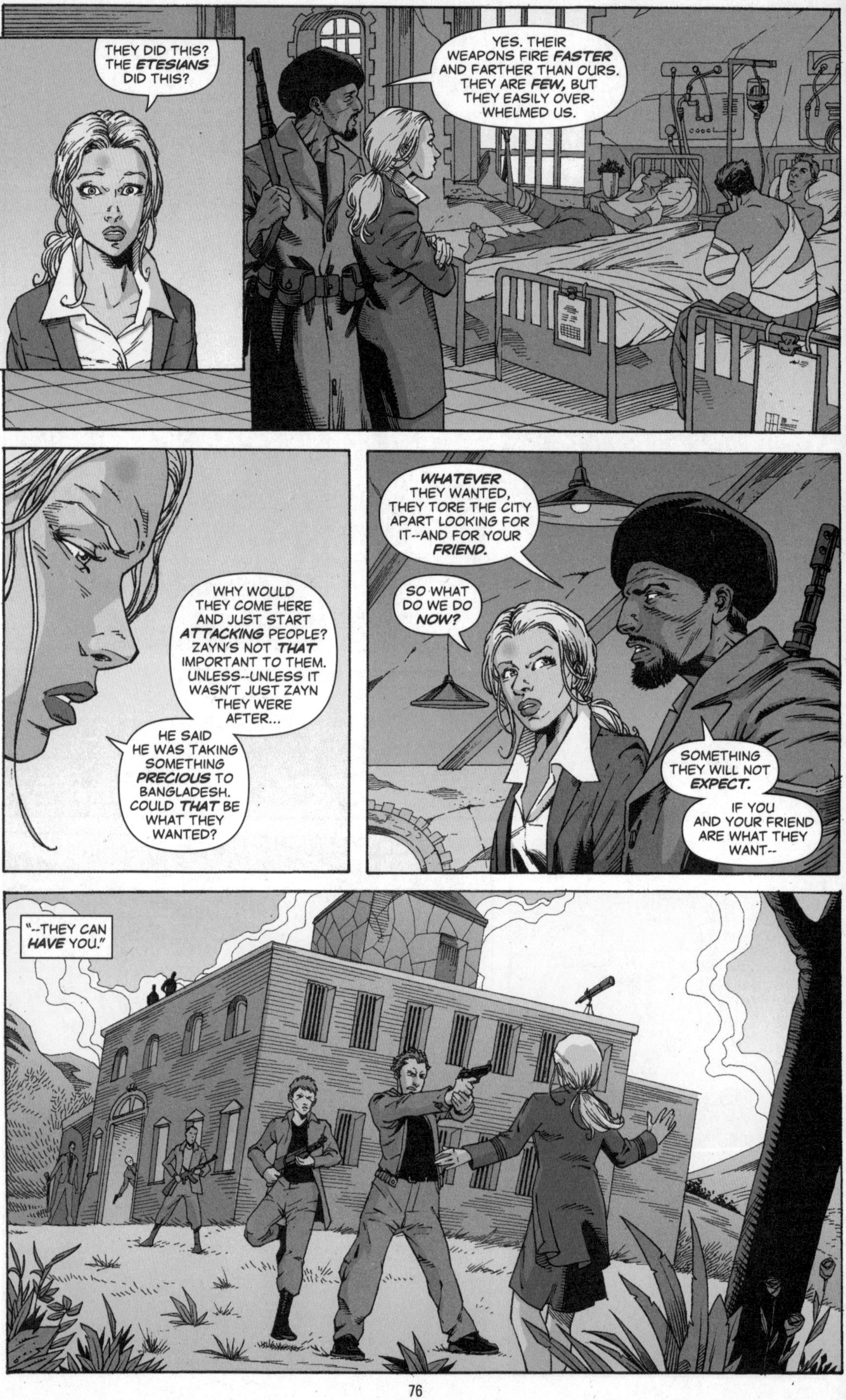
THEY DID THIS? THE ETESIANS DID THIS?
YES. THEIR WEAPONS FIRE FASTER AND FARTHER THAN OURS. THEY ARE FEW, BUT THEY EASILY OVER-WHELMED US.
WHY WOULD THEY COME HERE AND JUST START ATTACKING PEOPLE? ZAYN'S NOT THAT IMPORTANT TO THEM. UNLESS--UNLESS IT WASN'T JUST ZAYN THEY WERE AFTER...
HE SAID HE WAS TAKING SOMETHING PRECIOUS TO BANGLADESH. COULD THAT BE WHAT THEY WANTED?
WHATEVER THEY WANTED, THEY TORE THE CITY APART LOOKING FOR IT--AND FOR YOUR FRIEND.
SO WHAT DO WE DO NOW?
SOMETHING THEY WILL NOT EXPECT.
IF YOU AND YOUR FRIEND ARE WHAT THEY WANT--
"--THEY CAN HAVE YOU."

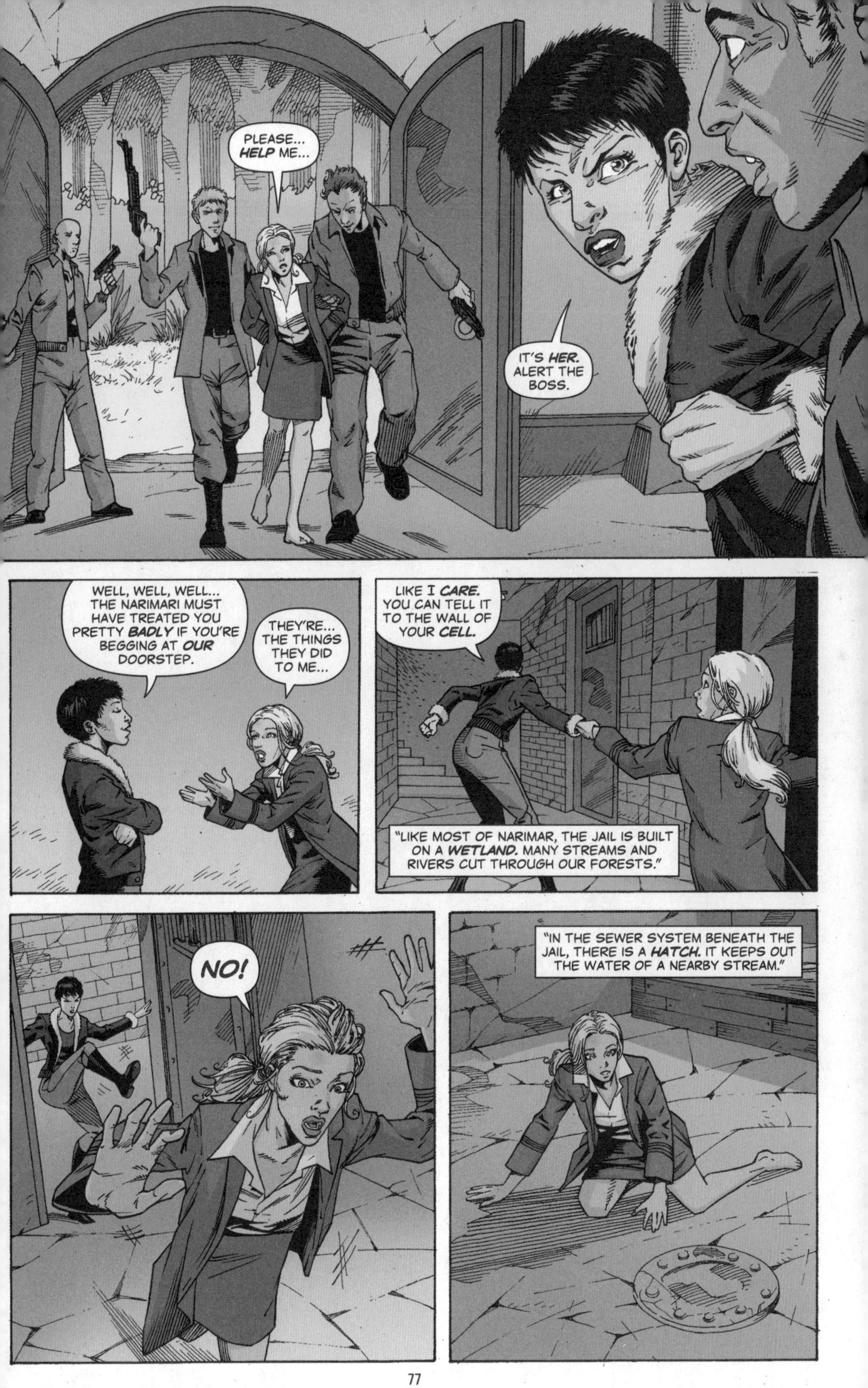
PLEASE... HELP ME...
IT'S HER. ALERT THE BOSS.
WELL, WELL, WELL... THE NARIMARI MUST HAVE TREATED YOU PRETTY BADLY IF YOU'RE BEGGING AT OUR DOORSTEP.
THEY'RE... THE THINGS THEY DID TO ME...
LIKE I CARE. YOU CAN TELL IT TO THE WALL OF YOUR CELL.
"LIKE MOST OF NARIMAR, THE JAIL IS BUILT ON A WETLAND. MANY STREAMS AND RIVERS CUT THROUGH OUR FORESTS."
NO!
"IN THE SEWER SYSTEM BENEATH THE JAIL, THERE IS A HATCH. IT KEEPS OUT THE WATER OF A NEARBY STREAM."

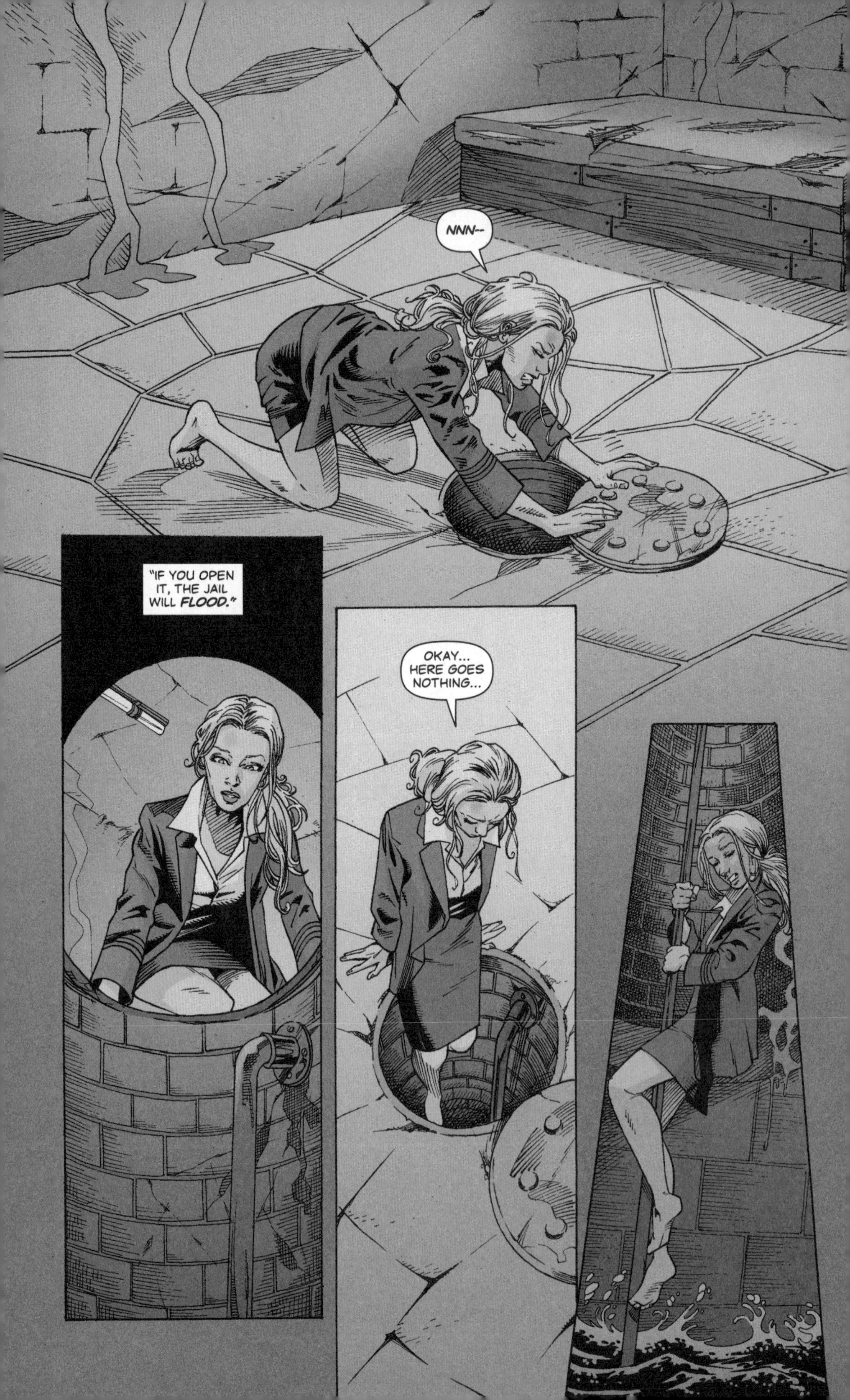
NNN--
"IF YOU OPEN IT, THE JAIL WILL FLOOD."
OKAY... HERE GOES NOTHING...

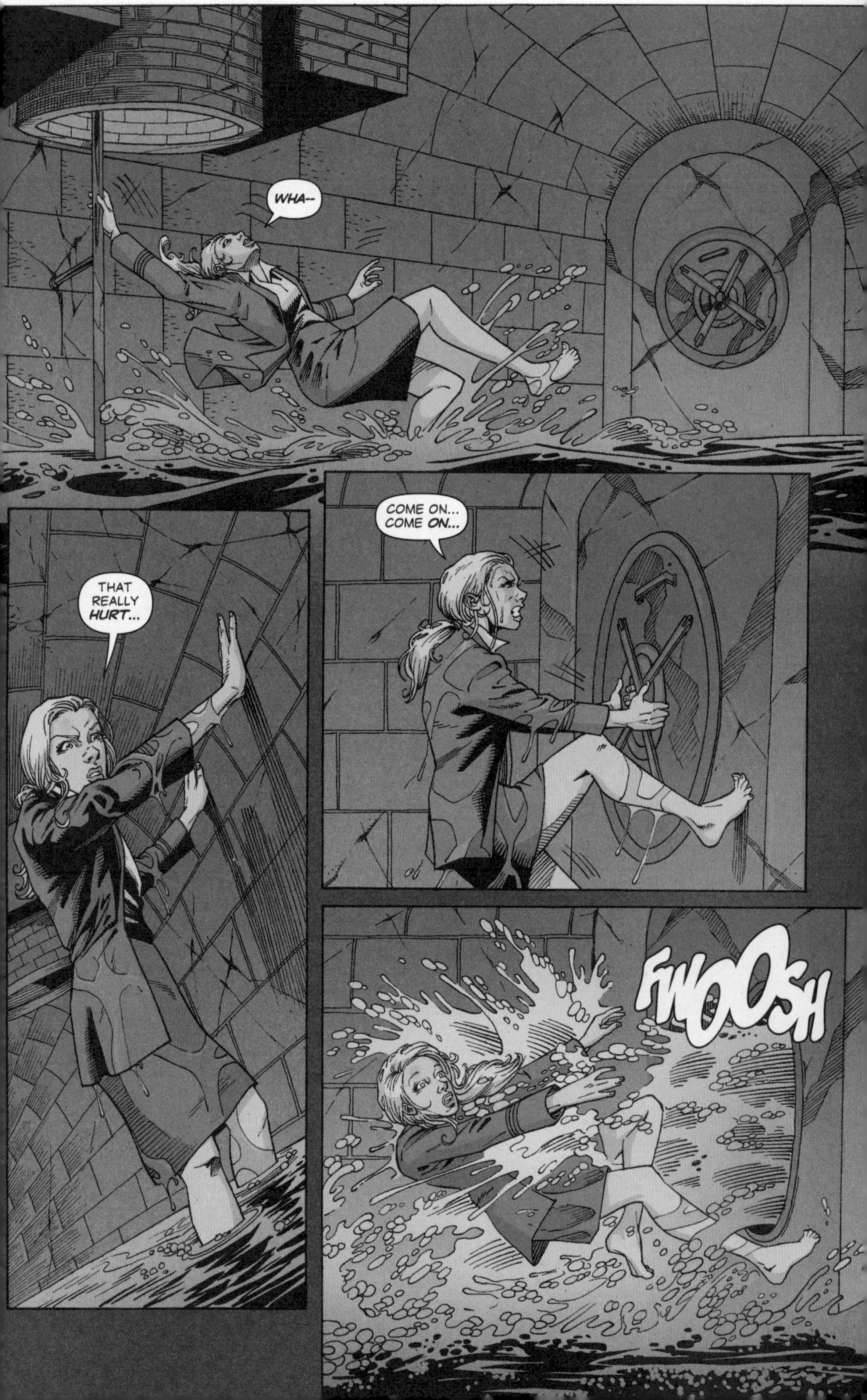
WHA--
THAT REALLY HURT...
COME ON... COME ON...
FWOOSH

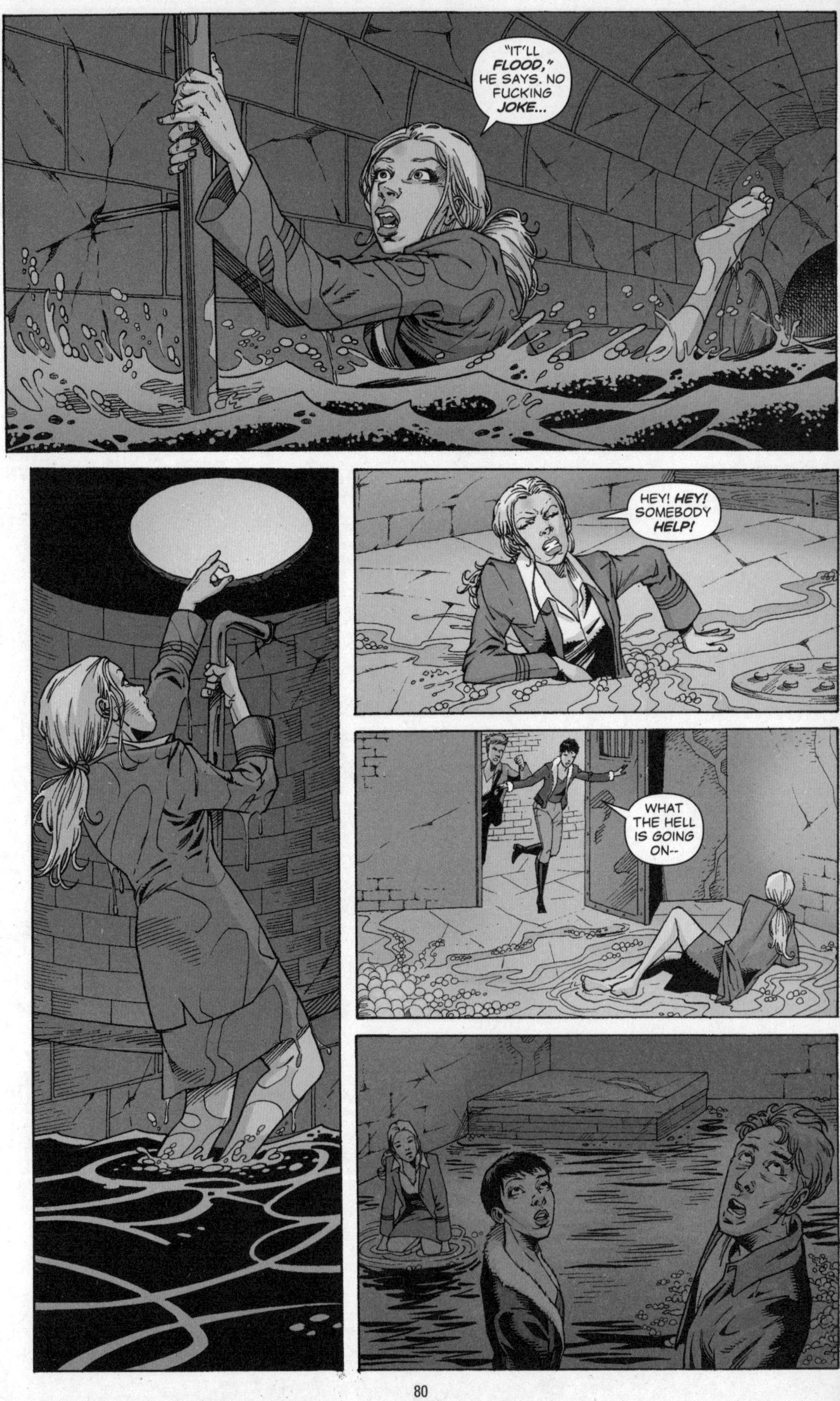
"IT'LL FLOOD," HE SAYS. NO FUCKING JOKE...
HEY! HEY! SOMEBODY HELP!
WHAT THE HELL IS GOING ON--

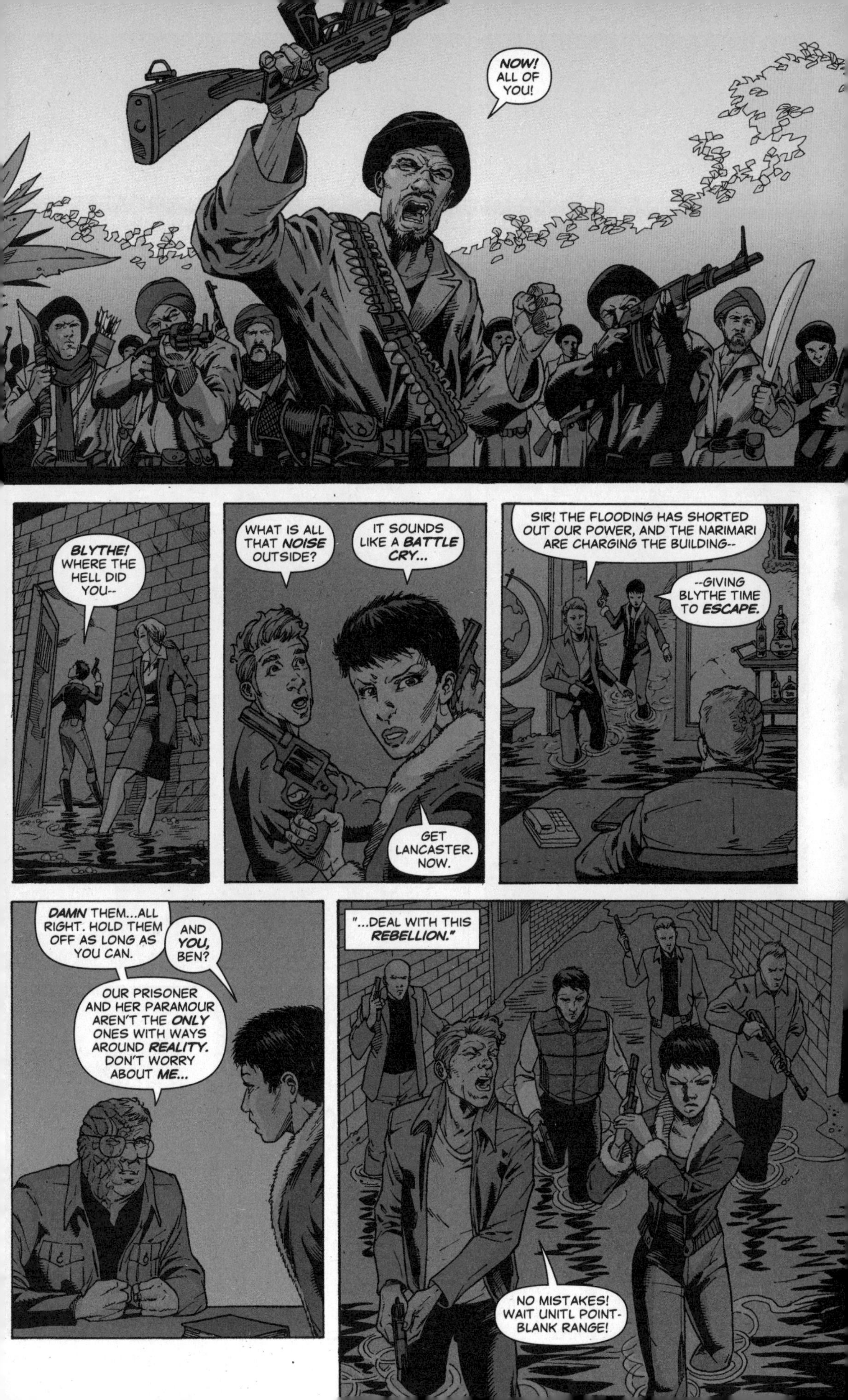
NOW! ALL OF YOU!
BLYTHE! WHERE THE HELL DID YOU--
WHAT IS ALL THAT NOISE OUTSIDE?
IT SOUNDS LIKE A BATTLE CRY...
GET LANCASTER. NOW.
SIR! THE FLOODING HAS SHORTED OUT OUR POWER, AND THE NARIMARI ARE CHARGING THE BUILDING--
--GIVING BLYTHE TIME TO ESCAPE.
DAMN THEM...ALL RIGHT. HOLD THEM OFF AS LONG AS YOU CAN.
AND YOU, BEN?
OUR PRISONER AND HER PARAMOUR AREN'T THE ONLY ONES WITH WAYS AROUND REALITY. DON'T WORRY ABOUT ME...
"...DEAL WITH THIS REBELLION."
NO MISTAKES! WAIT UNITL POINT-BLANK RANGE!

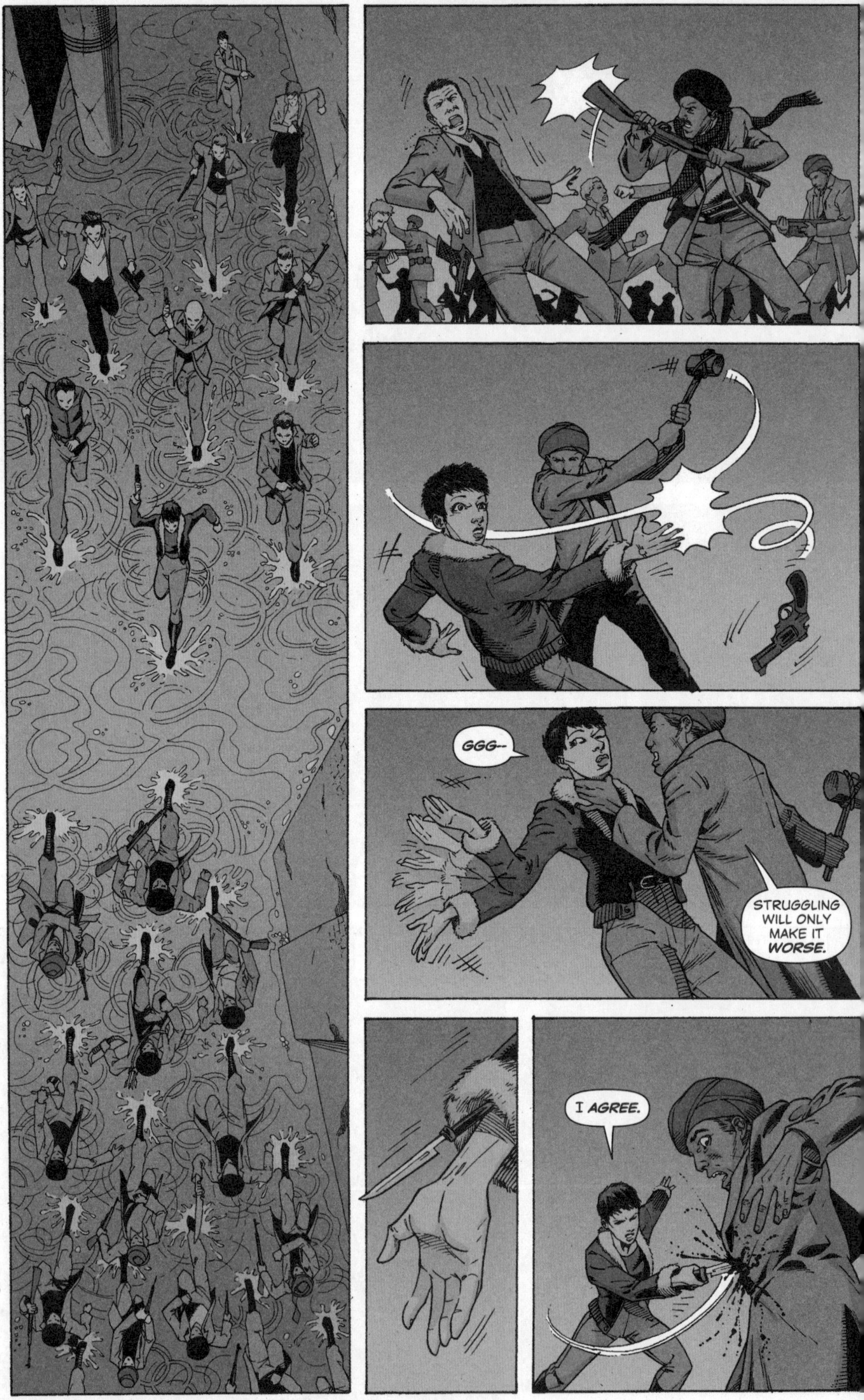
GGG--
STRUGGLING WILL ONLY MAKE IT WORSE.
I AGREE.

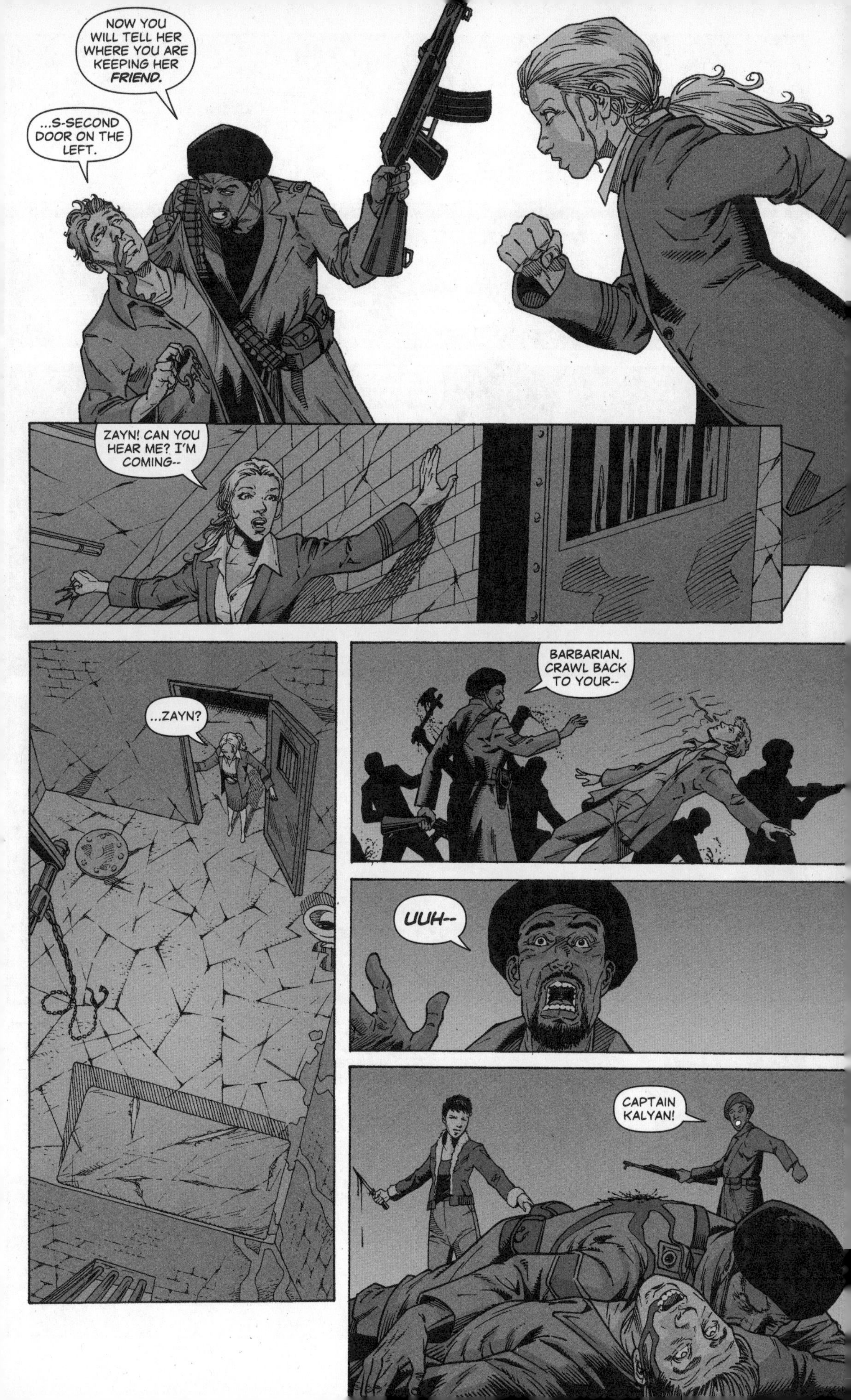
NOW YOU WILL TELL HER WHERE YOU ARE KEEPING HER FRIEND.
...S-SECOND DOOR ON THE LEFT.
ZAYN! CAN YOU HEAR ME? I'M COMING--
...ZAYN?
BARBARIAN. CRAWL BACK TO YOUR--
UUH--
CAPTAIN KALYAN!

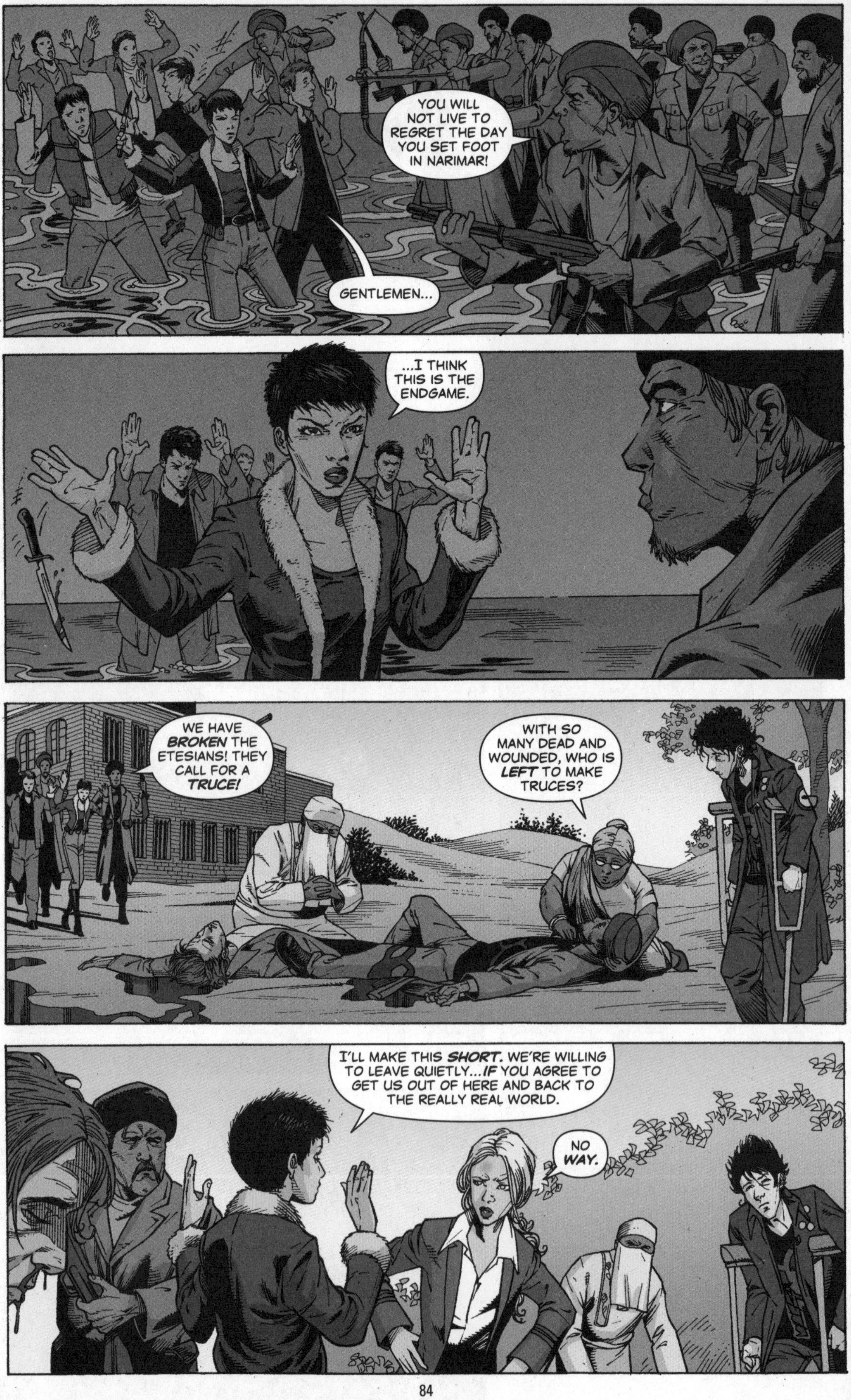

YOU WILL NOT LIVE TO REGRET THE DAY YOU SET FOOT IN NARIMAR!
GENTLEMEN...
...I THINK THIS IS THE ENDGAME.
WE HAVE BROKEN THE ETESIANS! THEY CALL FOR A TRUCE!
WITH SO MANY DEAD AND WOUNDED, WHO IS LEFT TO MAKE TRUCES?
I'LL MAKE THIS SHORT. WE'RE WILLING TO LEAVE QUIETLY...IF YOU AGREE TO GET US OUT OF HERE AND BACK TO THE REALLY REAL WORLD.
NO WAY.

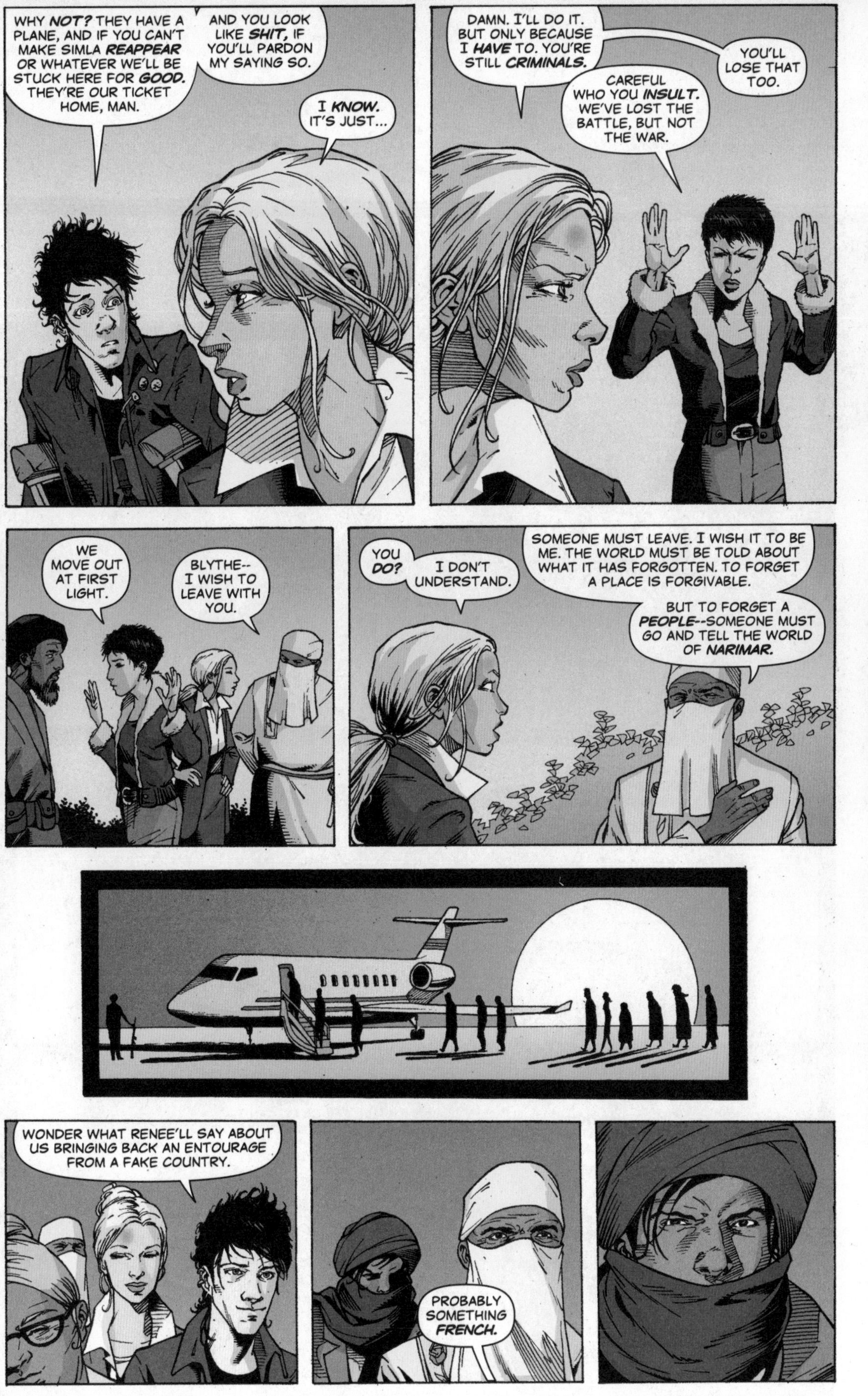
WHY NOT? THEY HAVE A PLANE, AND IF YOU CAN'T MAKE SIMLA REAPPEAR OR WHATEVER WE'LL BE STUCK HERE FOR GOOD. THEY'RE OUR TICKET HOME, MAN.
AND YOU LOOK LIKE SHIT, IF YOU'LL PARDON MY SAYING SO.
I KNOW. IT'S JUST...
DAMN. I'LL DO IT. BUT ONLY BECAUSE I HAVE TO. YOU'RE STILL CRIMINALS.
YOU'LL LOSE THAT TOO.
CAREFUL WHO YOU INSULT. WE'VE LOST THE BATTLE, BUT NOT THE WAR.
WE MOVE OUT AT FIRST LIGHT.
BLYTHE-- I WISH TO LEAVE WITH YOU.
YOU DO?
I DON'T UNDERSTAND.
SOMEONE MUST LEAVE. I WISH IT TO BE ME. THE WORLD MUST BE TOLD ABOUT WHAT IT HAS FORGOTTEN. TO FORGET A PLACE IS FORGIVABLE.
BUT TO FORGET A PEOPLE--SOMEONE MUST GO AND TELL THE WORLD OF NARIMAR.
WONDER WHAT RENEE'LL SAY ABOUT US BRINGING BACK AN ENTOURAGE FROM A FAKE COUNTRY.
PROBABLY SOMETHING FRENCH.

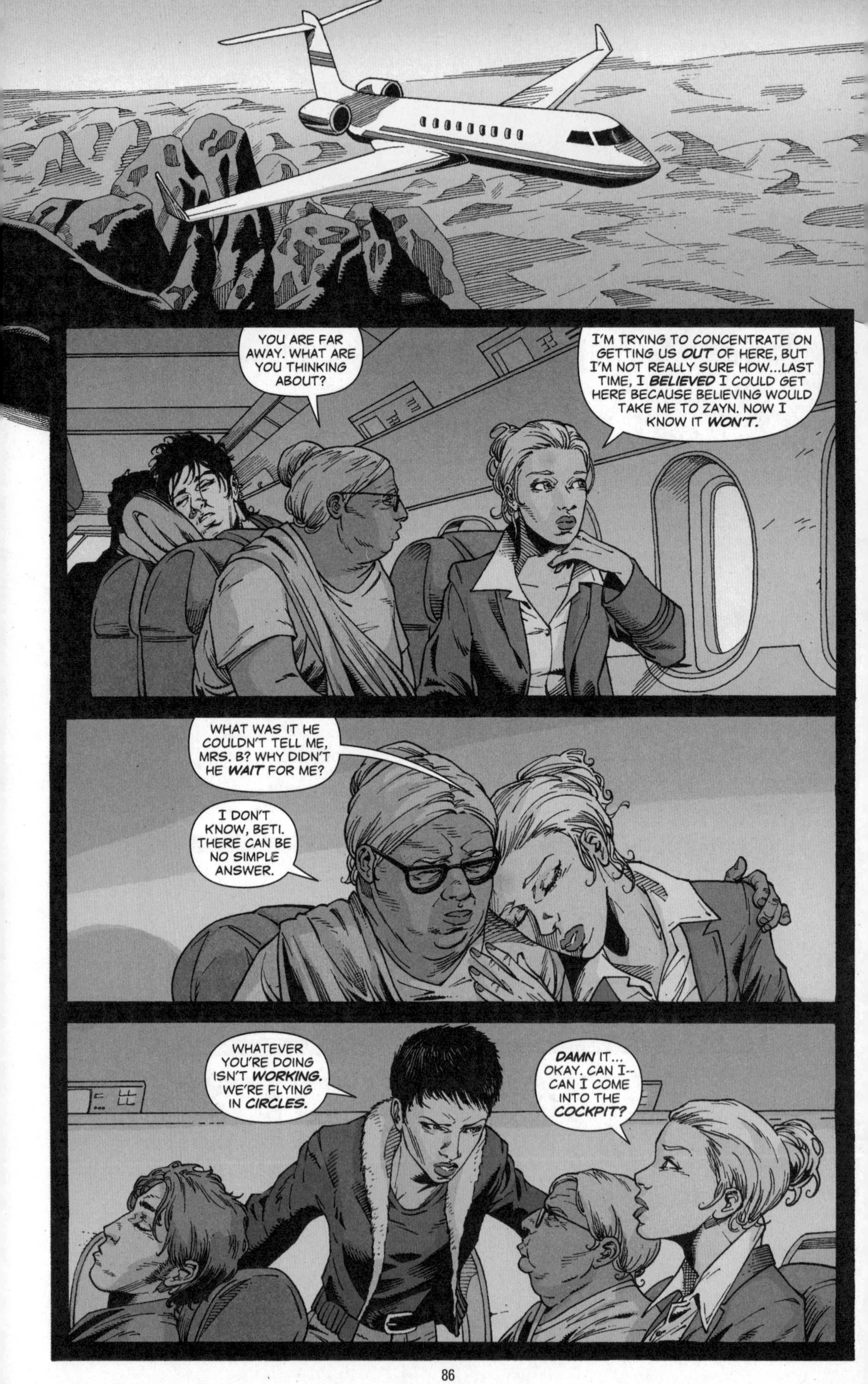
YOU ARE FAR AWAY. WHAT ARE YOU THINKING ABOUT?
I'M TRYING TO CONCENTRATE ON GETTING US OUT OF HERE, BUT I'M NOT REALLY SURE HOW...LAST TIME, I BELIEVED I COULD GET HERE BECAUSE BELIEVING WOULD TAKE ME TO ZAYN. NOW I KNOW IT WON'T.
WHAT WAS IT HE COULDN'T TELL ME, MRS. B? WHY DIDN'T HE WAIT FOR ME?
I DON'T KNOW, BETI. THERE CAN BE NO SIMPLE ANSWER.
WHATEVER YOU'RE DOING ISN'T WORKING. WE'RE FLYING IN CIRCLES.
DAMN IT... OKAY. CAN I-- CAN I COME INTO THE COCKPIT?

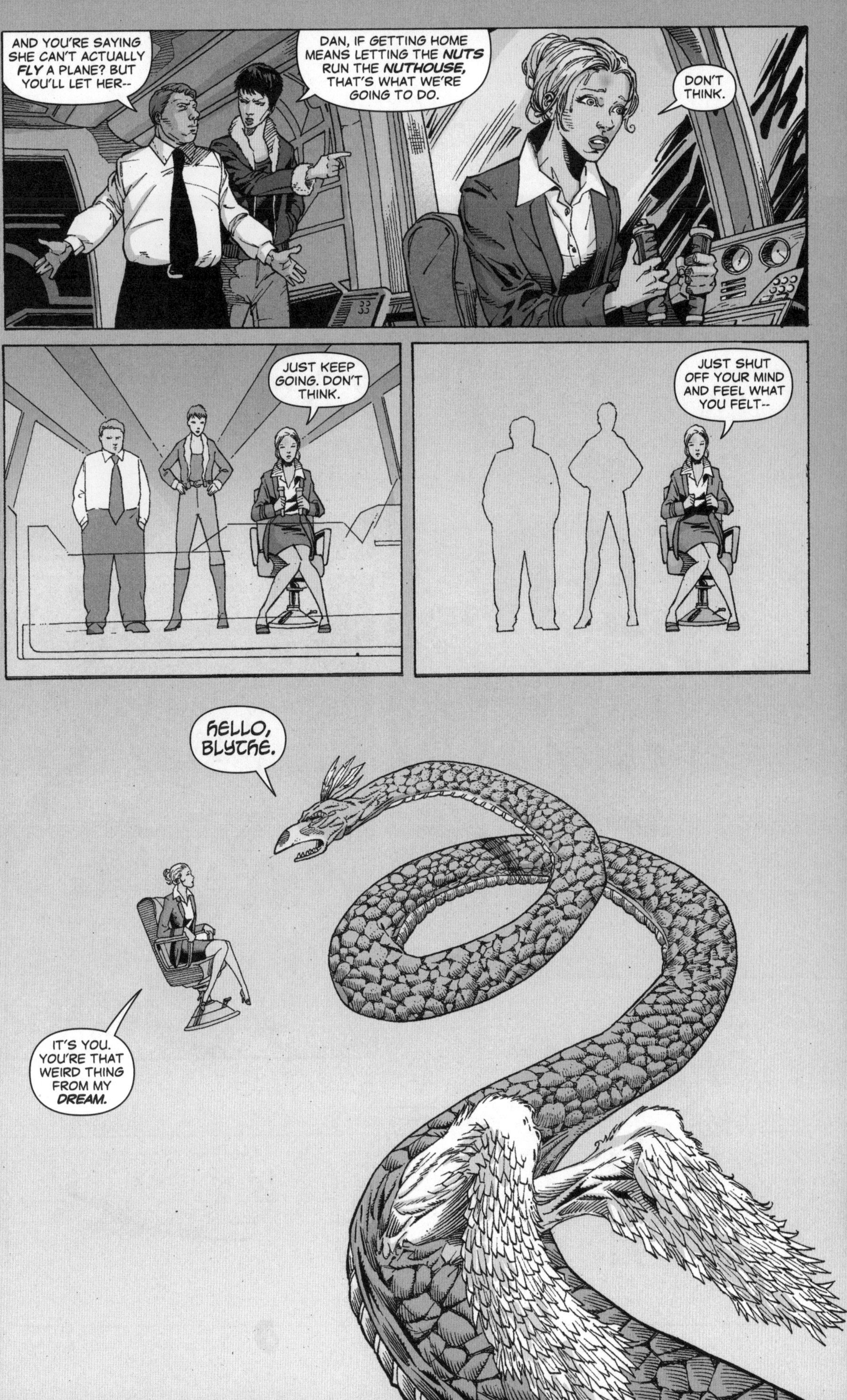
AND YOU'RE SAYING SHE CAN'T ACTUALLY FLY A PLANE? BUT YOU'LL LET HER--
DAN, IF GETTING HOME MEANS LETTING THE NUTS RUN THE NUTHOUSE, THAT'S WHAT WE'RE GOING TO DO.
DON'T THINK.
JUST KEEP GOING. DON'T THINK.
JUST SHUT OFF YOUR MIND AND FEEL WHAT YOU FELT--
HELLO, BLYTHE.
IT'S YOU. YOU'RE THAT WEIRD THING FROM MY DREAM.

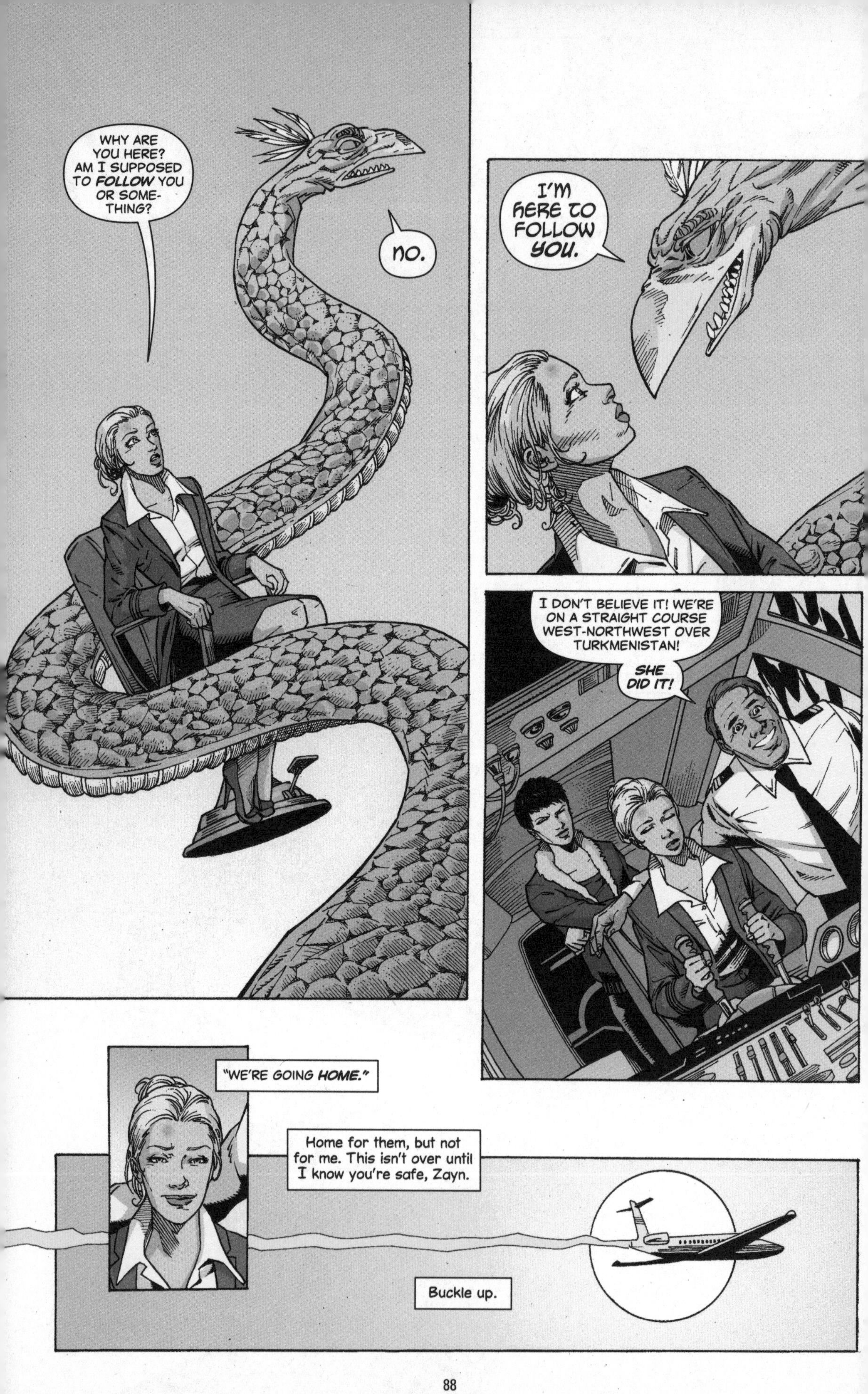
WHY ARE YOU HERE? AM I SUPPOSED TO FOLLOW YOU OR SOME-THING?
no.
I'M HERE TO FOLLOW YOU.
I DON'T BELIEVE IT! WE'RE ON A STRAIGHT COURSE WEST-NORTHWEST OVER TURKMENISTAN!
SHE DID IT!
"WE'RE GOING HOME."
Home for them, but not for me. This isn't over until I know you're safe, Zayn.
Buckle up.

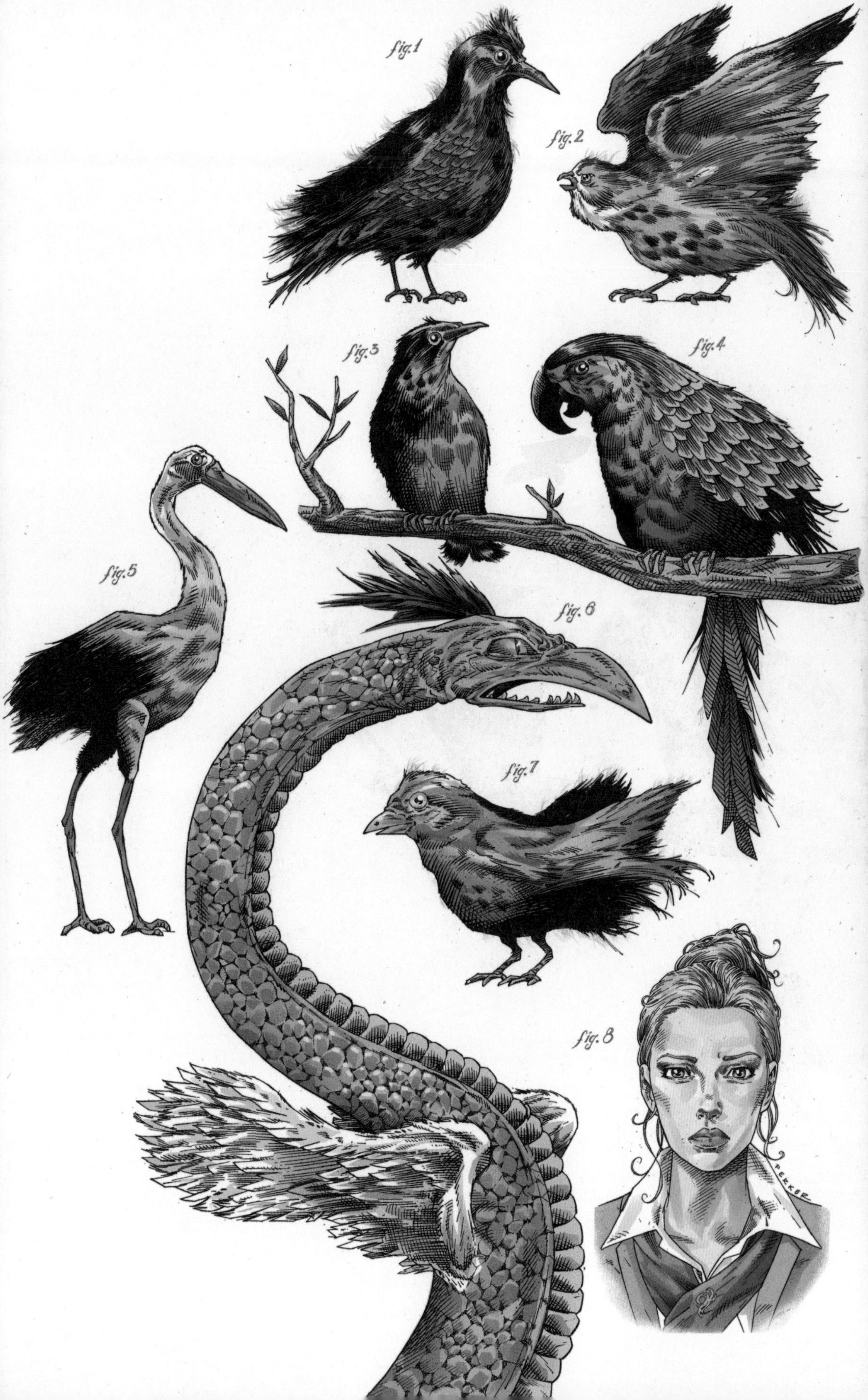
fig.1
fig.2
fig.3
fig.4
fig.5
fig.6
fig.7
fig.8
PEKKER

CHAPTER 4

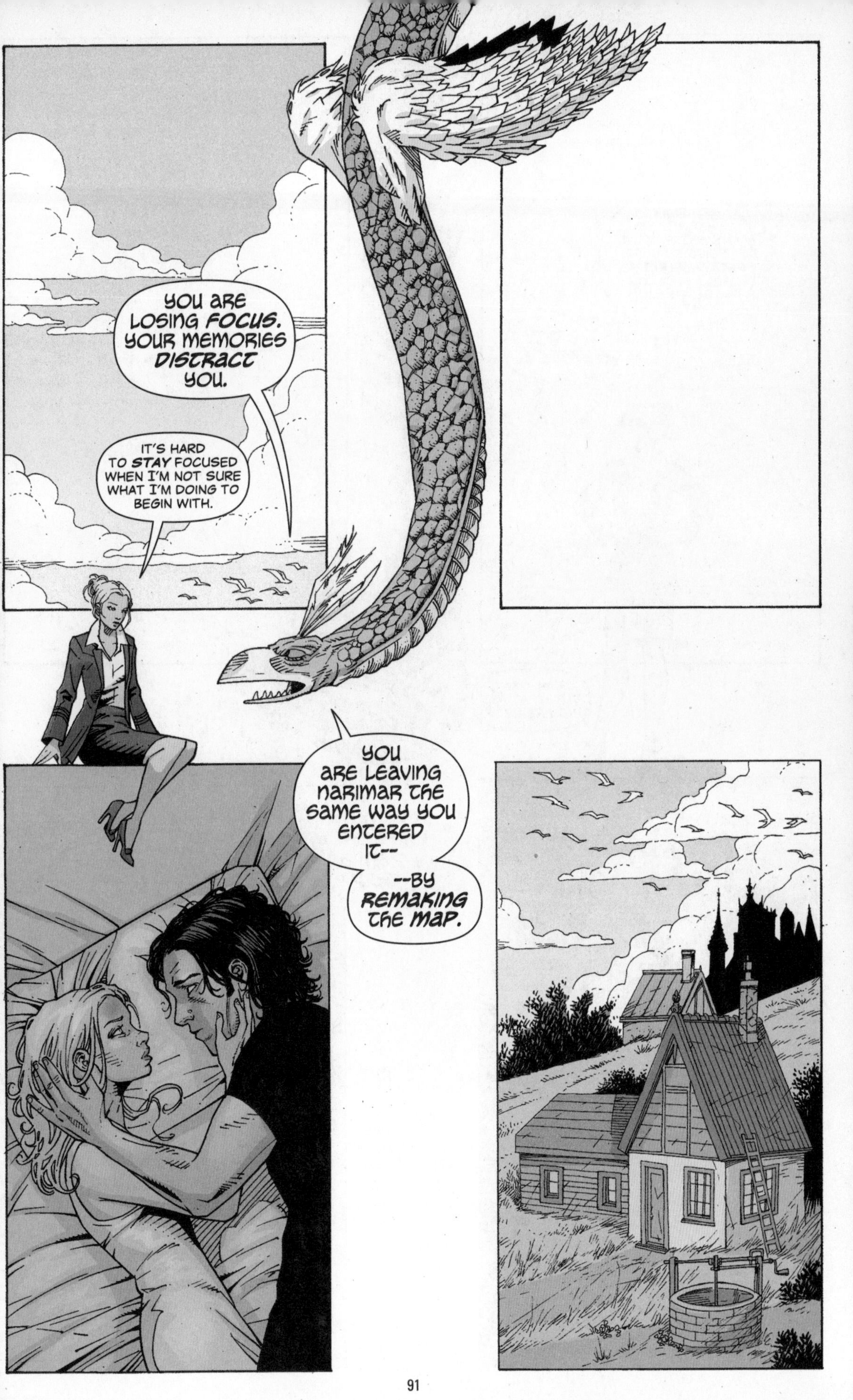
YOU ARE LOSING FOCUS. YOUR MEMORIES DISTRACT YOU.
IT'S HARD TO STAY FOCUSED WHEN I'M NOT SURE WHAT I'M DOING TO BEGIN WITH.
YOU ARE LEAVING NARIMAR THE SAME WAY YOU ENTERED IT--
--BY REMAKING THE MAP.

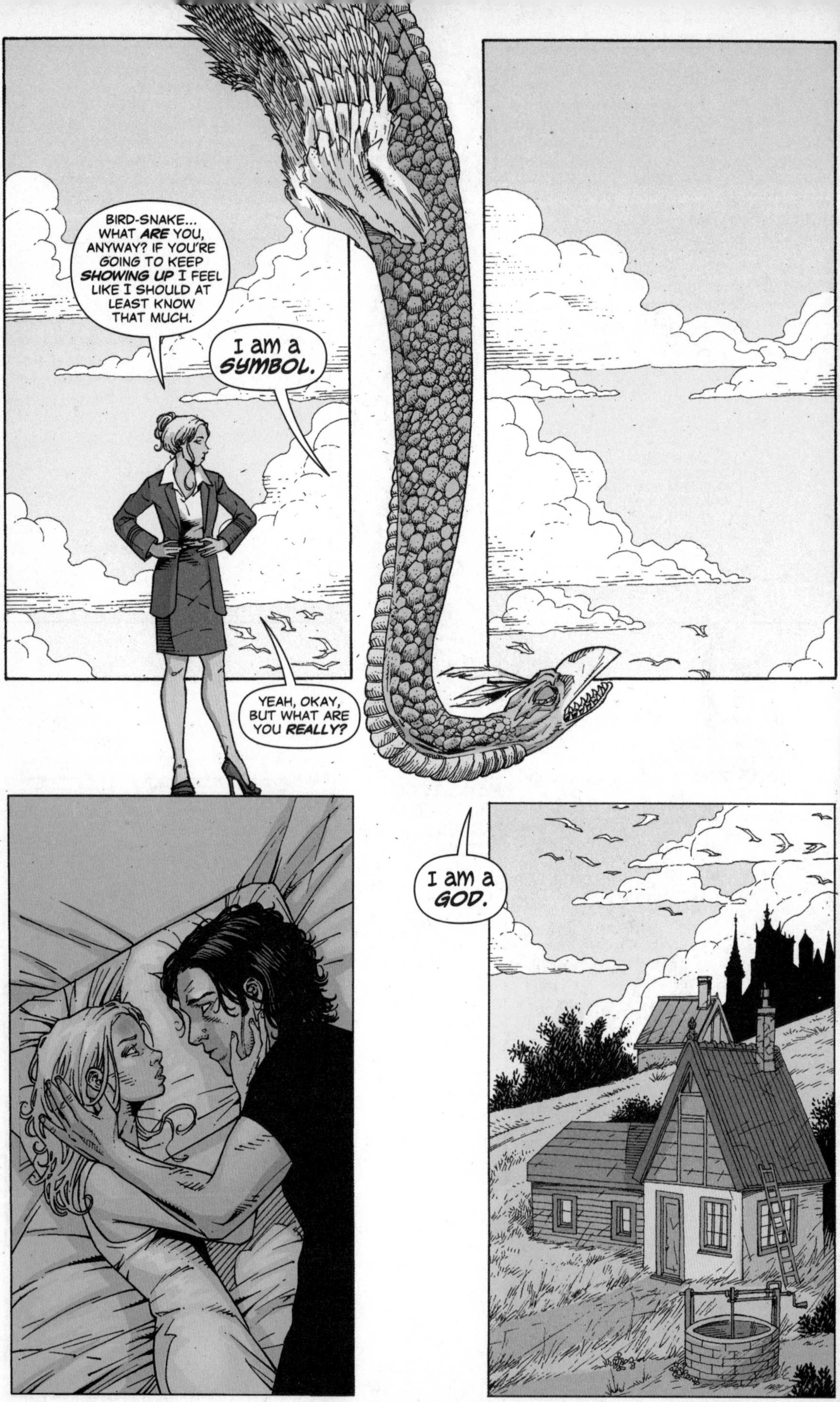
BIRD-SNAKE... WHAT ARE YOU, ANYWAY? IF YOU'RE GOING TO KEEP SHOWING UP I FEEL LIKE I SHOULD AT LEAST KNOW THAT MUCH.
I am a SYMBOL.
YEAH, OKAY, BUT WHAT ARE YOU REALLY?
I am a GOD.

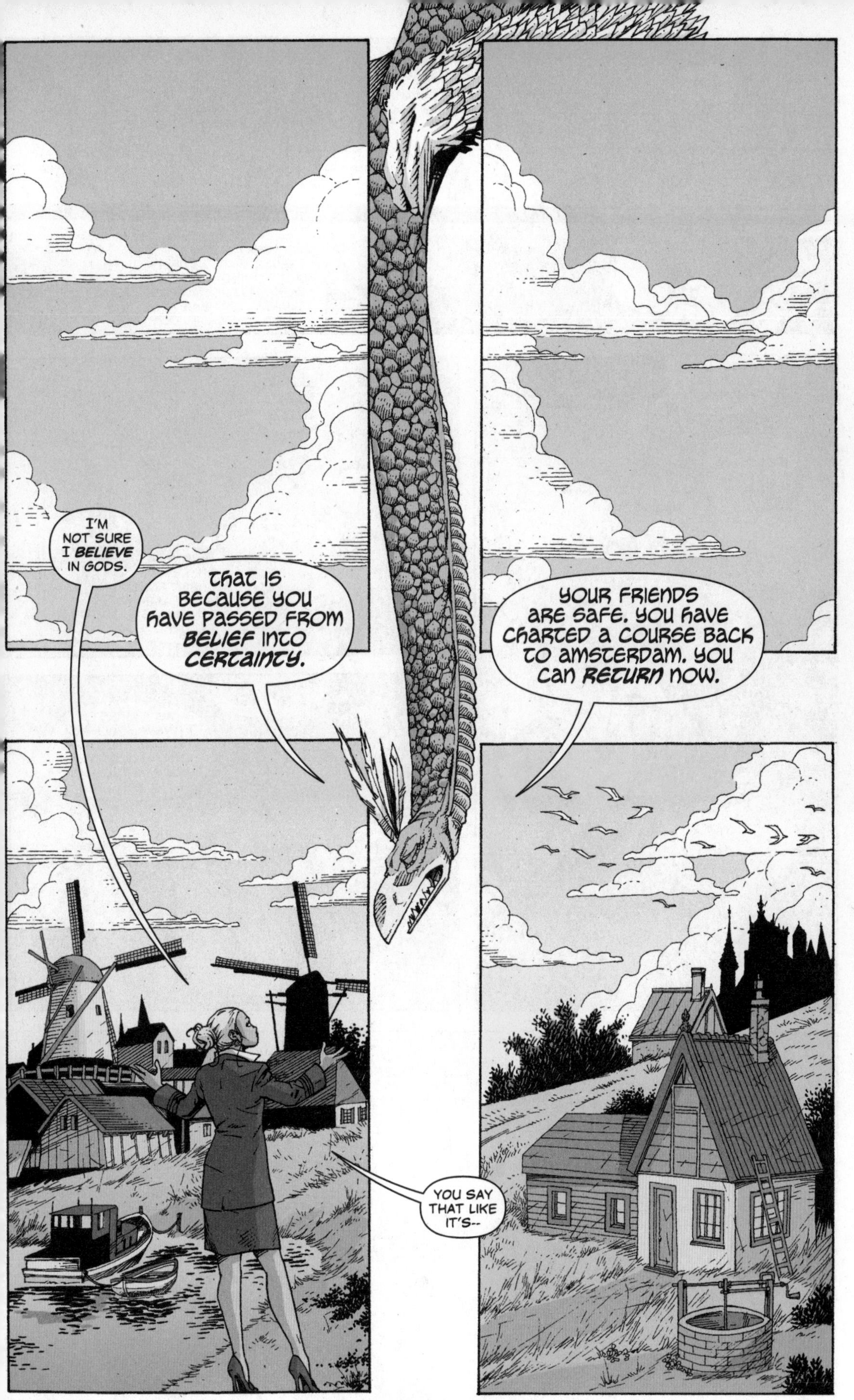
I'M NOT SURE I *BELIEVE* IN GODS.
THAT IS BECAUSE YOU HAVE PASSED FROM *BELIEF* INTO *CERTAINTY*.
YOUR FRIENDS ARE SAFE. YOU HAVE CHARTED A COURSE BACK TO AMSTERDAM. YOU CAN *RETURN* NOW.
YOU SAY THAT LIKE IT'S--

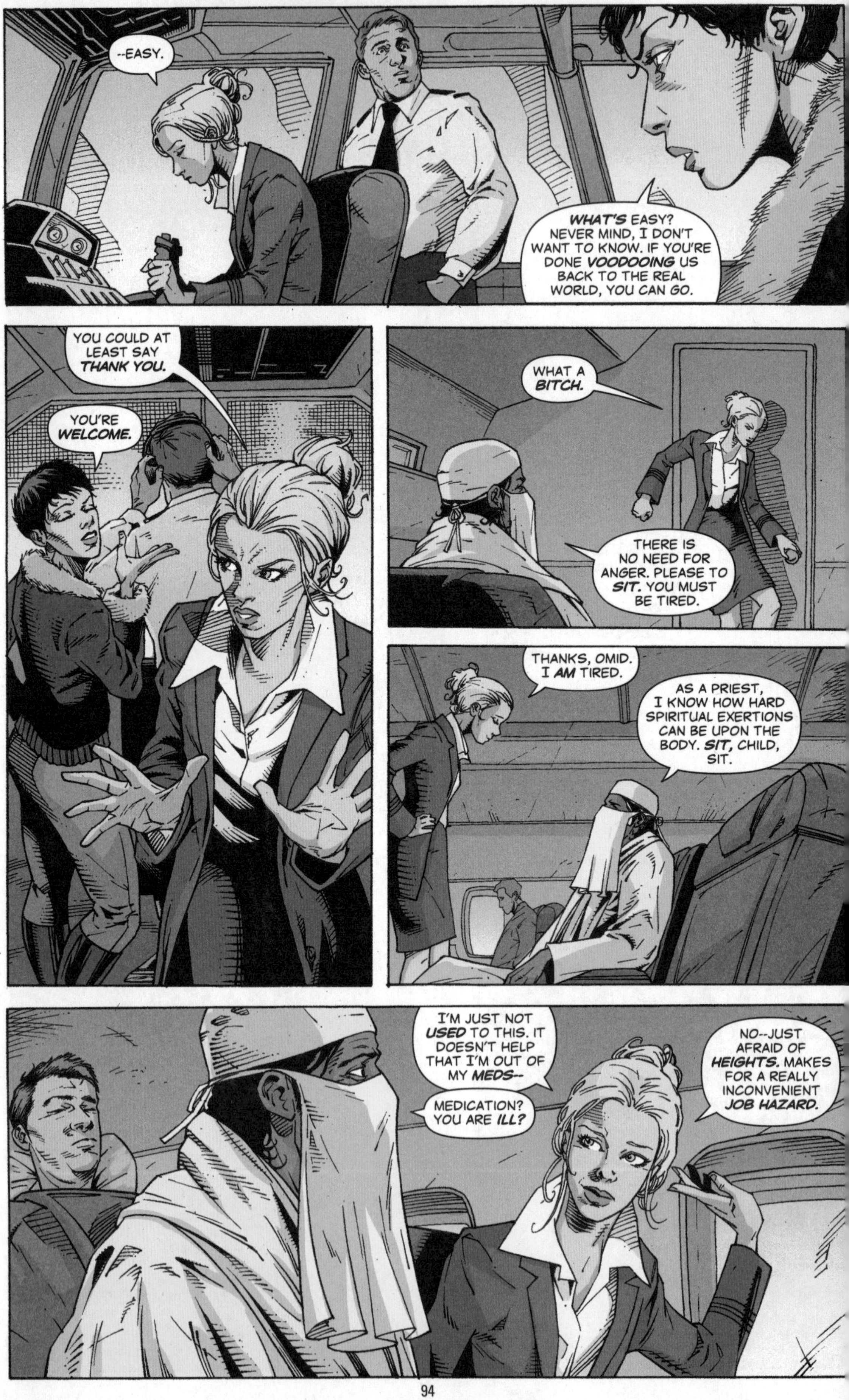
--EASY.
WHAT'S EASY? NEVER MIND, I DON'T WANT TO KNOW. IF YOU'RE DONE VOODOOING US BACK TO THE REAL WORLD, YOU CAN GO.
YOU COULD AT LEAST SAY THANK YOU.
YOU'RE WELCOME.
WHAT A BITCH.
THERE IS NO NEED FOR ANGER. PLEASE TO SIT. YOU MUST BE TIRED.
THANKS, OMID. I AM TIRED.
AS A PRIEST, I KNOW HOW HARD SPIRITUAL EXERTIONS CAN BE UPON THE BODY. SIT, CHILD, SIT.
I'M JUST NOT USED TO THIS. IT DOESN'T HELP THAT I'M OUT OF MY MEDS--
MEDICATION? YOU ARE ILL?
NO--JUST AFRAID OF HEIGHTS. MAKES FOR A REALLY INCONVENIENT JOB HAZARD.

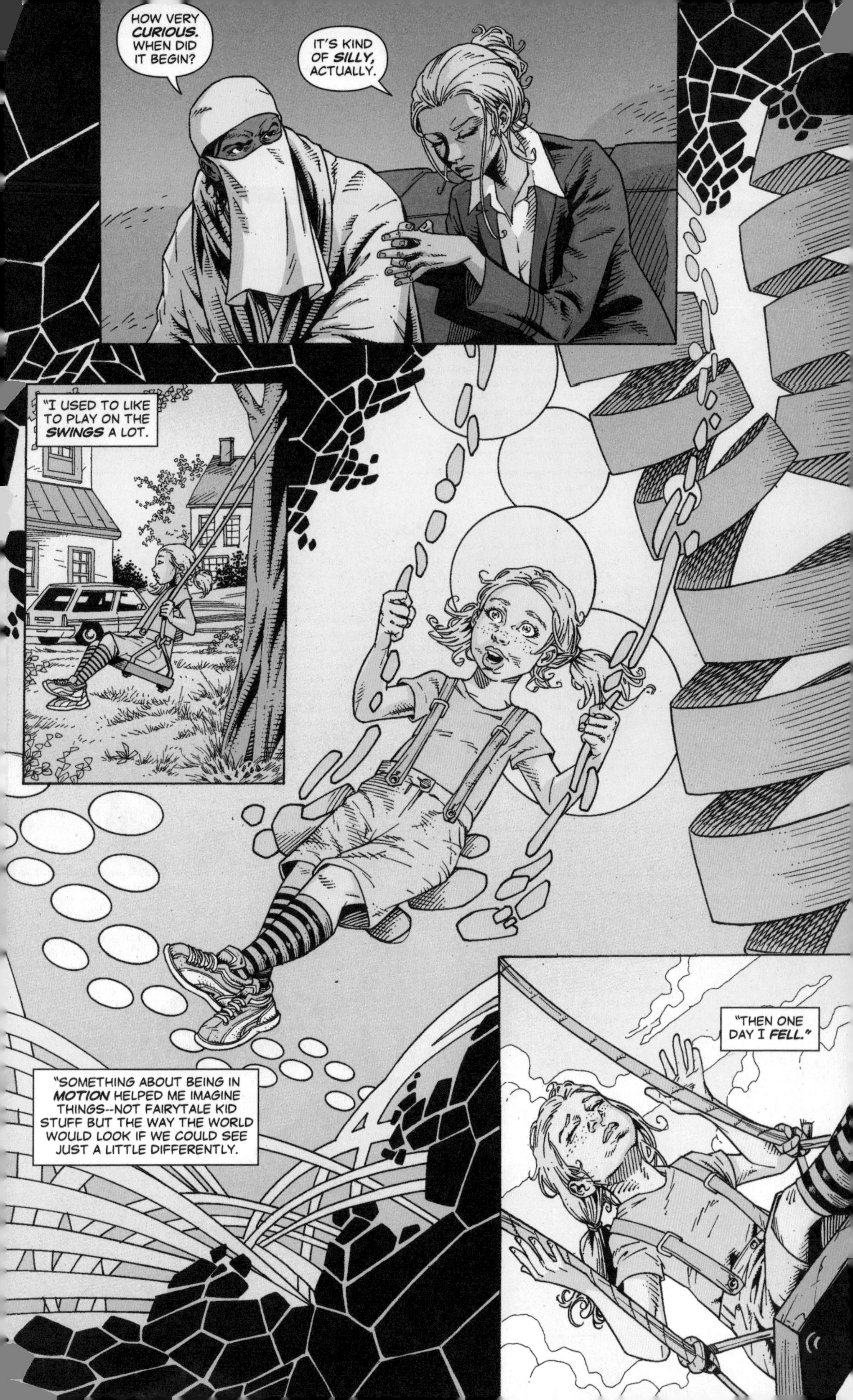
HOW VERY CURIOUS. WHEN DID IT BEGIN?
IT'S KIND OF SILLY, ACTUALLY.
"I USED TO LIKE TO PLAY ON THE SWINGS A LOT.
"SOMETHING ABOUT BEING IN MOTION HELPED ME IMAGINE THINGS--NOT FAIRYTALE KID STUFF BUT THE WAY THE WORLD WOULD LOOK IF WE COULD SEE JUST A LITTLE DIFFERENTLY.
"THEN ONE DAY I FELL."

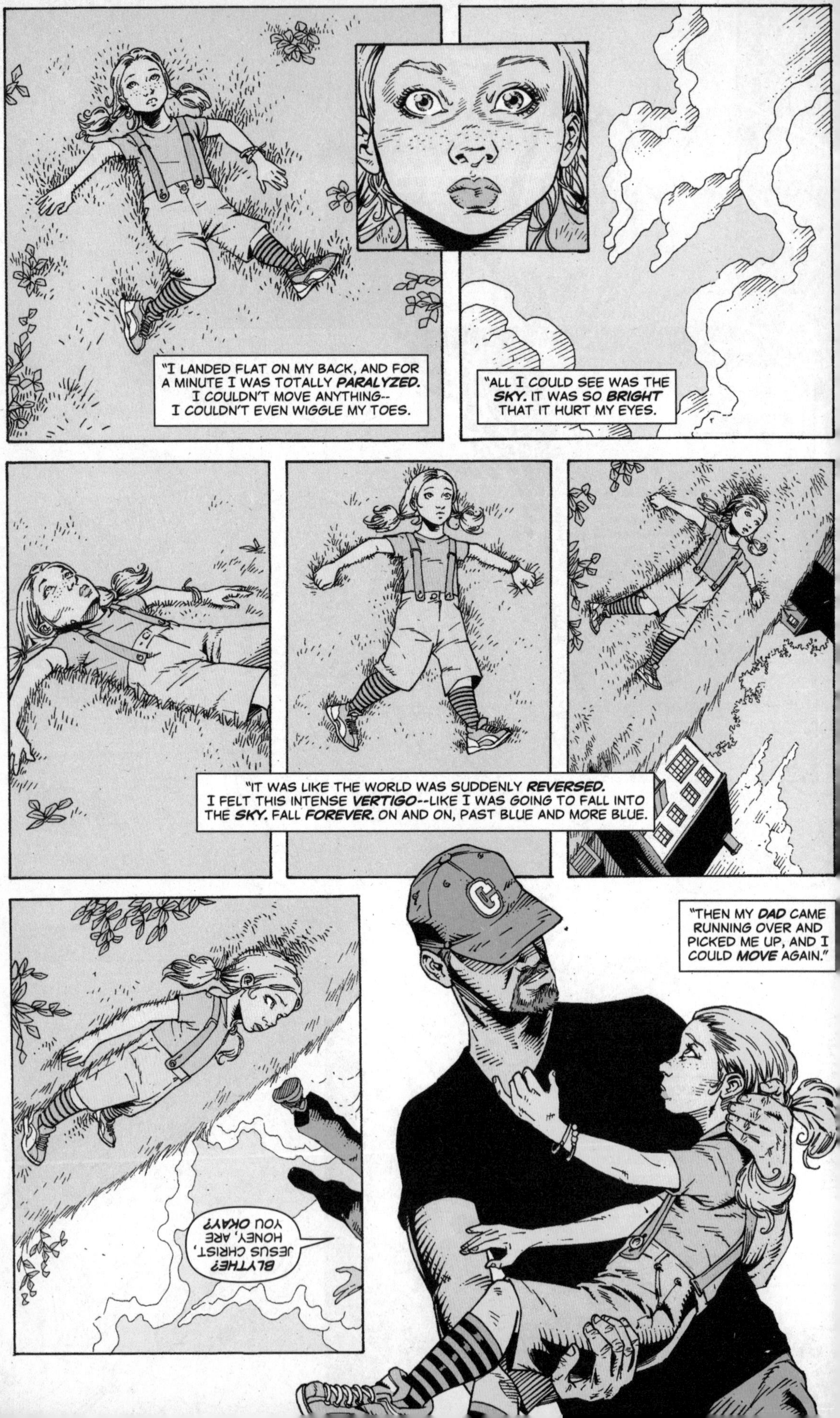
"I LANDED FLAT ON MY BACK, AND FOR A MINUTE I WAS TOTALLY PARALYZED. I COULDN'T MOVE ANYTHING-- I COULDN'T EVEN WIGGLE MY TOES.
"ALL I COULD SEE WAS THE SKY. IT WAS SO BRIGHT THAT IT HURT MY EYES.
"IT WAS LIKE THE WORLD WAS SUDDENLY REVERSED. I FELT THIS INTENSE VERTIGO--LIKE I WAS GOING TO FALL INTO THE SKY. FALL FOREVER. ON AND ON, PAST BLUE AND MORE BLUE.
BLYTHE? JESUS CHRIST, HONEY, ARE YOU OKAY?
"THEN MY DAD CAME RUNNING OVER AND PICKED ME UP, AND I COULD MOVE AGAIN."

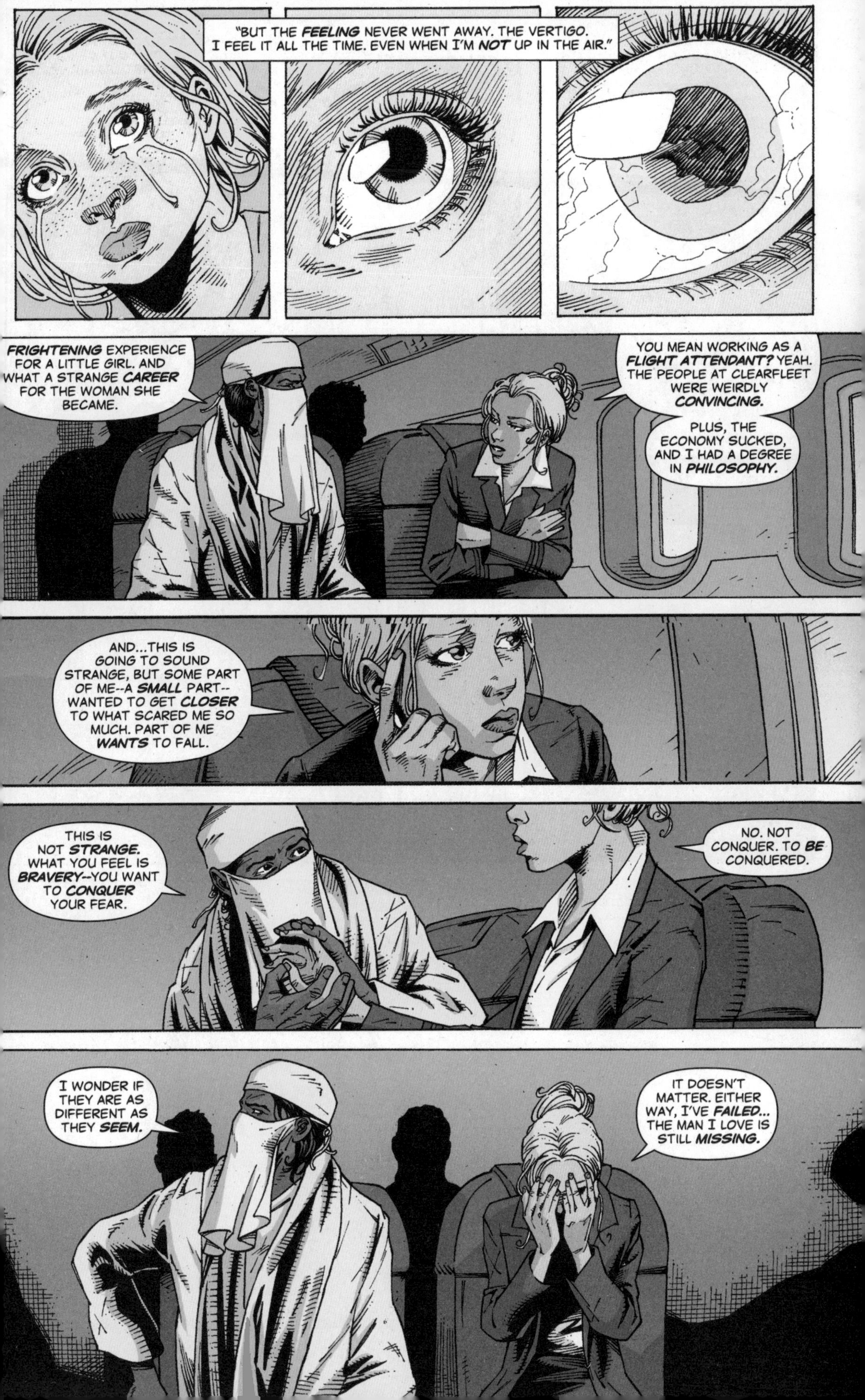
"BUT THE FEELING NEVER WENT AWAY. THE VERTIGO. I FEEL IT ALL THE TIME. EVEN WHEN I'M NOT UP IN THE AIR."
FRIGHTENING EXPERIENCE FOR A LITTLE GIRL. AND WHAT A STRANGE CAREER FOR THE WOMAN SHE BECAME.
YOU MEAN WORKING AS A FLIGHT ATTENDANT? YEAH. THE PEOPLE AT CLEARFLEET WERE WEIRDLY CONVINCING.
PLUS, THE ECONOMY SUCKED, AND I HAD A DEGREE IN PHILOSOPHY.
AND...THIS IS GOING TO SOUND STRANGE, BUT SOME PART OF ME--A SMALL PART--WANTED TO GET CLOSER TO WHAT SCARED ME SO MUCH. PART OF ME WANTS TO FALL.
THIS IS NOT STRANGE. WHAT YOU FEEL IS BRAVERY--YOU WANT TO CONQUER YOUR FEAR.
NO. NOT CONQUER. TO BE CONQUERED.
I WONDER IF THEY ARE AS DIFFERENT AS THEY SEEM.
IT DOESN'T MATTER. EITHER WAY, I'VE FAILED... THE MAN I LOVE IS STILL MISSING.

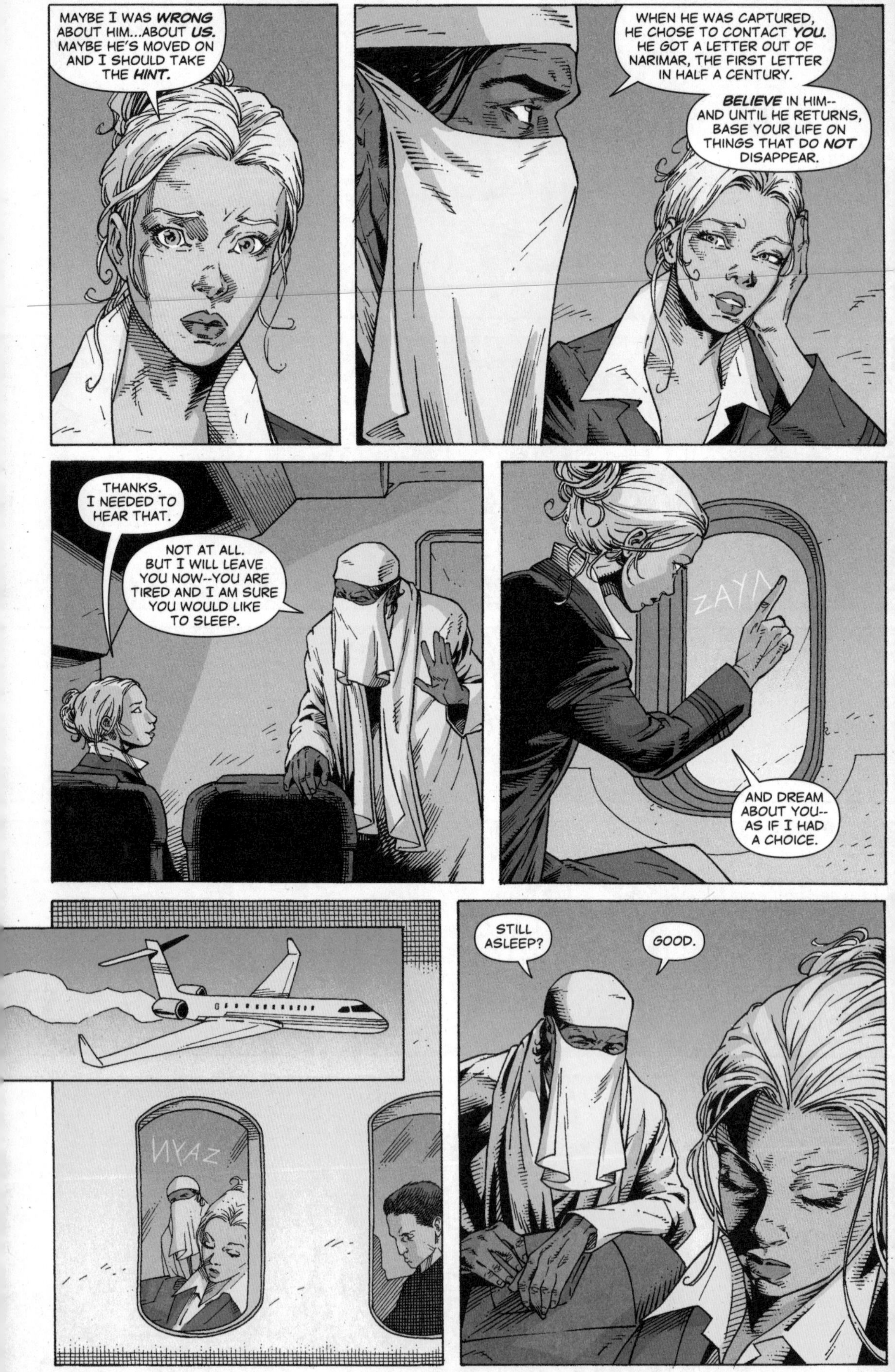
MAYBE I WAS WRONG ABOUT HIM...ABOUT US. MAYBE HE'S MOVED ON AND I SHOULD TAKE THE HINT.
WHEN HE WAS CAPTURED, HE CHOSE TO CONTACT YOU. HE GOT A LETTER OUT OF NARIMAR, THE FIRST LETTER IN HALF A CENTURY.
BELIEVE IN HIM-- AND UNTIL HE RETURNS, BASE YOUR LIFE ON THINGS THAT DO NOT DISAPPEAR.
THANKS. I NEEDED TO HEAR THAT.
NOT AT ALL. BUT I WILL LEAVE YOU NOW--YOU ARE TIRED AND I AM SURE YOU WOULD LIKE TO SLEEP.
AND DREAM ABOUT YOU-- AS IF I HAD A CHOICE.
STILL ASLEEP?
GOOD.

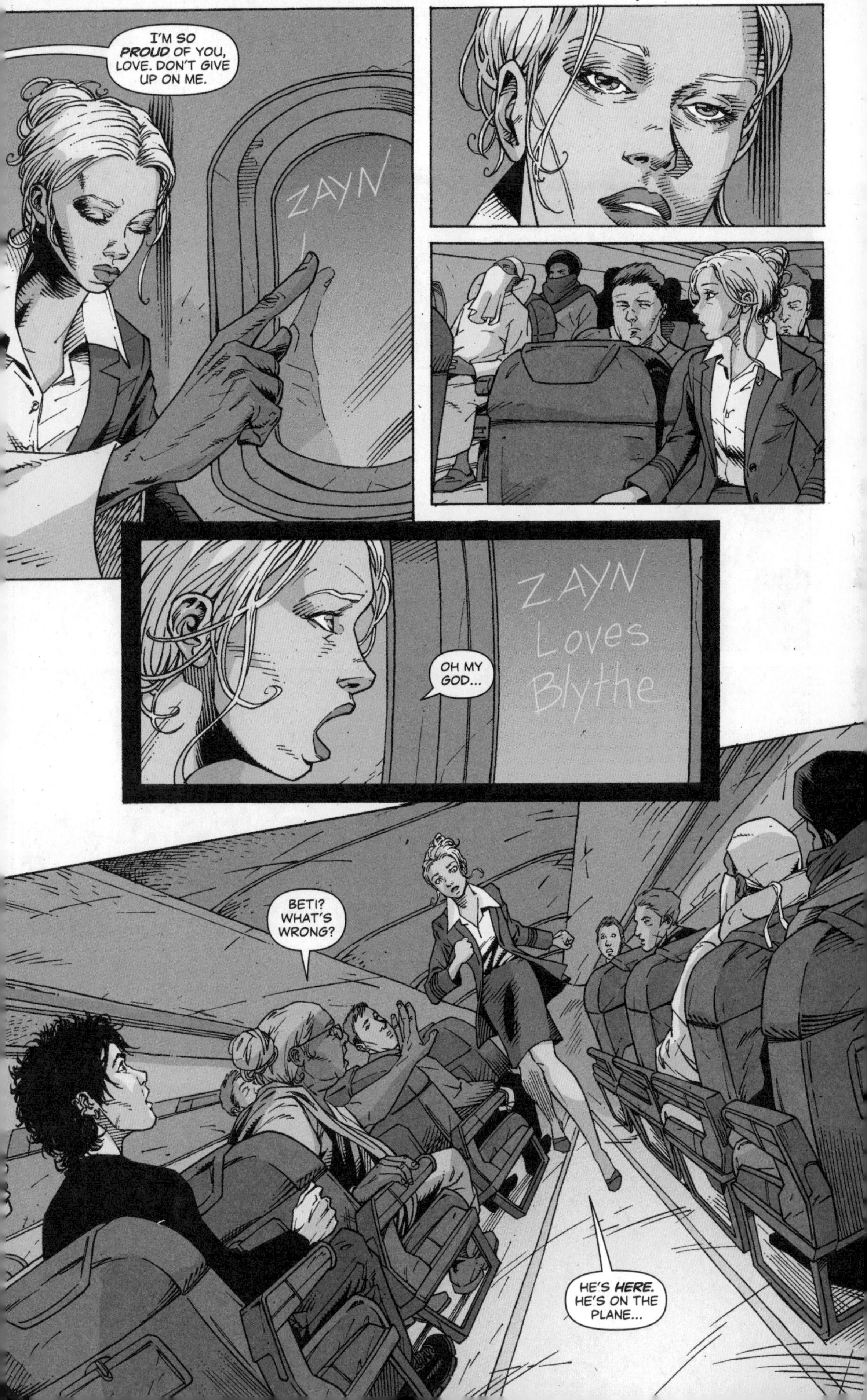
I'M SO **PROUD** OF YOU, LOVE. DON'T GIVE UP ON ME.
ZAYN
ZAYN Loves Blythe
OH MY GOD...
BETI? WHAT'S WRONG?
HE'S **HERE.** HE'S ON THE PLANE...

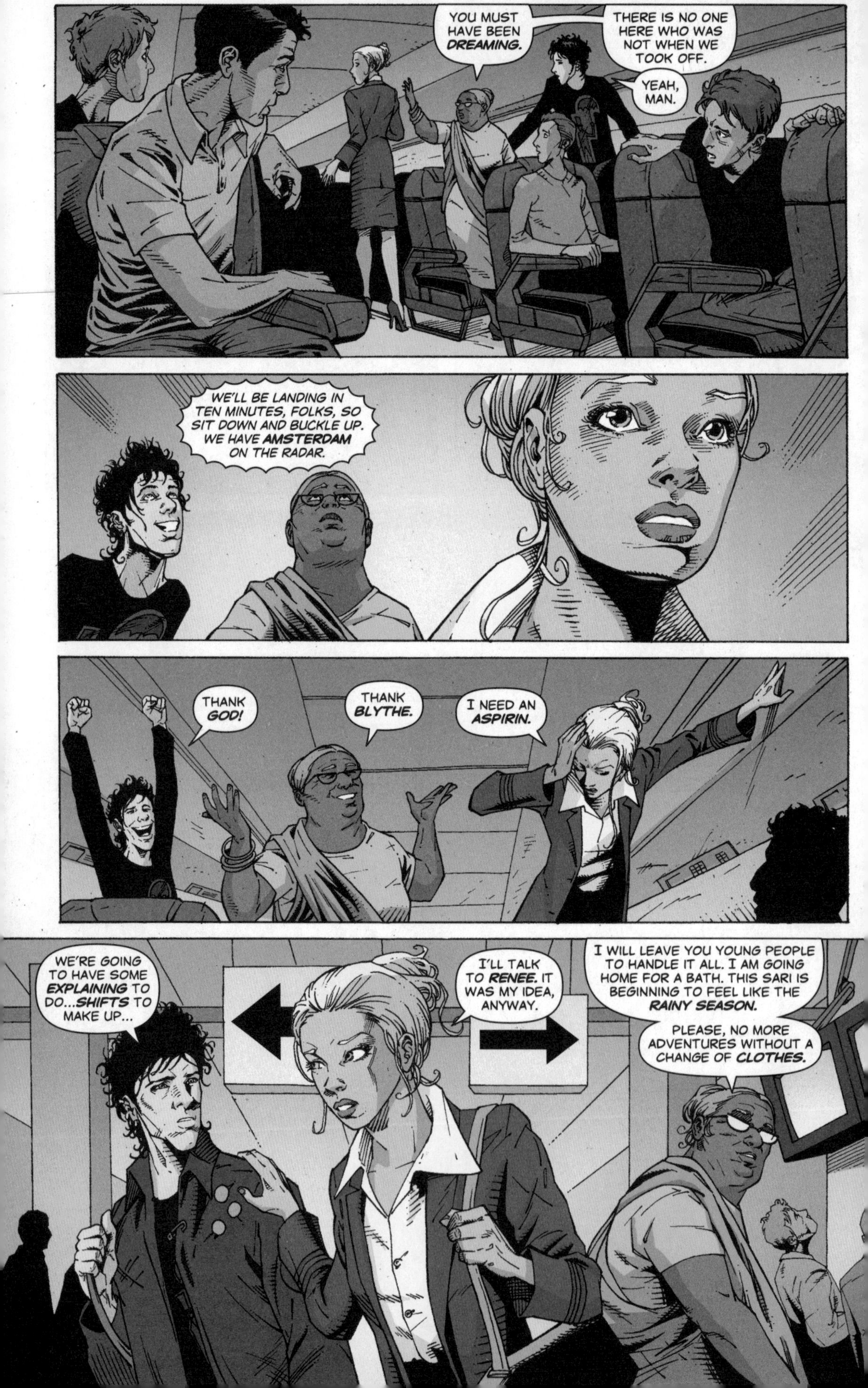
YOU MUST HAVE BEEN DREAMING.
THERE IS NO ONE HERE WHO WAS NOT WHEN WE TOOK OFF.
YEAH, MAN.
WE'LL BE LANDING IN TEN MINUTES, FOLKS, SO SIT DOWN AND BUCKLE UP. WE HAVE AMSTERDAM ON THE RADAR.
THANK GOD!
THANK BLYTHE.
I NEED AN ASPIRIN.
WE'RE GOING TO HAVE SOME EXPLAINING TO DO...SHIFTS TO MAKE UP...
I'LL TALK TO RENEE. IT WAS MY IDEA, ANYWAY.
I WILL LEAVE YOU YOUNG PEOPLE TO HANDLE IT ALL. I AM GOING HOME FOR A BATH. THIS SARI IS BEGINNING TO FEEL LIKE THE RAINY SEASON.
PLEASE, NO MORE ADVENTURES WITHOUT A CHANGE OF CLOTHES.

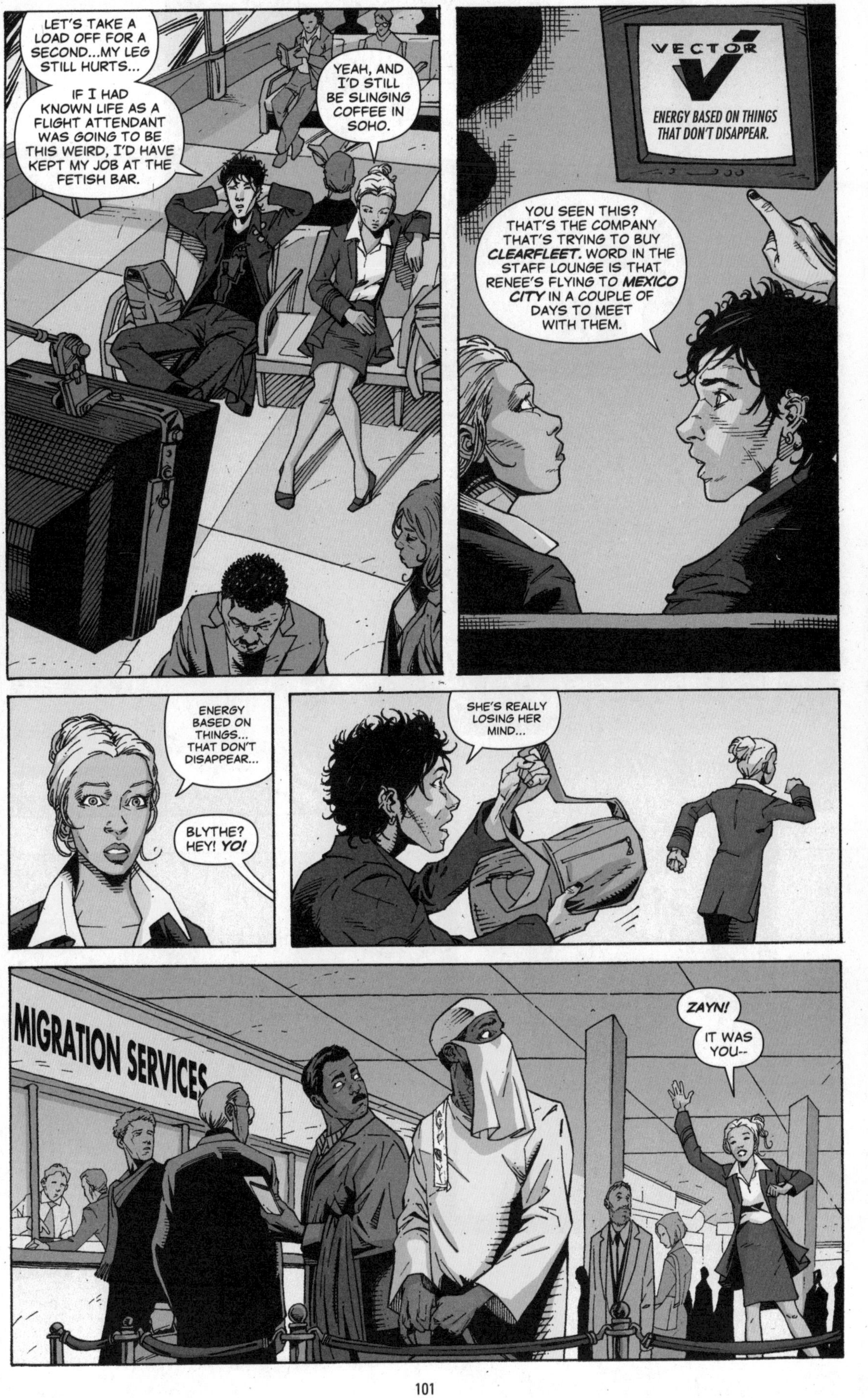
LET'S TAKE A LOAD OFF FOR A SECOND...MY LEG STILL HURTS...
IF I HAD KNOWN LIFE AS A FLIGHT ATTENDANT WAS GOING TO BE THIS WEIRD, I'D HAVE KEPT MY JOB AT THE FETISH BAR.
YEAH, AND I'D STILL BE SLINGING COFFEE IN SOHO.
VECTOR V
ENERGY BASED ON THINGS THAT DON'T DISAPPEAR.
YOU SEEN THIS? THAT'S THE COMPANY THAT'S TRYING TO BUY CLEARFLEET. WORD IN THE STAFF LOUNGE IS THAT RENEE'S FLYING TO MEXICO CITY IN A COUPLE OF DAYS TO MEET WITH THEM.
ENERGY BASED ON THINGS... THAT DON'T DISAPPEAR...
BLYTHE? HEY! YO!
SHE'S REALLY LOSING HER MIND...
MIGRATION SERVICES
ZAYN!
IT WAS YOU--

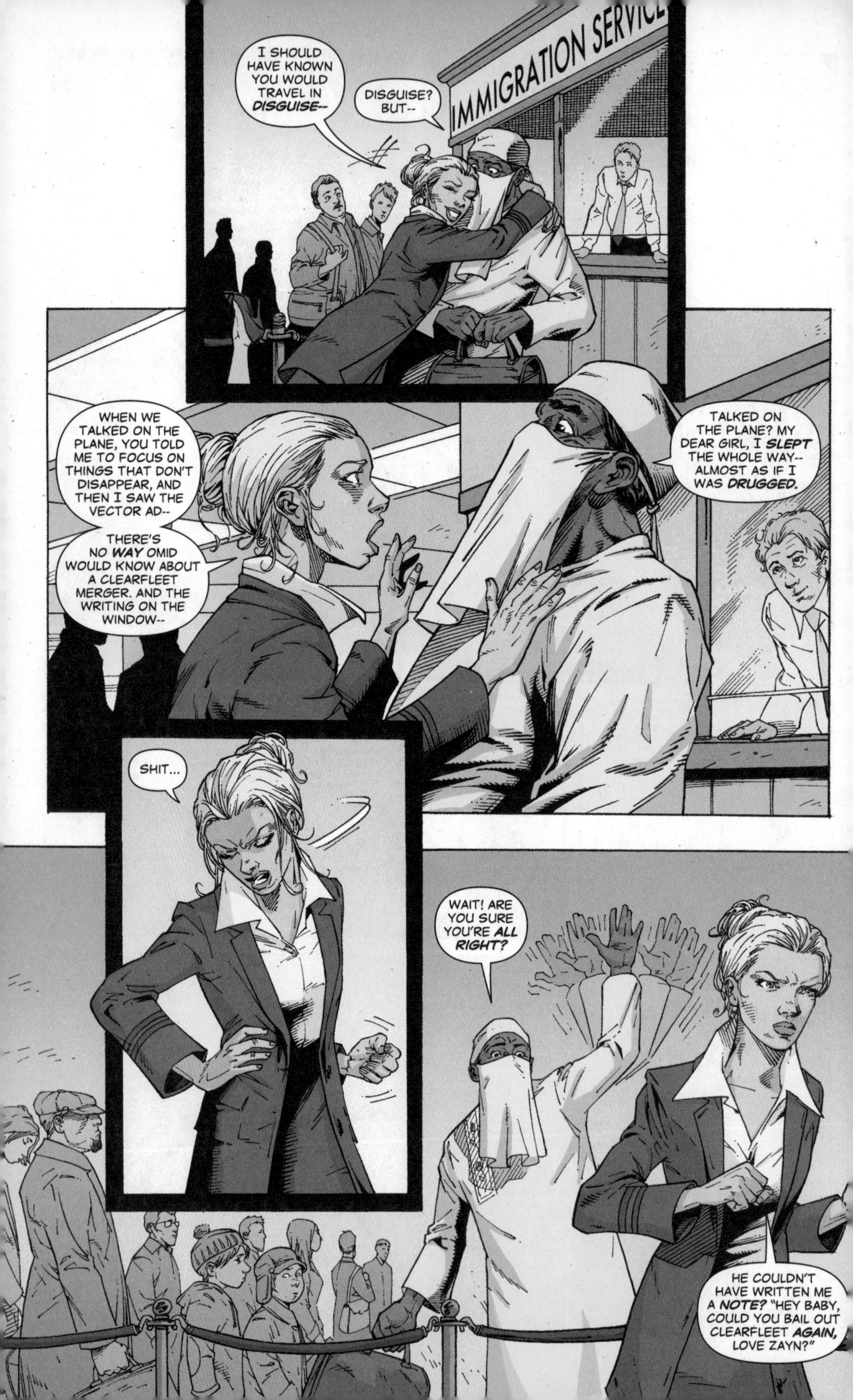
IMMIGRATION SERVICE
I SHOULD HAVE KNOWN YOU WOULD TRAVEL IN DISGUISE--
DISGUISE? BUT--
WHEN WE TALKED ON THE PLANE, YOU TOLD ME TO FOCUS ON THINGS THAT DON'T DISAPPEAR, AND THEN I SAW THE VECTOR AD--
THERE'S NO WAY OMID WOULD KNOW ABOUT A CLEARFLEET MERGER. AND THE WRITING ON THE WINDOW--
TALKED ON THE PLANE? MY DEAR GIRL, I SLEPT THE WHOLE WAY-- ALMOST AS IF I WAS DRUGGED.
SHIT...
WAIT! ARE YOU SURE YOU'RE ALL RIGHT?
HE COULDN'T HAVE WRITTEN ME A NOTE? "HEY BABY, COULD YOU BAIL OUT CLEARFLEET AGAIN, LOVE ZAYN?"

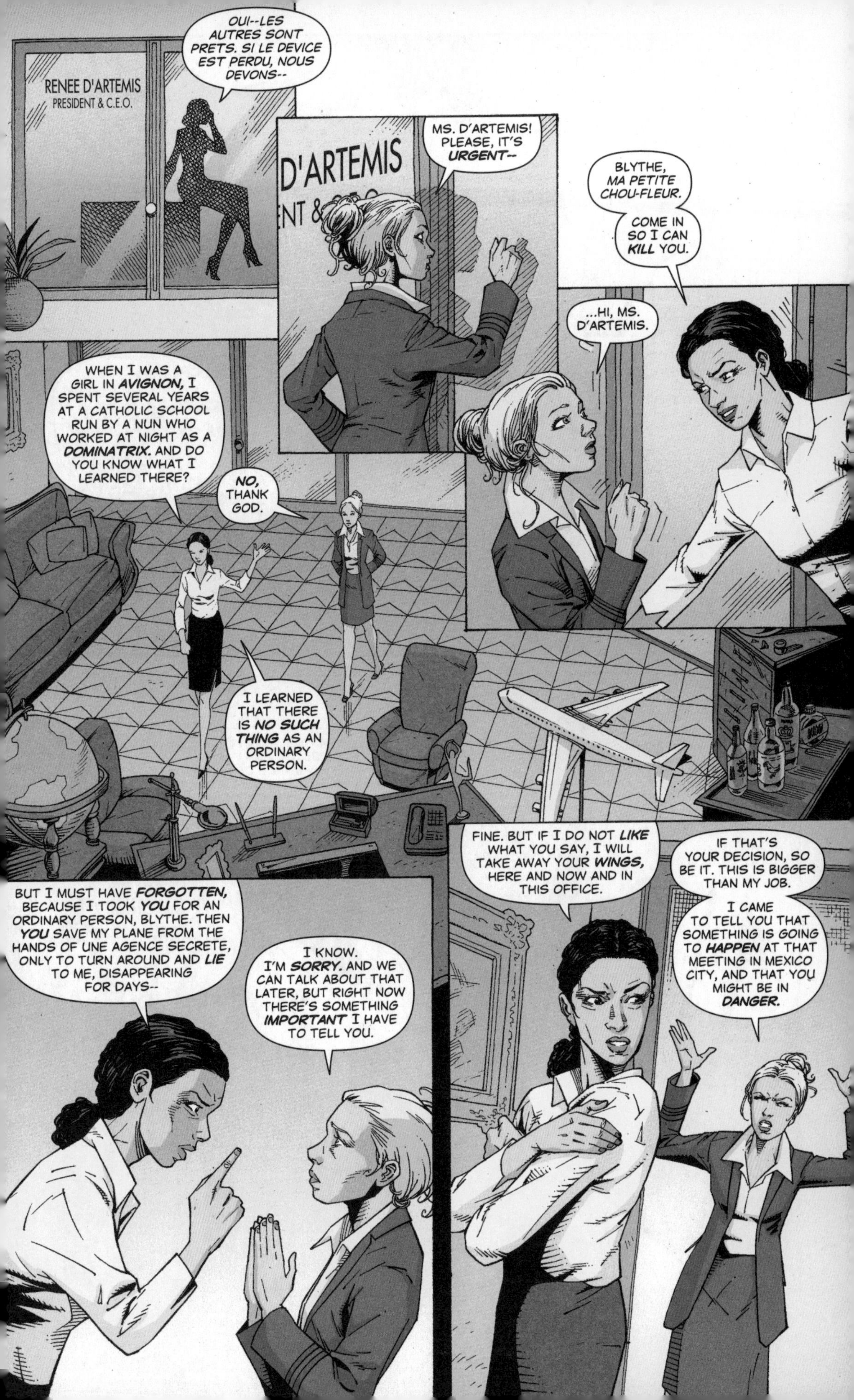
RENEE D'ARTEMIS
PRESIDENT & C.E.O.
OUI--LES AUTRES SONT PRETS. SI LE DEVICE EST PERDU, NOUS DEVONS--
D'ARTEMIS
MS. D'ARTEMIS! PLEASE, IT'S URGENT--
BLYTHE, MA PETITE CHOU-FLEUR.
COME IN SO I CAN KILL YOU.
...HI, MS. D'ARTEMIS.
WHEN I WAS A GIRL IN AVIGNON, I SPENT SEVERAL YEARS AT A CATHOLIC SCHOOL RUN BY A NUN WHO WORKED AT NIGHT AS A DOMINATRIX. AND DO YOU KNOW WHAT I LEARNED THERE?
NO, THANK GOD.
I LEARNED THAT THERE IS NO SUCH THING AS AN ORDINARY PERSON.
BUT I MUST HAVE FORGOTTEN, BECAUSE I TOOK YOU FOR AN ORDINARY PERSON, BLYTHE. THEN YOU SAVE MY PLANE FROM THE HANDS OF UNE AGENCE SECRETE, ONLY TO TURN AROUND AND LIE TO ME, DISAPPEARING FOR DAYS--
I KNOW. I'M SORRY. AND WE CAN TALK ABOUT THAT LATER, BUT RIGHT NOW THERE'S SOMETHING IMPORTANT I HAVE TO TELL YOU.
FINE. BUT IF I DO NOT LIKE WHAT YOU SAY, I WILL TAKE AWAY YOUR WINGS, HERE AND NOW AND IN THIS OFFICE.
IF THAT'S YOUR DECISION, SO BE IT. THIS IS BIGGER THAN MY JOB.
I CAME TO TELL YOU THAT SOMETHING IS GOING TO HAPPEN AT THAT MEETING IN MEXICO CITY, AND THAT YOU MIGHT BE IN DANGER.

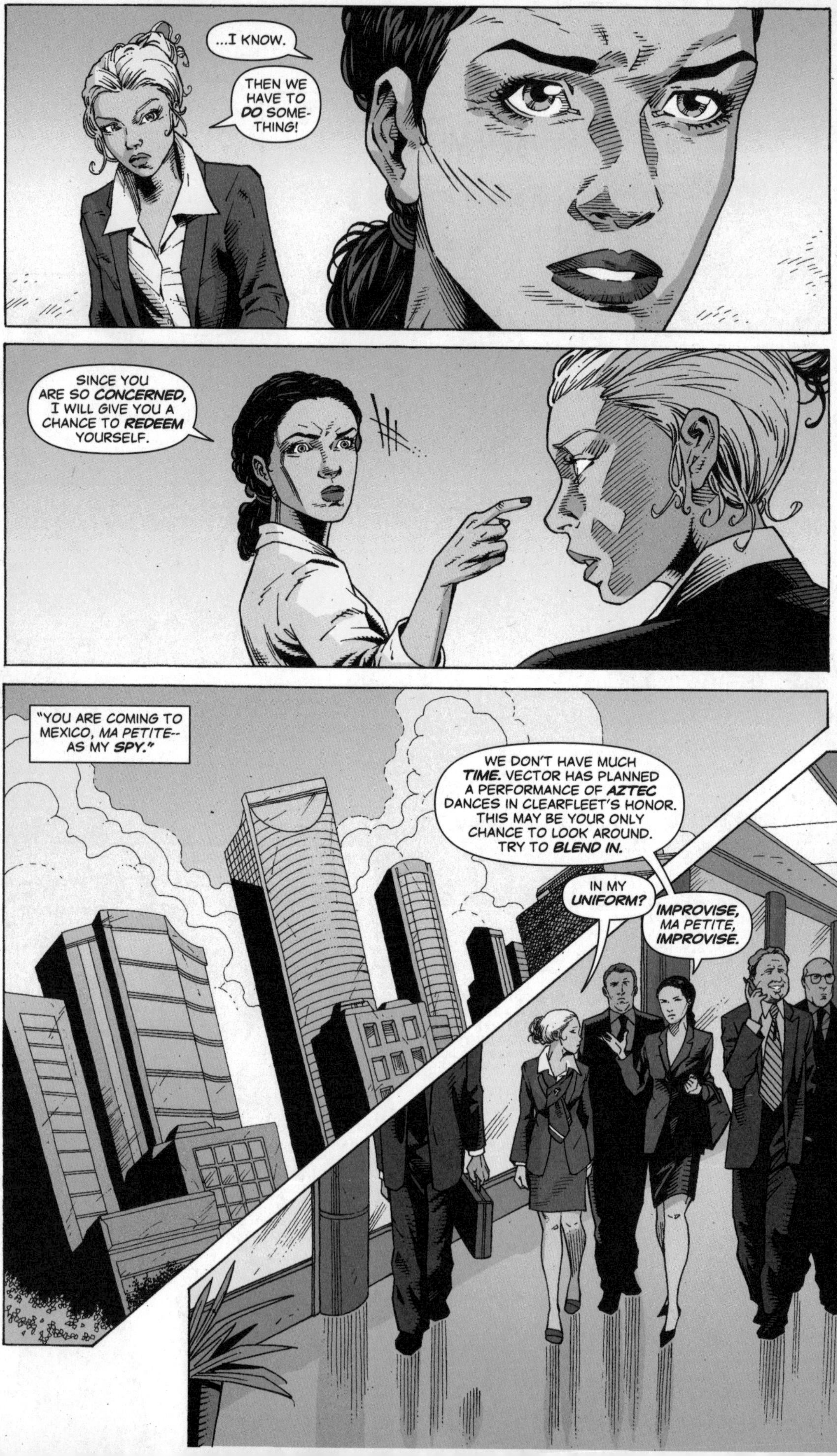
...I KNOW.
THEN WE HAVE TO *DO* SOMETHING!
SINCE YOU ARE SO *CONCERNED,* I WILL GIVE YOU A CHANCE TO *REDEEM* YOURSELF.
"YOU ARE COMING TO MEXICO, MA PETITE-- AS MY *SPY.*"
WE DON'T HAVE MUCH *TIME.* VECTOR HAS PLANNED A PERFORMANCE OF *AZTEC* DANCES IN CLEARFLEET'S HONOR. THIS MAY BE YOUR ONLY CHANCE TO LOOK AROUND. TRY TO *BLEND IN.*
IN MY *UNIFORM?*
IMPROVISE, MA PETITE, *IMPROVISE.*

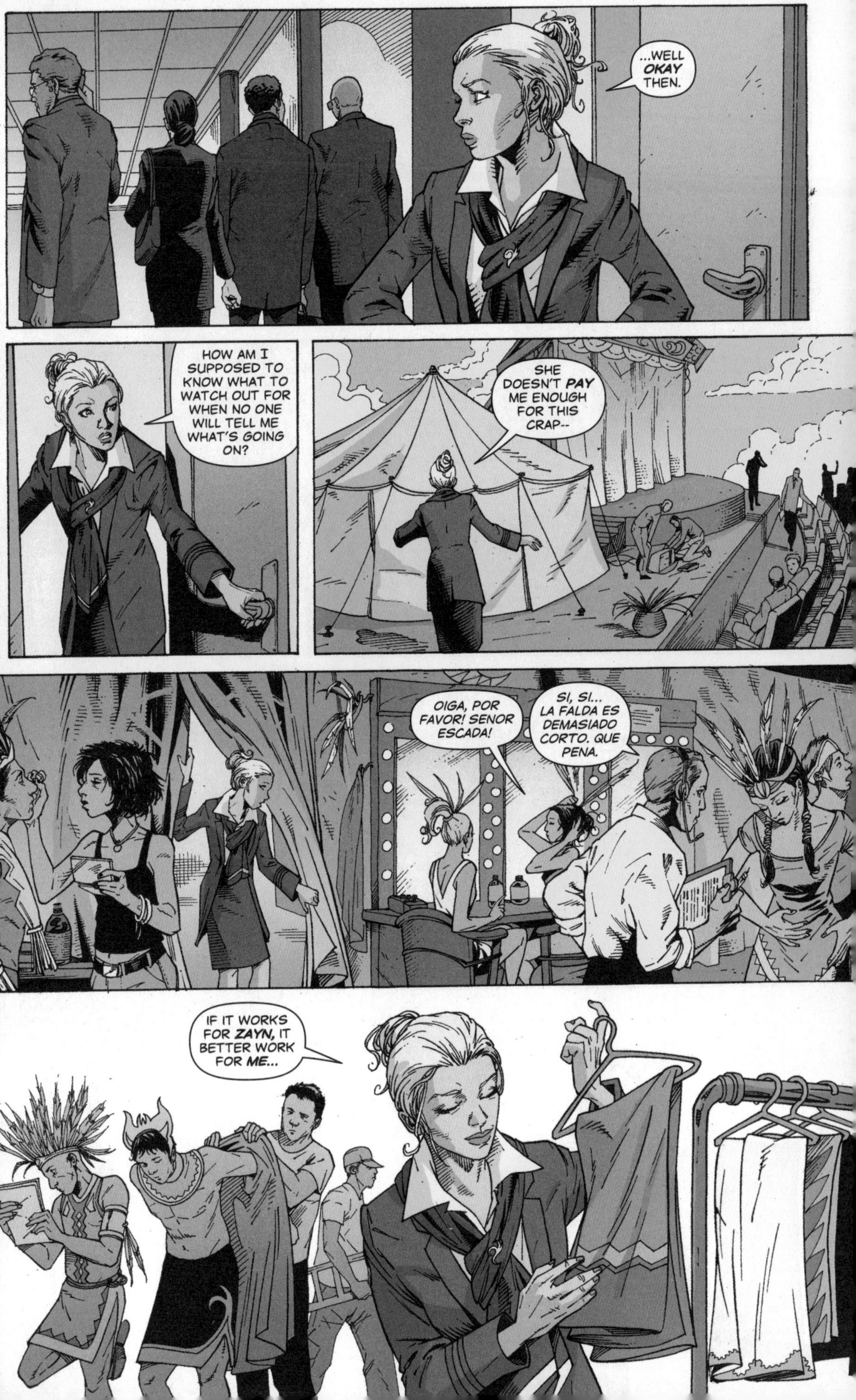
...WELL OKAY THEN.
HOW AM I SUPPOSED TO KNOW WHAT TO WATCH OUT FOR WHEN NO ONE WILL TELL ME WHAT'S GOING ON?
SHE DOESN'T PAY ME ENOUGH FOR THIS CRAP--
OIGA, POR FAVOR! SENOR ESCADA!
SI, SI... LA FALDA ES DEMASIADO CORTO. QUE PENA.
IF IT WORKS FOR ZAYN, IT BETTER WORK FOR ME...

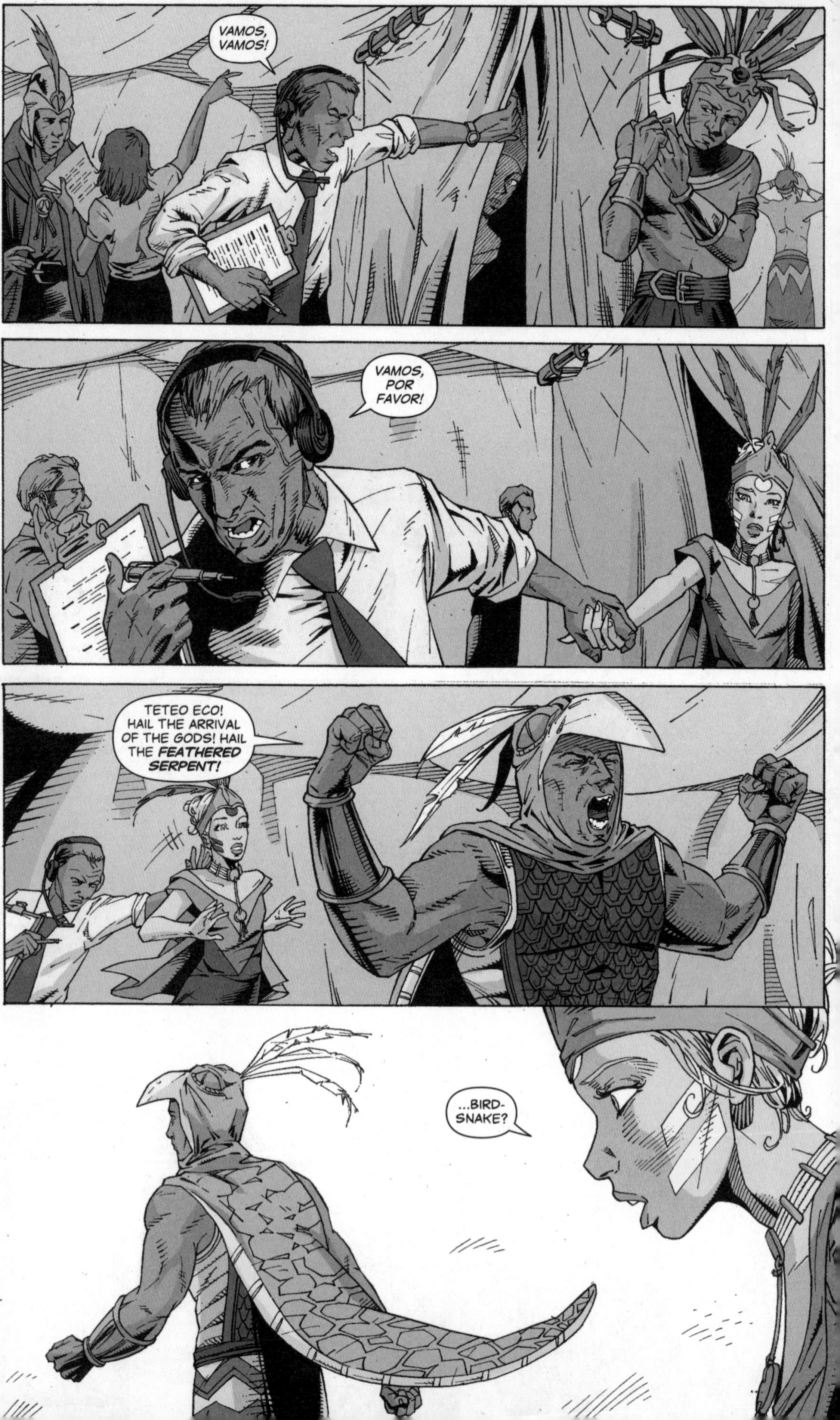
VAMOS, VAMOS!
VAMOS, POR FAVOR!
TETEO ECO! HAIL THE ARRIVAL OF THE GODS! HAIL THE **FEATHERED SERPENT!**
...BIRD-SNAKE?

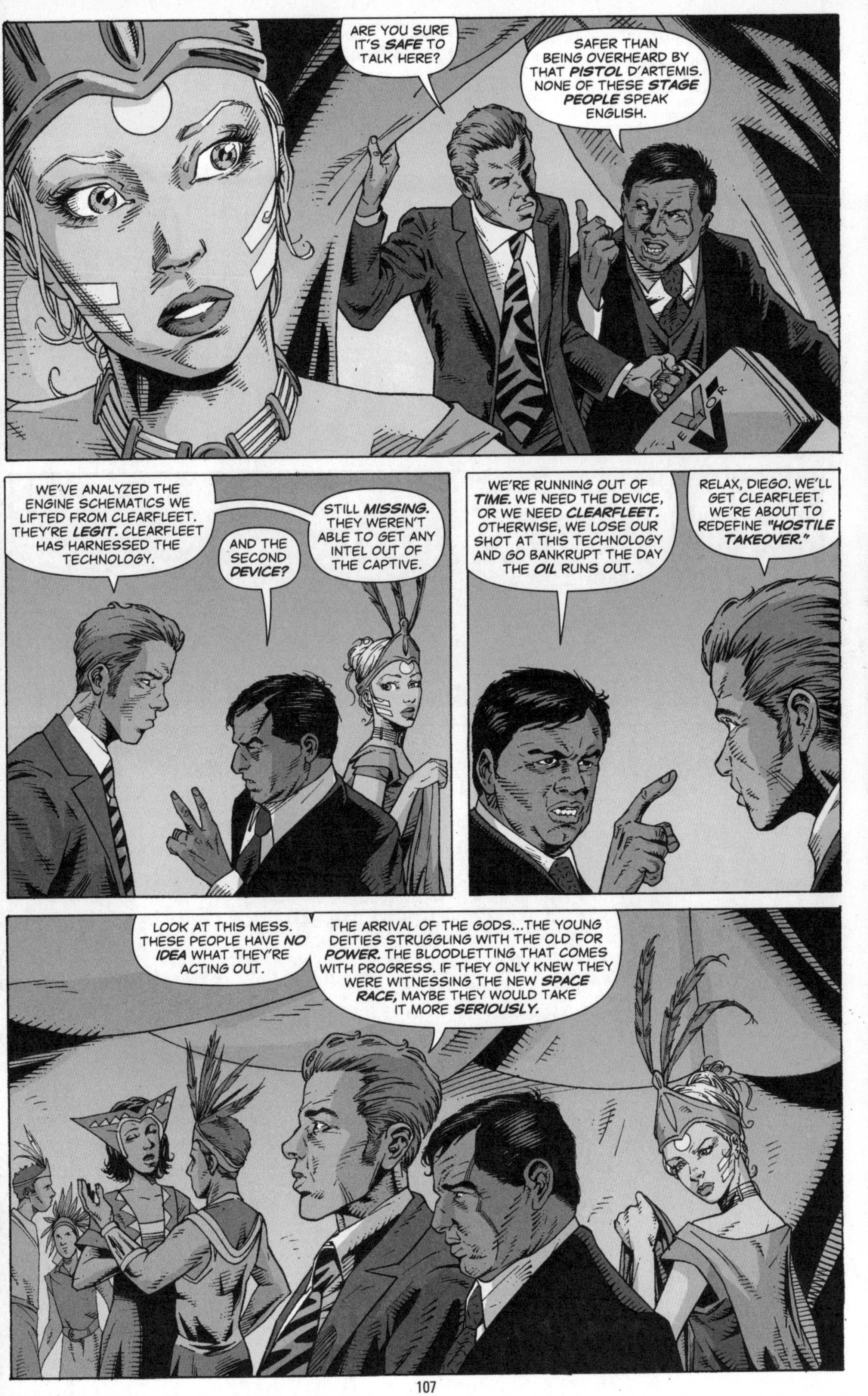
ARE YOU SURE IT'S *SAFE* TO TALK HERE?
SAFER THAN BEING OVERHEARD BY THAT *PISTOL* D'ARTEMIS. NONE OF THESE *STAGE PEOPLE* SPEAK ENGLISH.
WE'VE ANALYZED THE ENGINE SCHEMATICS WE LIFTED FROM CLEARFLEET. THEY'RE *LEGIT.* CLEARFLEET HAS HARNESSED THE TECHNOLOGY.
AND THE SECOND *DEVICE?*
STILL *MISSING.* THEY WEREN'T ABLE TO GET ANY INTEL OUT OF THE CAPTIVE.
WE'RE RUNNING OUT OF *TIME.* WE NEED THE DEVICE, OR WE NEED *CLEARFLEET.* OTHERWISE, WE LOSE OUR SHOT AT THIS TECHNOLOGY AND GO BANKRUPT THE DAY THE *OIL* RUNS OUT.
RELAX, DIEGO. WE'LL GET CLEARFLEET. WE'RE ABOUT TO REDEFINE *"HOSTILE TAKEOVER."*
LOOK AT THIS MESS. THESE PEOPLE HAVE *NO IDEA* WHAT THEY'RE ACTING OUT.
THE ARRIVAL OF THE GODS...THE YOUNG DEITIES STRUGGLING WITH THE OLD FOR *POWER.* THE BLOODLETTING THAT COMES WITH PROGRESS. IF THEY ONLY KNEW THEY WERE WITNESSING THE NEW *SPACE RACE,* MAYBE THEY WOULD TAKE IT MORE *SERIOUSLY.*

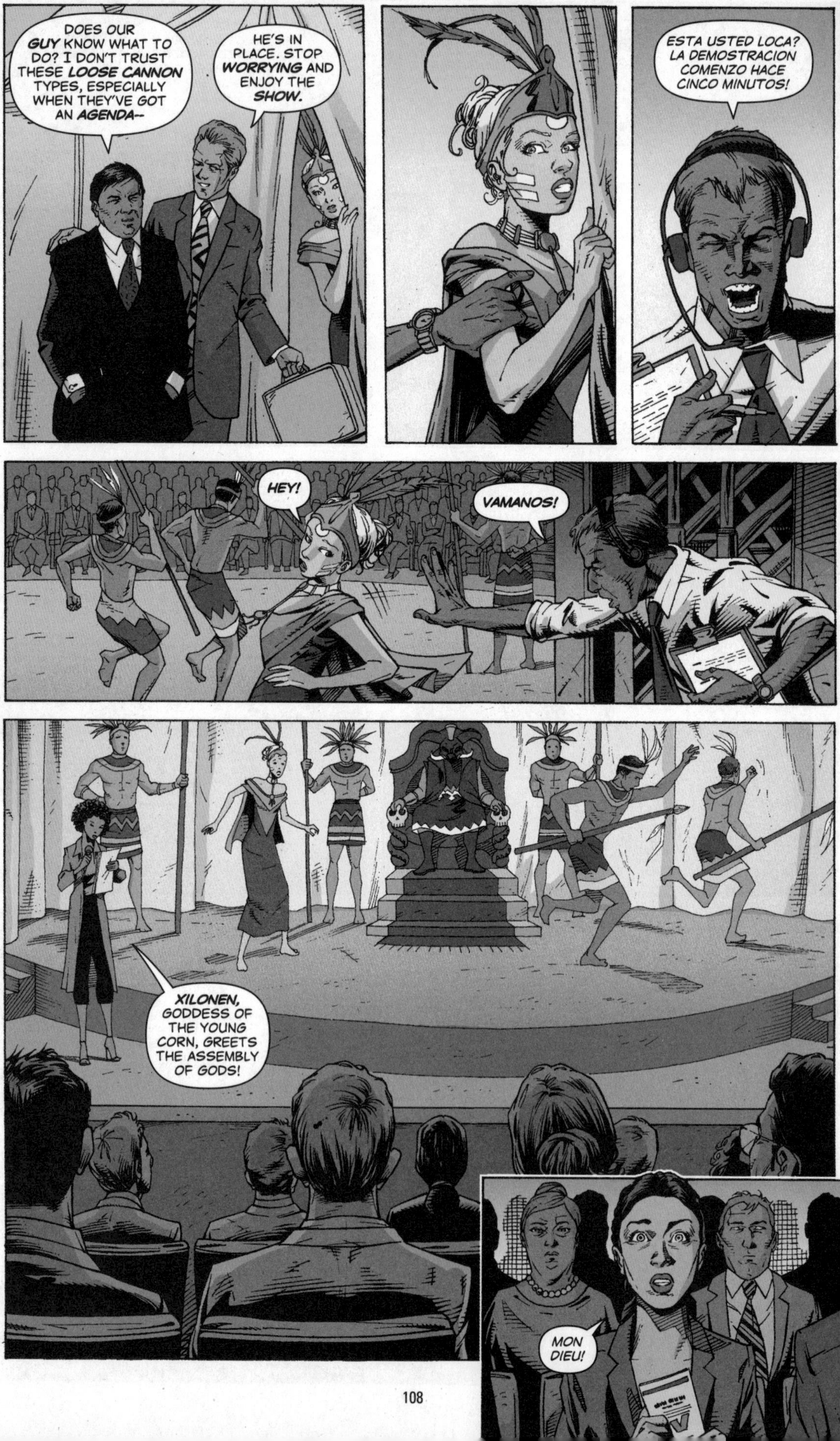

DOES OUR GUY KNOW WHAT TO DO? I DON'T TRUST THESE LOOSE CANNON TYPES, ESPECIALLY WHEN THEY'VE GOT AN AGENDA--
HE'S IN PLACE. STOP WORRYING AND ENJOY THE SHOW.
ESTA USTED LOCA? LA DEMOSTRACION COMENZO HACE CINCO MINUTOS!
HEY!
VAMANOS!
XILONEN, GODDESS OF THE YOUNG CORN, GREETS THE ASSEMBLY OF GODS!
MON DIEU!

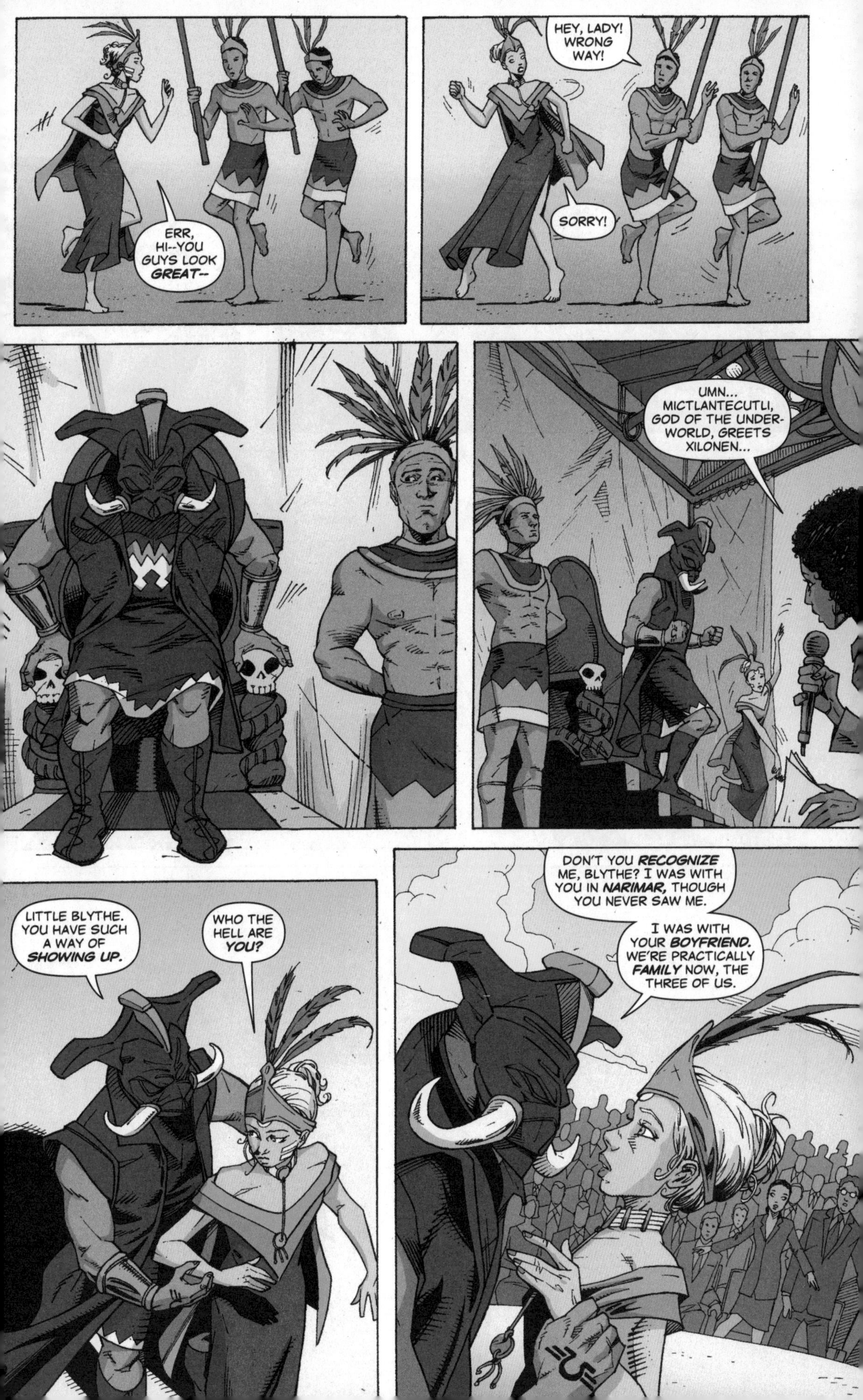
ERR, HI--YOU GUYS LOOK **GREAT--**
HEY, LADY! WRONG WAY!
SORRY!
UMN... MICTLANTECUTLI, GOD OF THE UNDER-WORLD, GREETS XILONEN...
LITTLE BLYTHE. YOU HAVE SUCH A WAY OF **SHOWING UP.**
WHO THE HELL ARE **YOU?**
DON'T YOU **RECOGNIZE** ME, BLYTHE? I WAS WITH YOU IN **NARIMAR,** THOUGH YOU NEVER SAW ME.
I WAS WITH YOUR **BOYFRIEND.** WE'RE PRACTICALLY **FAMILY** NOW, THE THREE OF US.

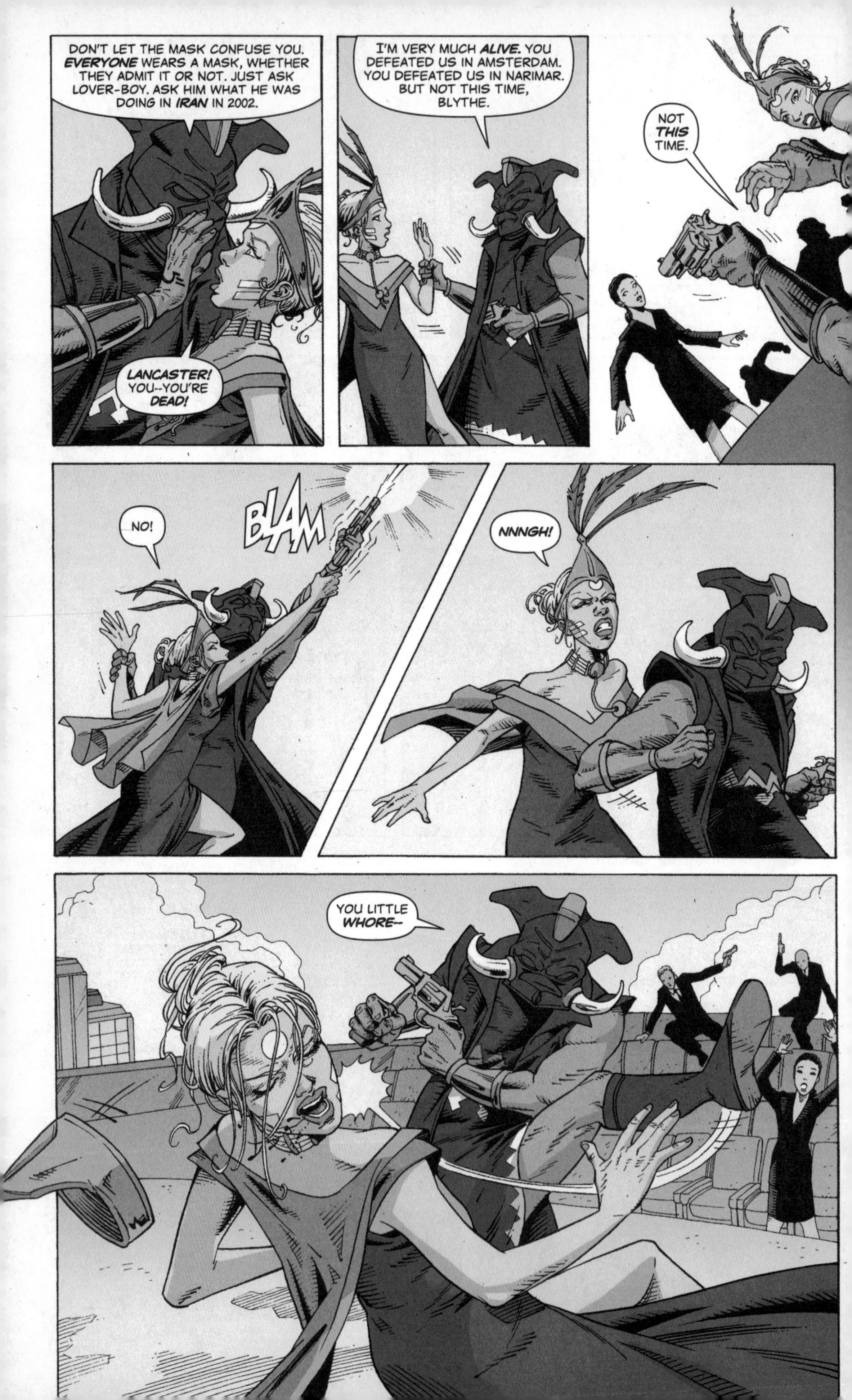
DON'T LET THE MASK CONFUSE YOU. **EVERYONE** WEARS A MASK, WHETHER THEY ADMIT IT OR NOT. JUST ASK LOVER-BOY. ASK HIM WHAT HE WAS DOING IN **IRAN** IN 2002.
LANCASTER! YOU--YOU'RE **DEAD!**
I'M VERY MUCH **ALIVE.** YOU DEFEATED US IN AMSTERDAM. YOU DEFEATED US IN NARIMAR. BUT NOT THIS TIME, BLYTHE.
NOT **THIS** TIME.
NO!
BLAM
NNNGH!
YOU LITTLE **WHORE--**

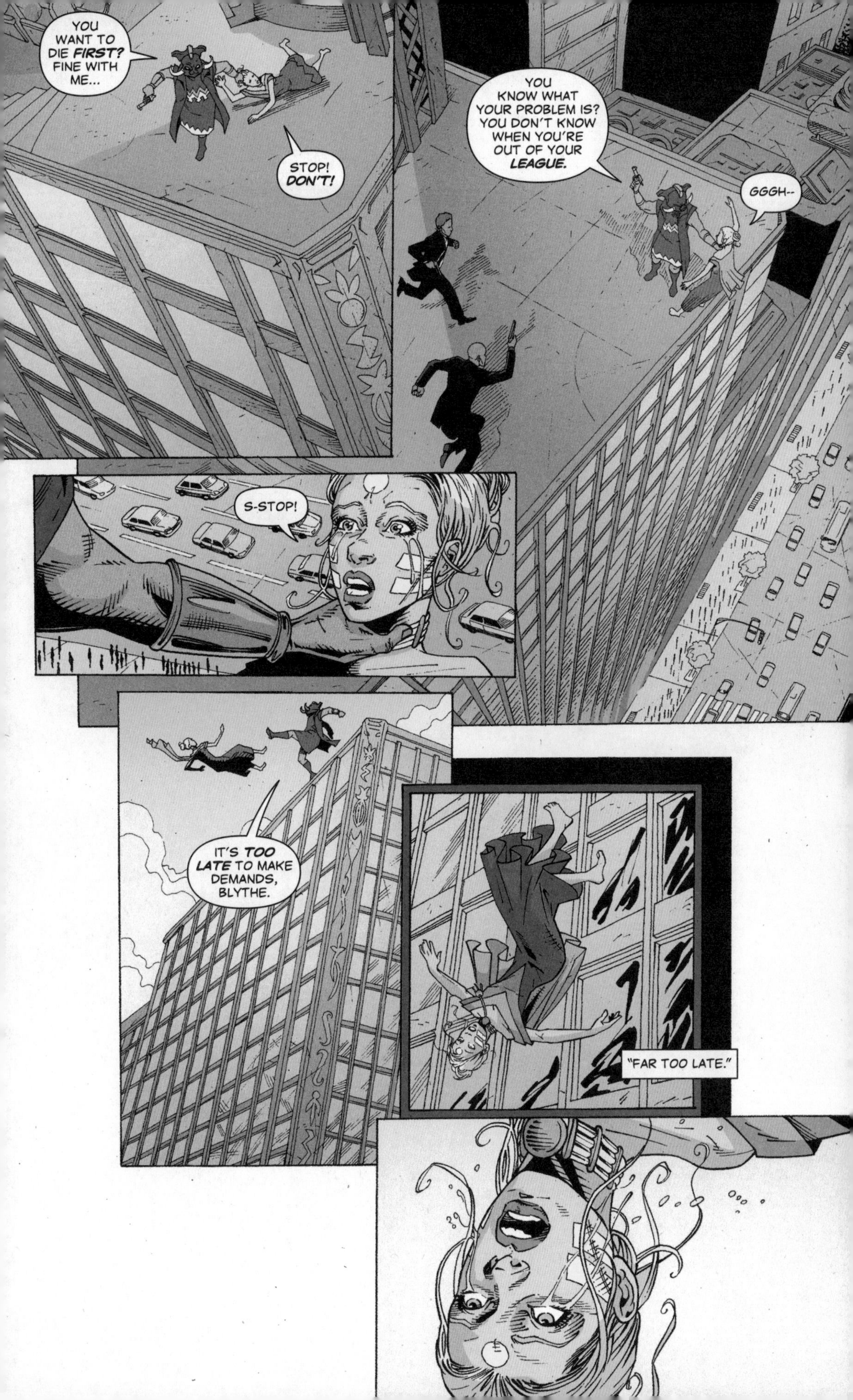
YOU WANT TO DIE FIRST? FINE WITH ME...
STOP! DON'T!
YOU KNOW WHAT YOUR PROBLEM IS? YOU DON'T KNOW WHEN YOU'RE OUT OF YOUR LEAGUE.
GGGH--
S-STOP!
IT'S TOO LATE TO MAKE DEMANDS, BLYTHE.
"FAR TOO LATE."

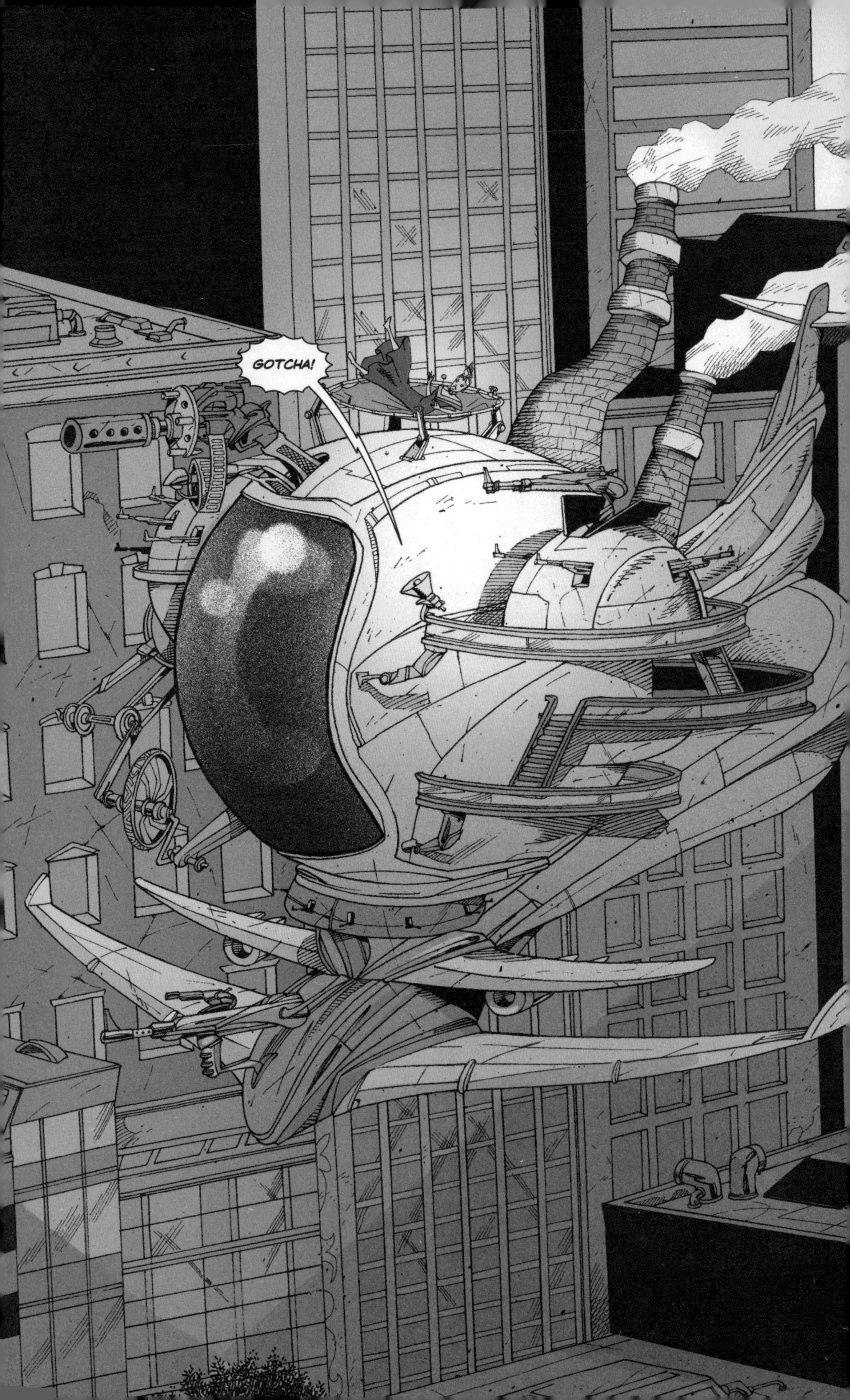
GOTCHA!

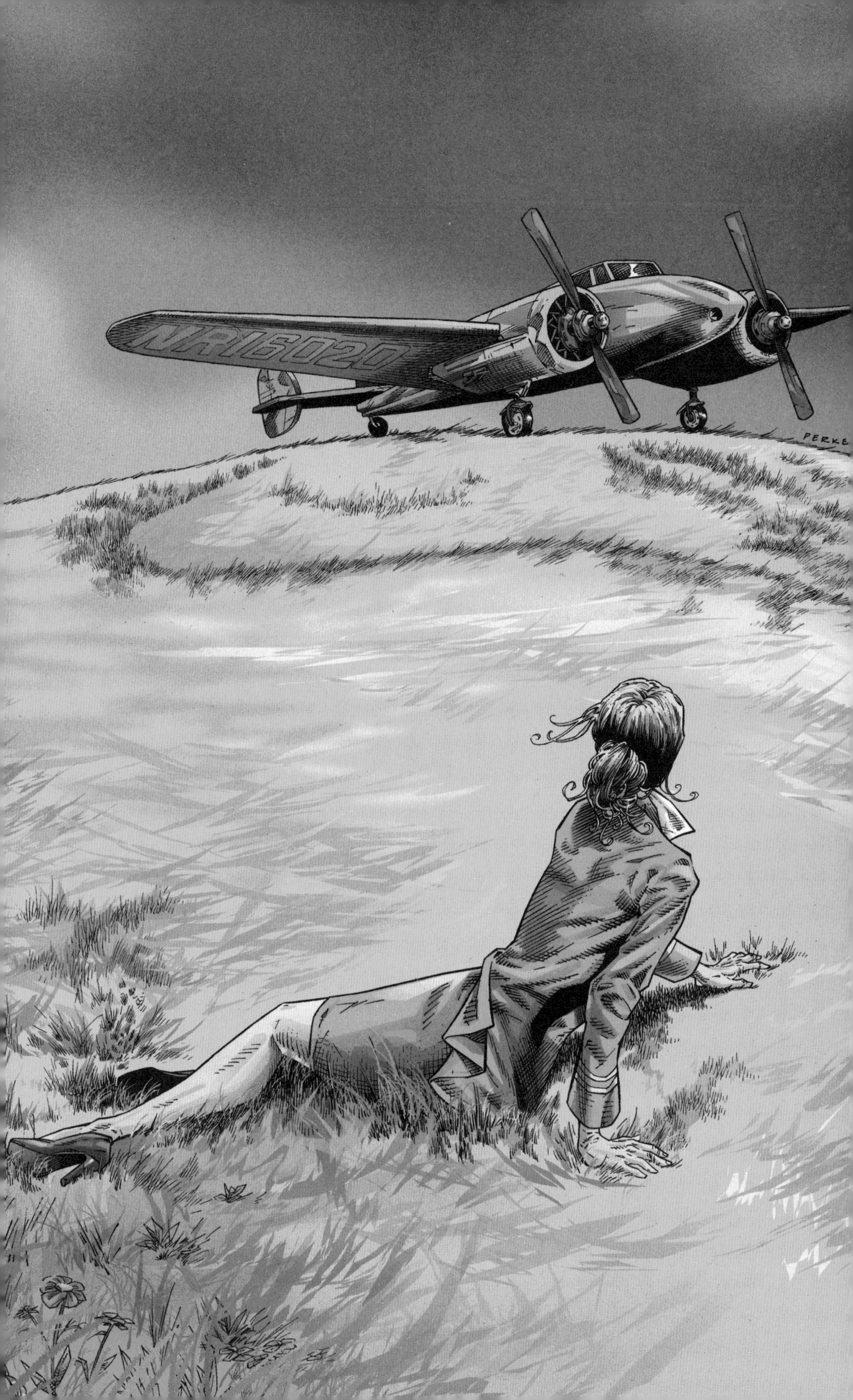
NR16020
PERKE

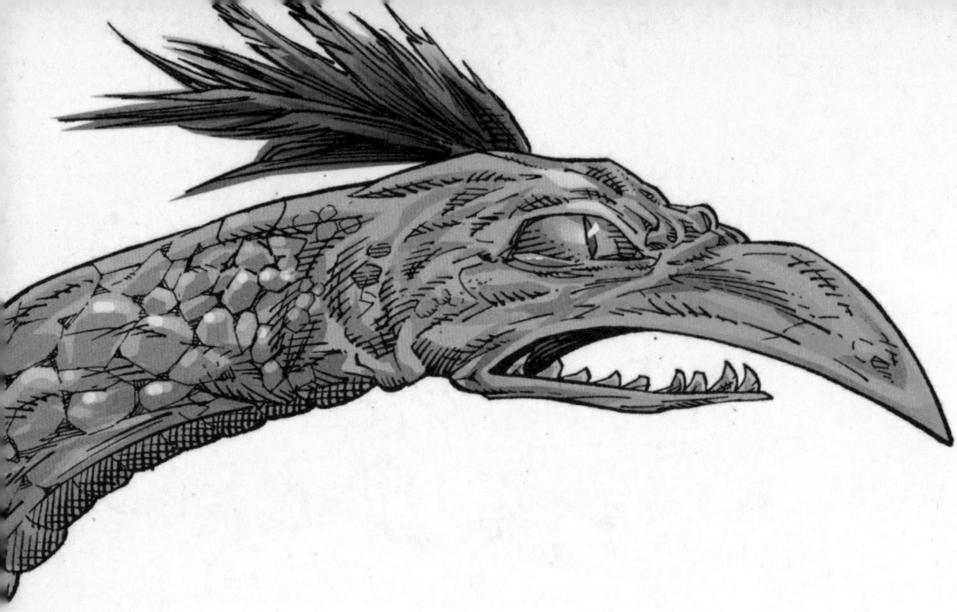

CHAPTER 5

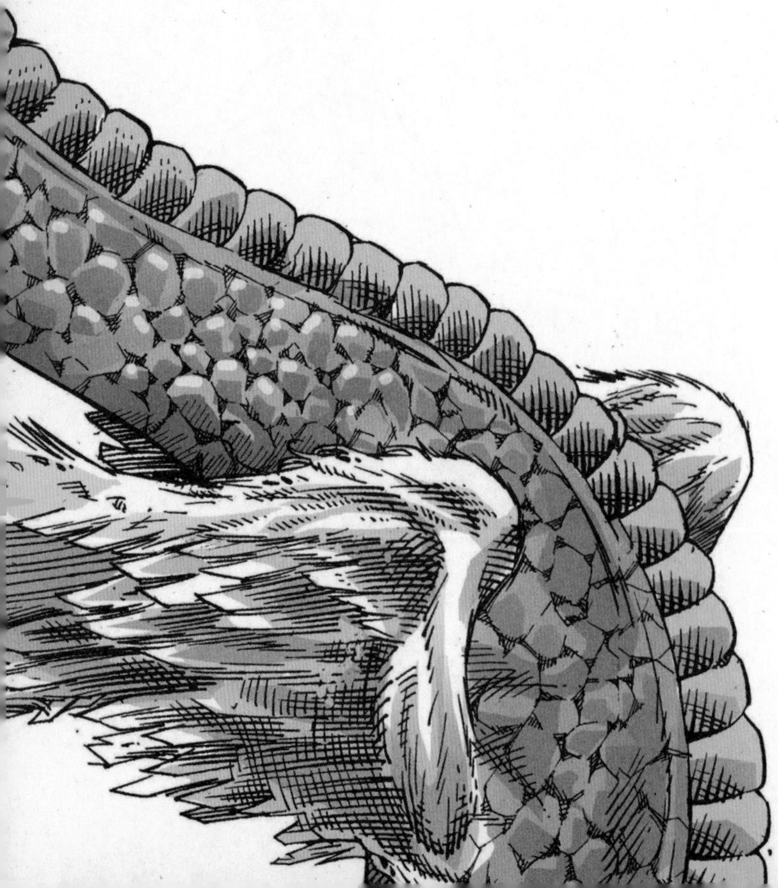

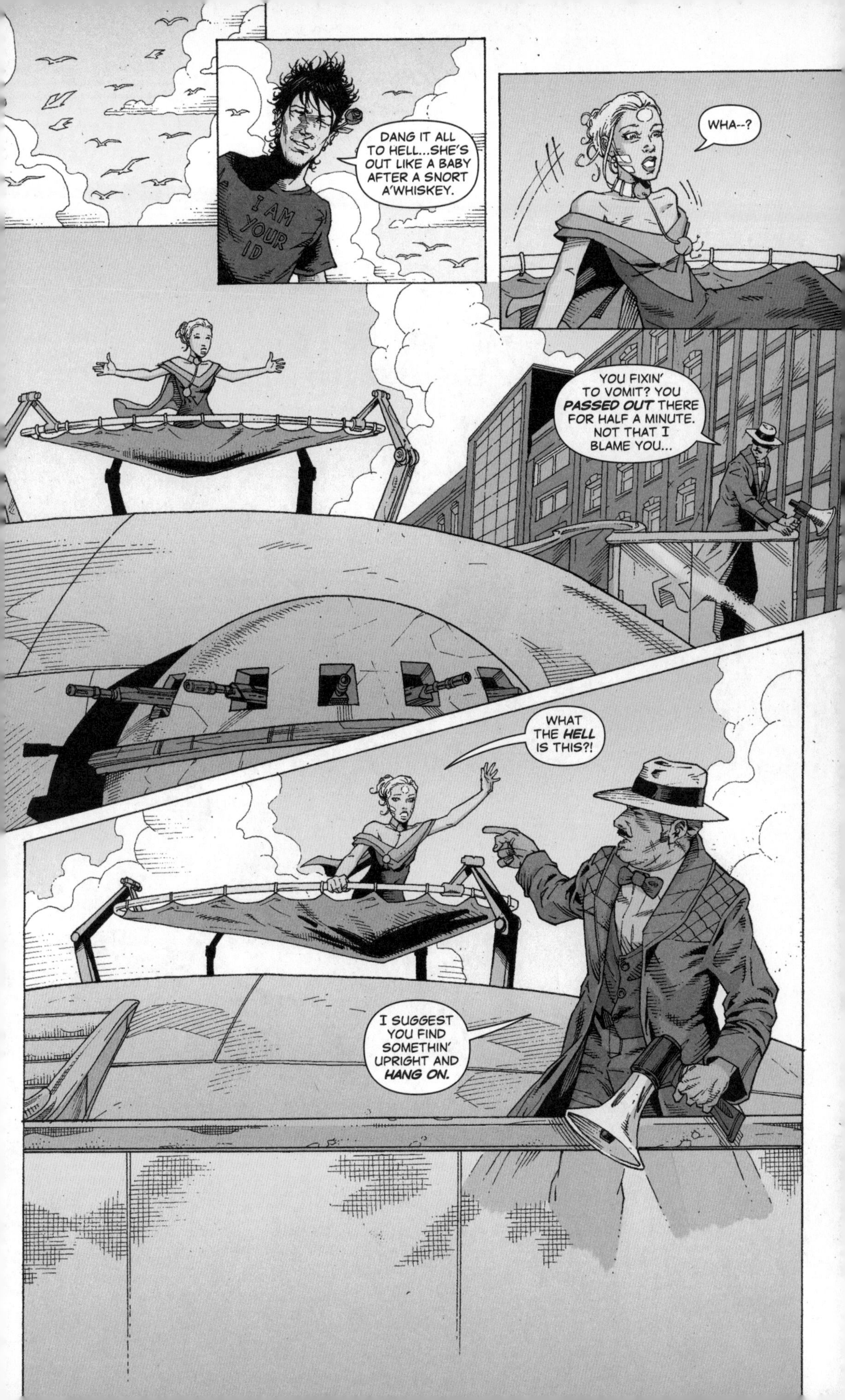
DANG IT ALL TO HELL...SHE'S OUT LIKE A BABY AFTER A SNORT A'WHISKEY.
I AM YOUR ID
WHA--?
YOU FIXIN' TO VOMIT? YOU **PASSED OUT** THERE FOR HALF A MINUTE. NOT THAT I BLAME YOU...
WHAT THE **HELL** IS THIS?!
I SUGGEST YOU FIND SOMETHIN' UPRIGHT AND **HANG ON.**

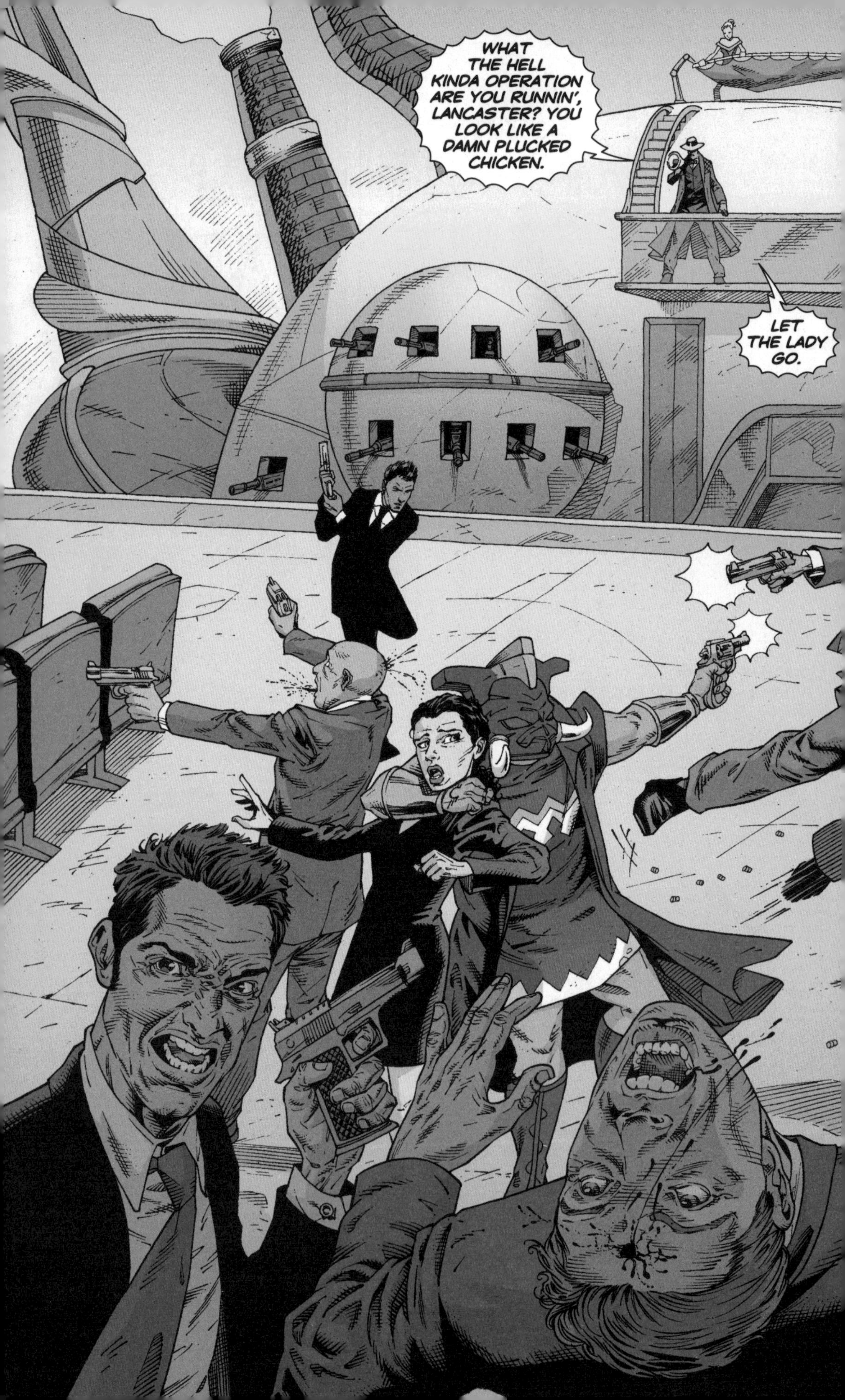
WHAT THE HELL KINDA OPERATION ARE YOU RUNNIN', LANCASTER? YOU LOOK LIKE A DAMN PLUCKED CHICKEN.
LET THE LADY GO.

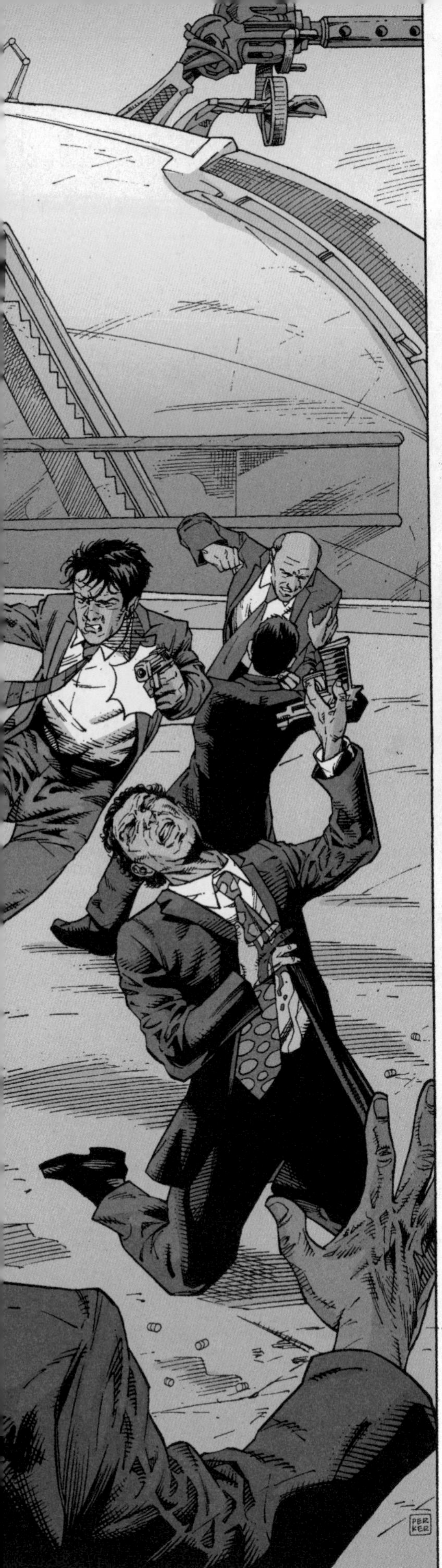

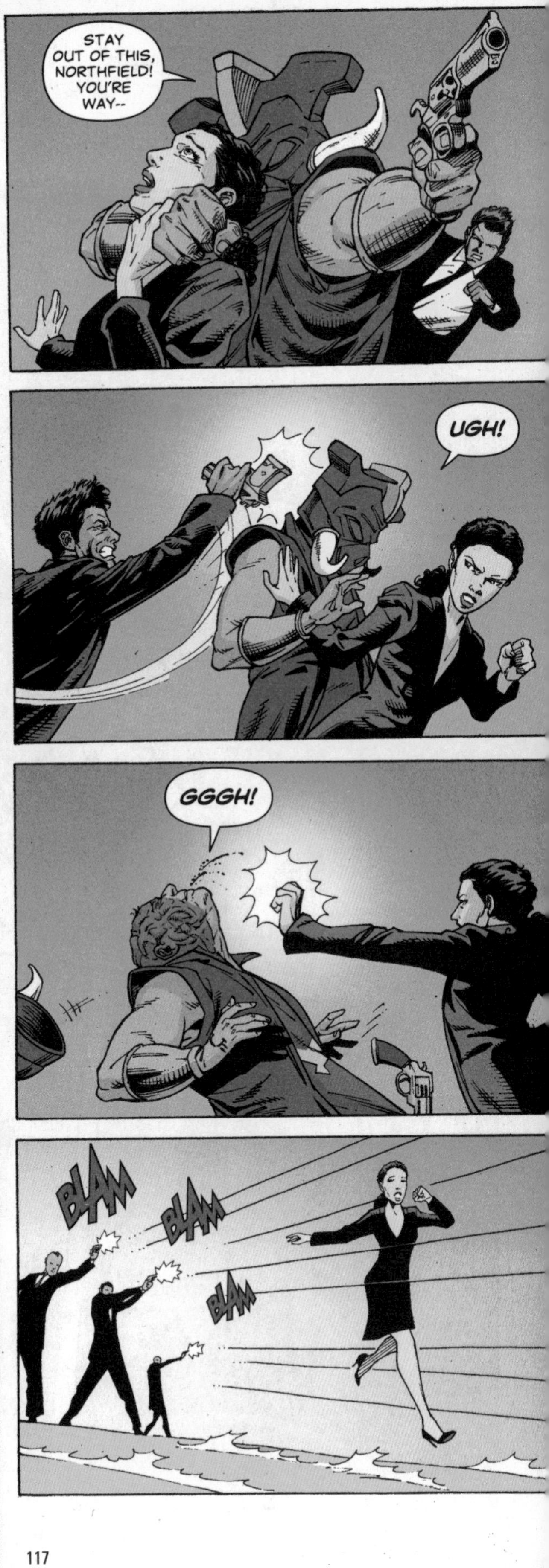
STAY OUT OF THIS, NORTHFIELD! YOU'RE WAY--
UGH!
GGGH!
BLAM
BLAM
BLAM

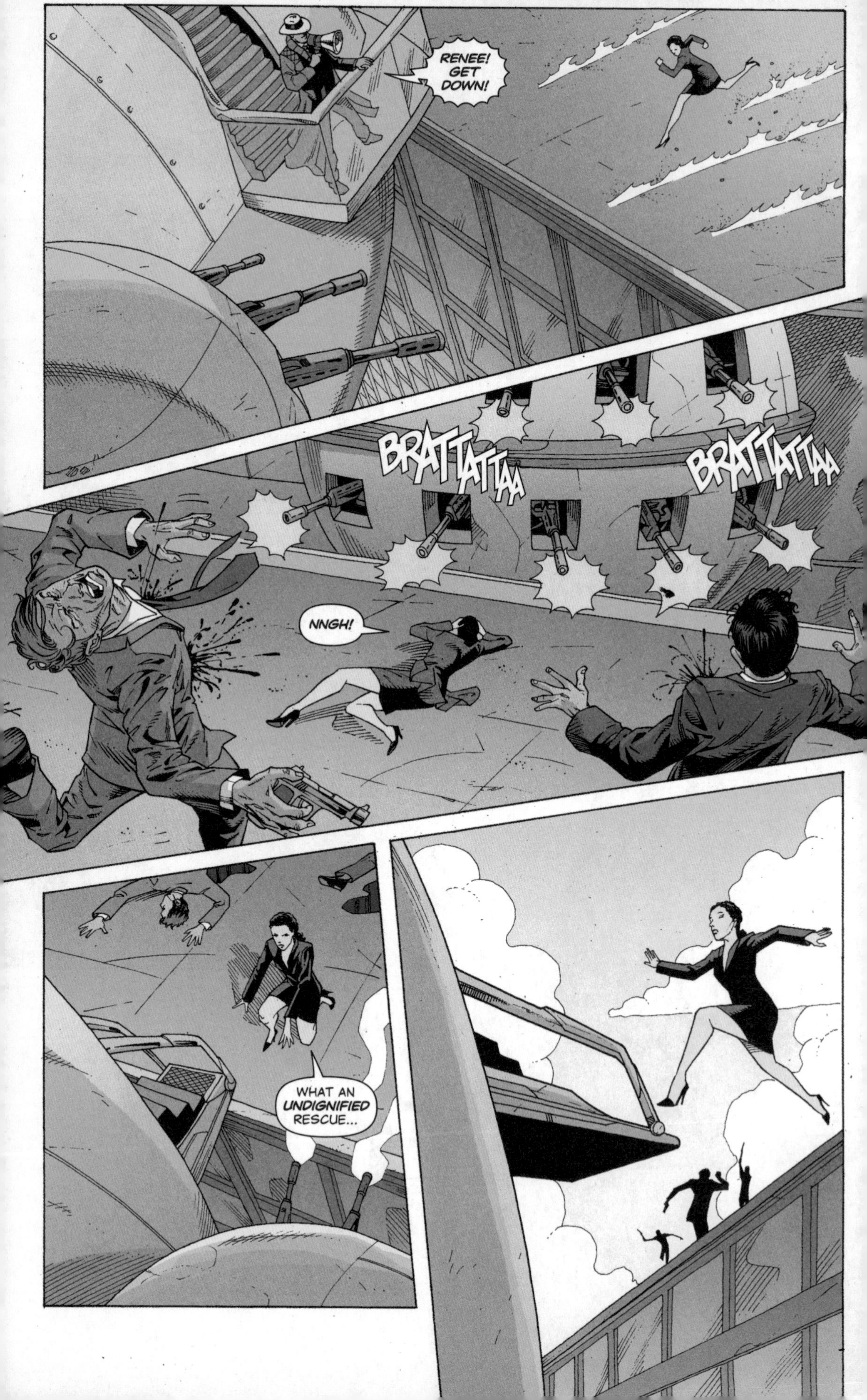
RENEE! GET DOWN!
BRATTATTAA
BRATTATTAA
NNGH!
WHAT AN UNDIGNIFIED RESCUE...

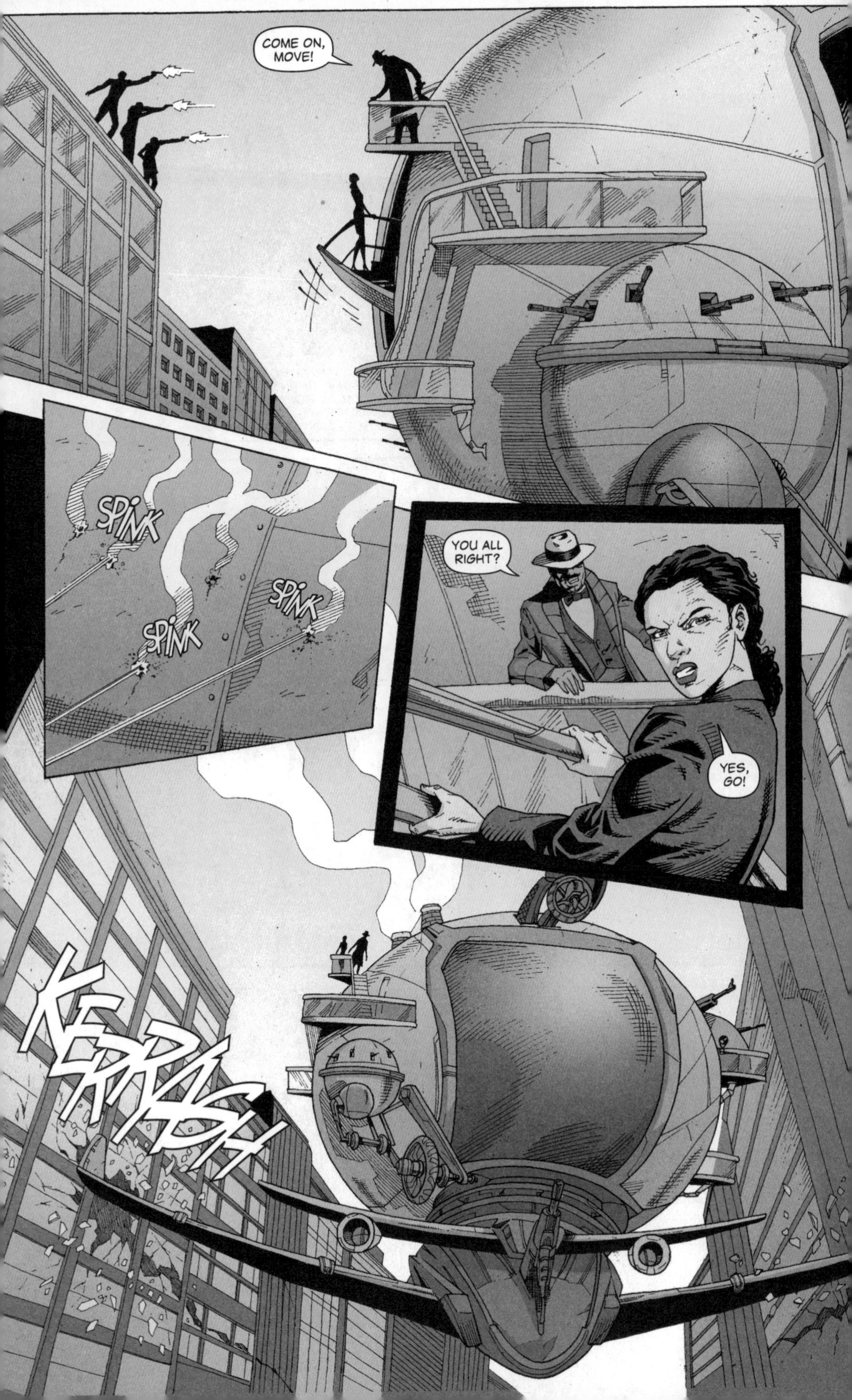
COME ON, MOVE!
SPINK
SPINK
SPINK
YOU ALL RIGHT?
YES, GO!
KERRASH

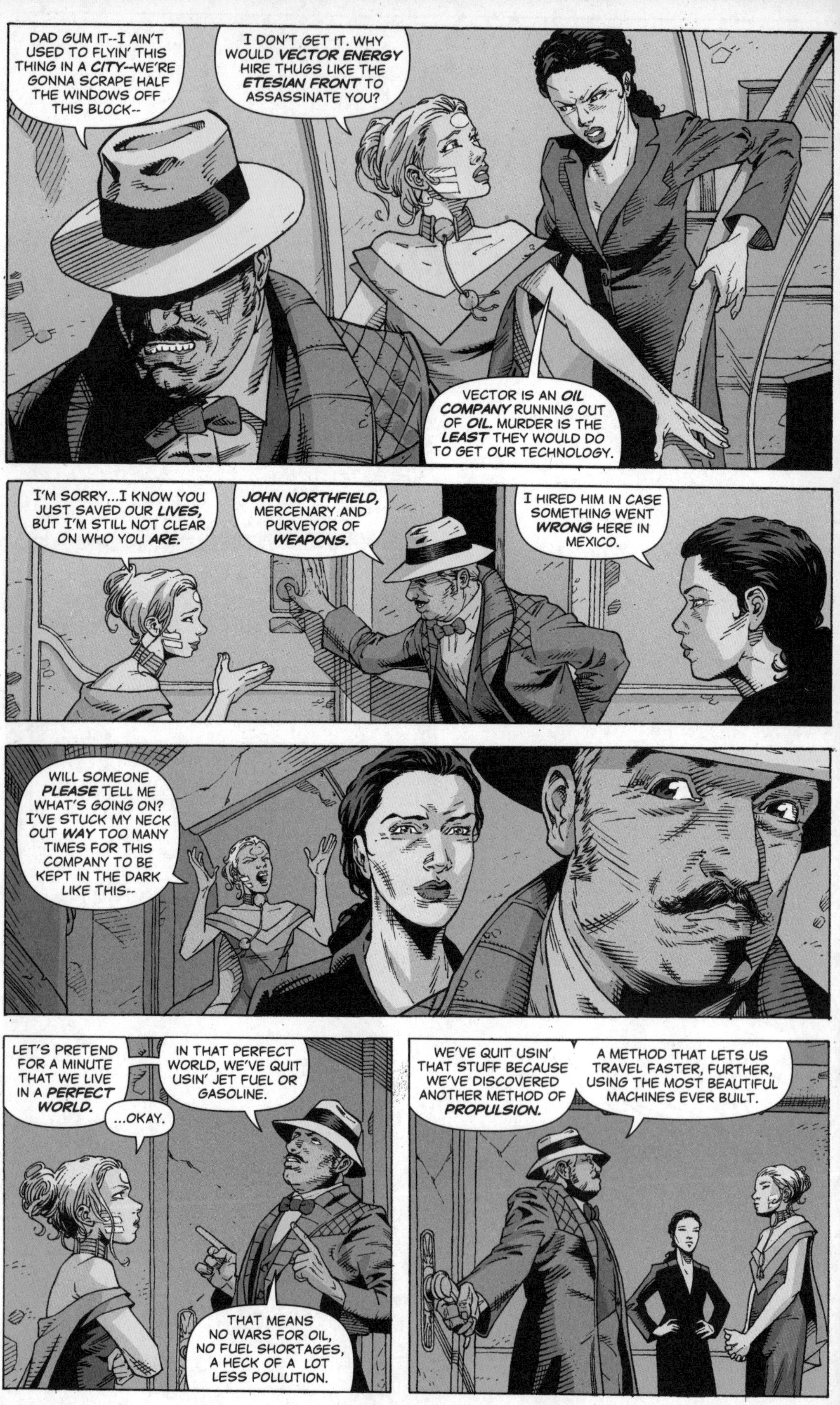
DAD GUM IT--I AIN'T USED TO FLYIN' THIS THING IN A CITY--WE'RE GONNA SCRAPE HALF THE WINDOWS OFF THIS BLOCK--
I DON'T GET IT. WHY WOULD VECTOR ENERGY HIRE THUGS LIKE THE ETESIAN FRONT TO ASSASSINATE YOU?
VECTOR IS AN OIL COMPANY RUNNING OUT OF OIL. MURDER IS THE LEAST THEY WOULD DO TO GET OUR TECHNOLOGY.
I'M SORRY...I KNOW YOU JUST SAVED OUR LIVES, BUT I'M STILL NOT CLEAR ON WHO YOU ARE.
JOHN NORTHFIELD, MERCENARY AND PURVEYOR OF WEAPONS.
I HIRED HIM IN CASE SOMETHING WENT WRONG HERE IN MEXICO.
WILL SOMEONE PLEASE TELL ME WHAT'S GOING ON? I'VE STUCK MY NECK OUT WAY TOO MANY TIMES FOR THIS COMPANY TO BE KEPT IN THE DARK LIKE THIS--
LET'S PRETEND FOR A MINUTE THAT WE LIVE IN A PERFECT WORLD.
...OKAY.
IN THAT PERFECT WORLD, WE'VE QUIT USIN' JET FUEL OR GASOLINE.
THAT MEANS NO WARS FOR OIL, NO FUEL SHORTAGES, A HECK OF A LOT LESS POLLUTION.
WE'VE QUIT USIN' THAT STUFF BECAUSE WE'VE DISCOVERED ANOTHER METHOD OF PROPULSION.
A METHOD THAT LETS US TRAVEL FASTER, FURTHER, USING THE MOST BEAUTIFUL MACHINES EVER BUILT.

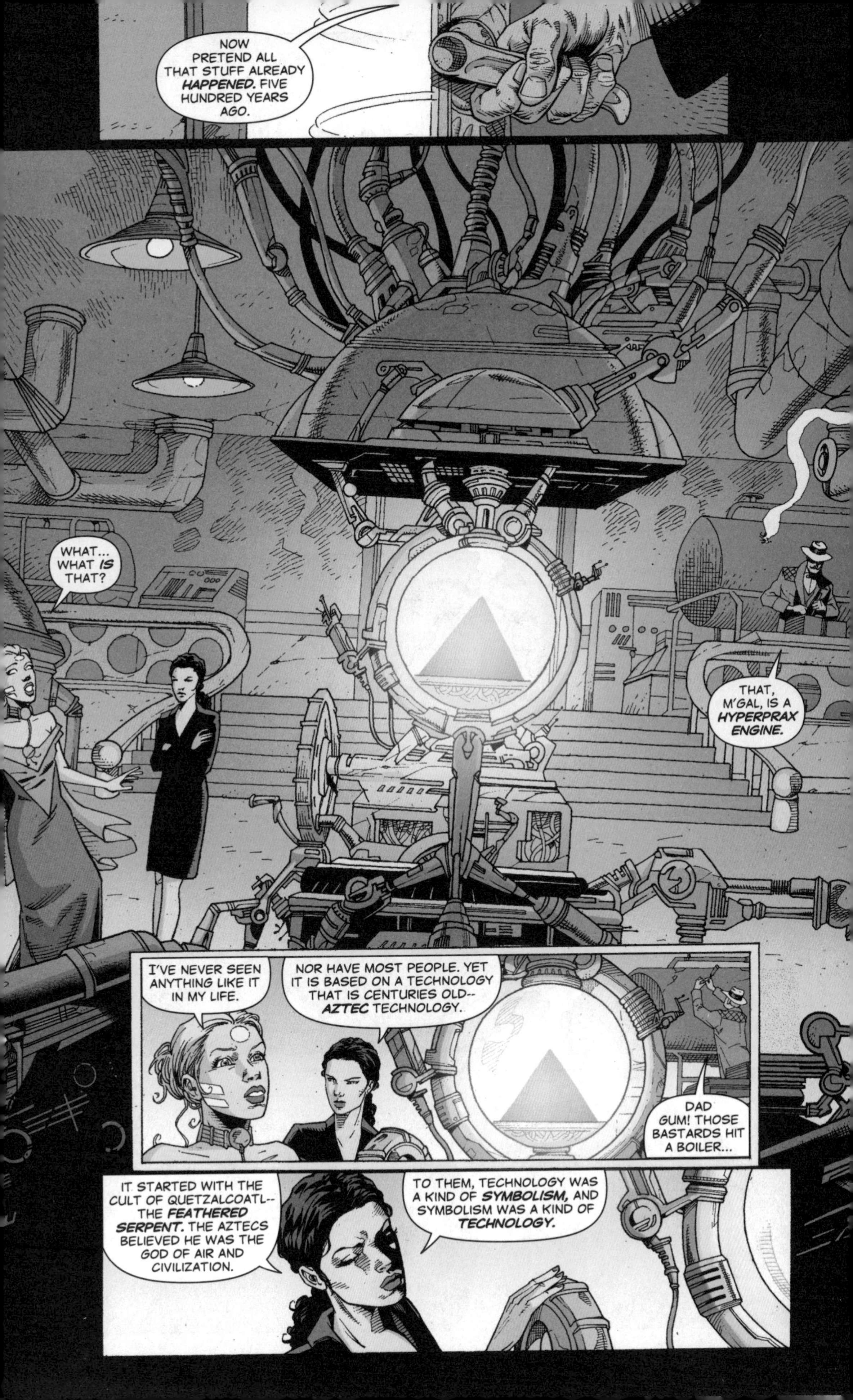
NOW PRETEND ALL THAT STUFF ALREADY HAPPENED. FIVE HUNDRED YEARS AGO.
WHAT... WHAT IS THAT?
THAT, M'GAL, IS A HYPERPRAX ENGINE.
I'VE NEVER SEEN ANYTHING LIKE IT IN MY LIFE.
NOR HAVE MOST PEOPLE. YET IT IS BASED ON A TECHNOLOGY THAT IS CENTURIES OLD-- AZTEC TECHNOLOGY.
DAD GUM! THOSE BASTARDS HIT A BOILER...
IT STARTED WITH THE CULT OF QUETZALCOATL-- THE FEATHERED SERPENT. THE AZTECS BELIEVED HE WAS THE GOD OF AIR AND CIVILIZATION.
TO THEM, TECHNOLOGY WAS A KIND OF SYMBOLISM, AND SYMBOLISM WAS A KIND OF TECHNOLOGY.

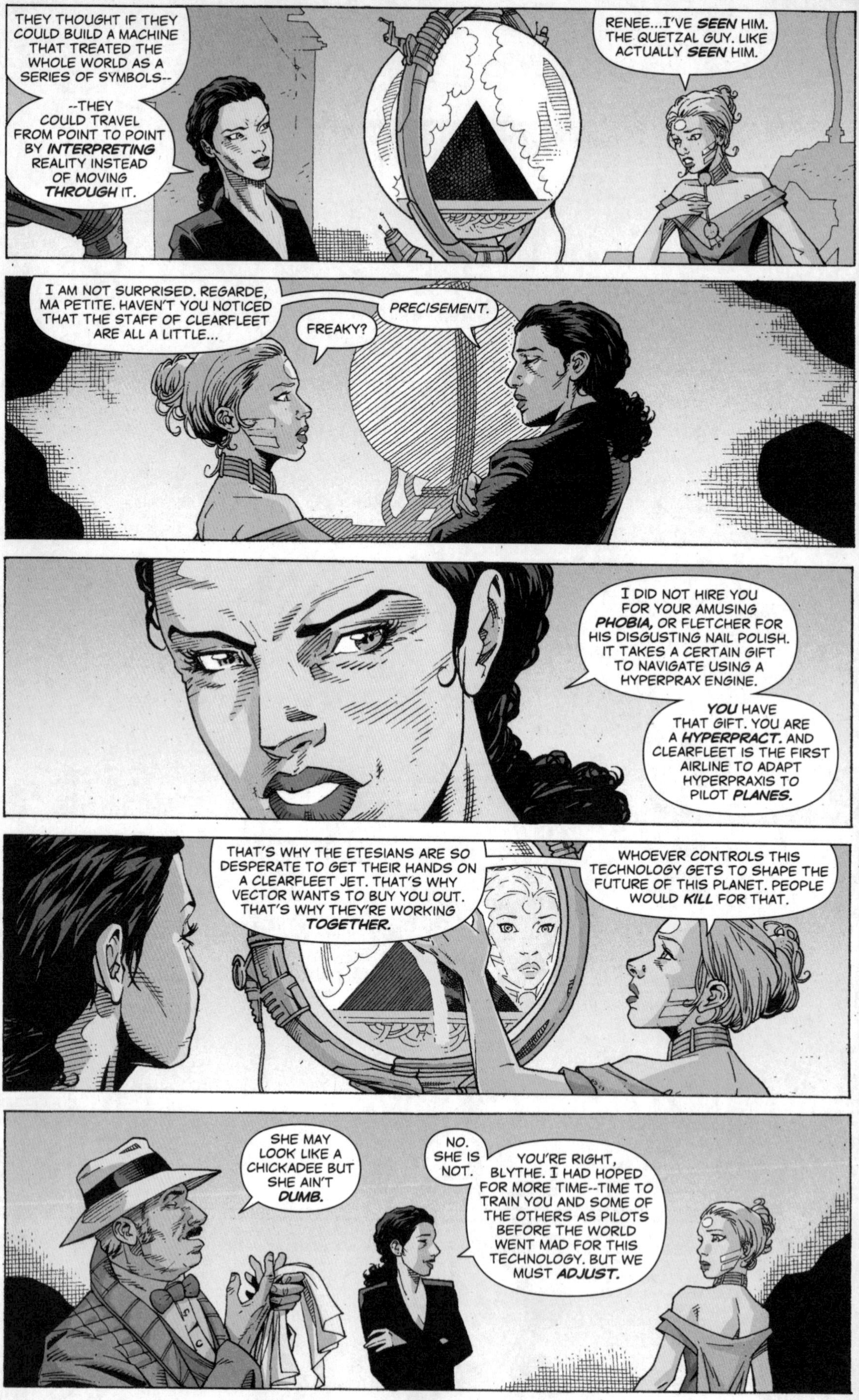
THEY THOUGHT IF THEY COULD BUILD A MACHINE THAT TREATED THE WHOLE WORLD AS A SERIES OF SYMBOLS--
--THEY COULD TRAVEL FROM POINT TO POINT BY INTERPRETING REALITY INSTEAD OF MOVING THROUGH IT.
RENEE...I'VE SEEN HIM. THE QUETZAL GUY. LIKE ACTUALLY SEEN HIM.
I AM NOT SURPRISED. REGARDE, MA PETITE. HAVEN'T YOU NOTICED THAT THE STAFF OF CLEARFLEET ARE ALL A LITTLE...
FREAKY?
PRECISEMENT.
I DID NOT HIRE YOU FOR YOUR AMUSING PHOBIA, OR FLETCHER FOR HIS DISGUSTING NAIL POLISH. IT TAKES A CERTAIN GIFT TO NAVIGATE USING A HYPERPRAX ENGINE.
YOU HAVE THAT GIFT. YOU ARE A HYPERPRACT. AND CLEARFLEET IS THE FIRST AIRLINE TO ADAPT HYPERPRAXIS TO PILOT PLANES.
THAT'S WHY THE ETESIANS ARE SO DESPERATE TO GET THEIR HANDS ON A CLEARFLEET JET. THAT'S WHY VECTOR WANTS TO BUY YOU OUT. THAT'S WHY THEY'RE WORKING TOGETHER.
WHOEVER CONTROLS THIS TECHNOLOGY GETS TO SHAPE THE FUTURE OF THIS PLANET. PEOPLE WOULD KILL FOR THAT.
SHE MAY LOOK LIKE A CHICKADEE BUT SHE AIN'T DUMB.
NO. SHE IS NOT.
YOU'RE RIGHT, BLYTHE. I HAD HOPED FOR MORE TIME--TIME TO TRAIN YOU AND SOME OF THE OTHERS AS PILOTS BEFORE THE WORLD WENT MAD FOR THIS TECHNOLOGY. BUT WE MUST ADJUST.

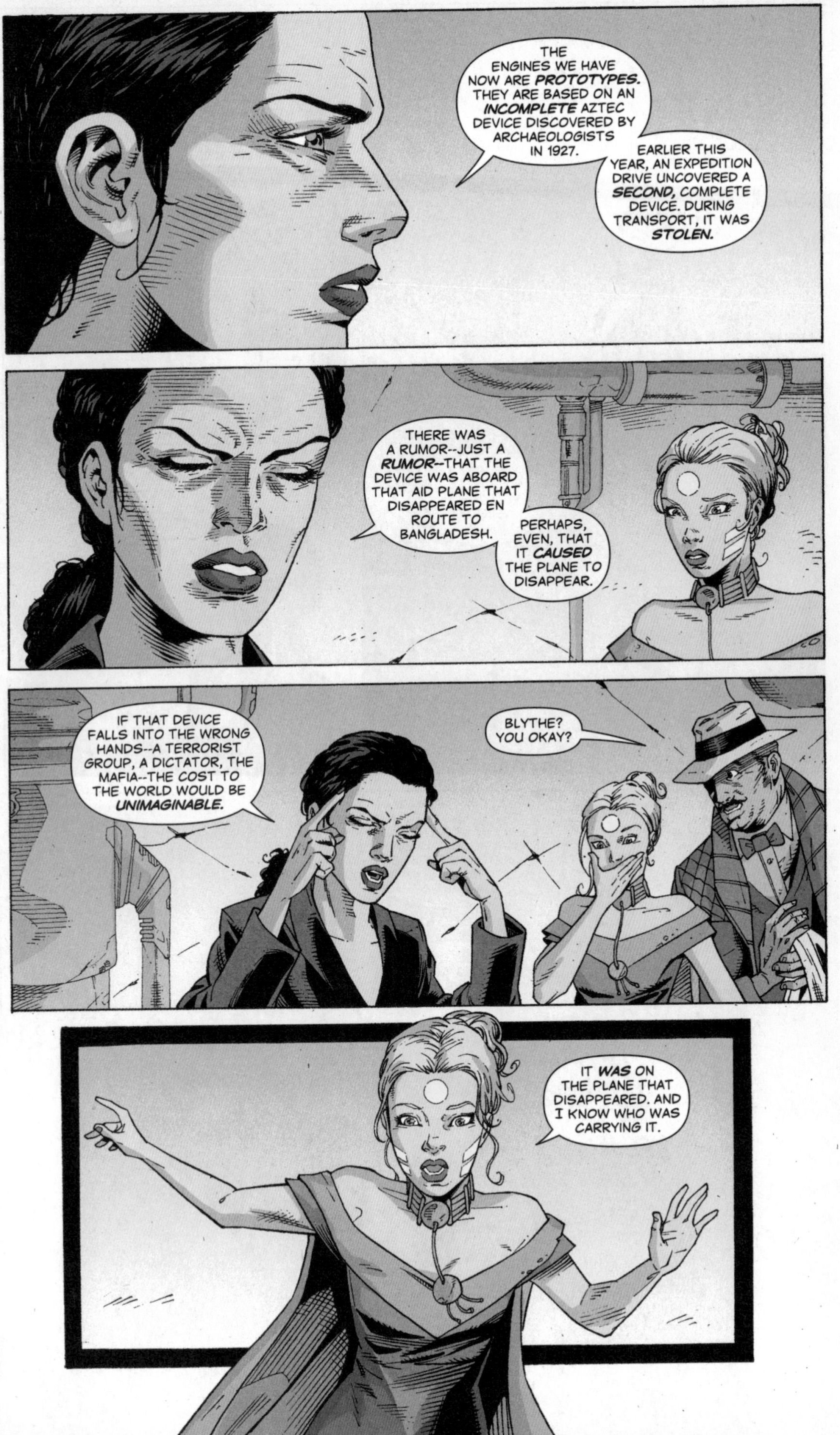
THE ENGINES WE HAVE NOW ARE PROTOTYPES. THEY ARE BASED ON AN INCOMPLETE AZTEC DEVICE DISCOVERED BY ARCHAEOLOGISTS IN 1927.
EARLIER THIS YEAR, AN EXPEDITION DRIVE UNCOVERED A SECOND, COMPLETE DEVICE. DURING TRANSPORT, IT WAS STOLEN.
THERE WAS A RUMOR--JUST A RUMOR--THAT THE DEVICE WAS ABOARD THAT AID PLANE THAT DISAPPEARED EN ROUTE TO BANGLADESH.
PERHAPS, EVEN, THAT IT CAUSED THE PLANE TO DISAPPEAR.
IF THAT DEVICE FALLS INTO THE WRONG HANDS--A TERRORIST GROUP, A DICTATOR, THE MAFIA--THE COST TO THE WORLD WOULD BE UNIMAGINABLE.
BLYTHE? YOU OKAY?
IT WAS ON THE PLANE THAT DISAPPEARED. AND I KNOW WHO WAS CARRYING IT.

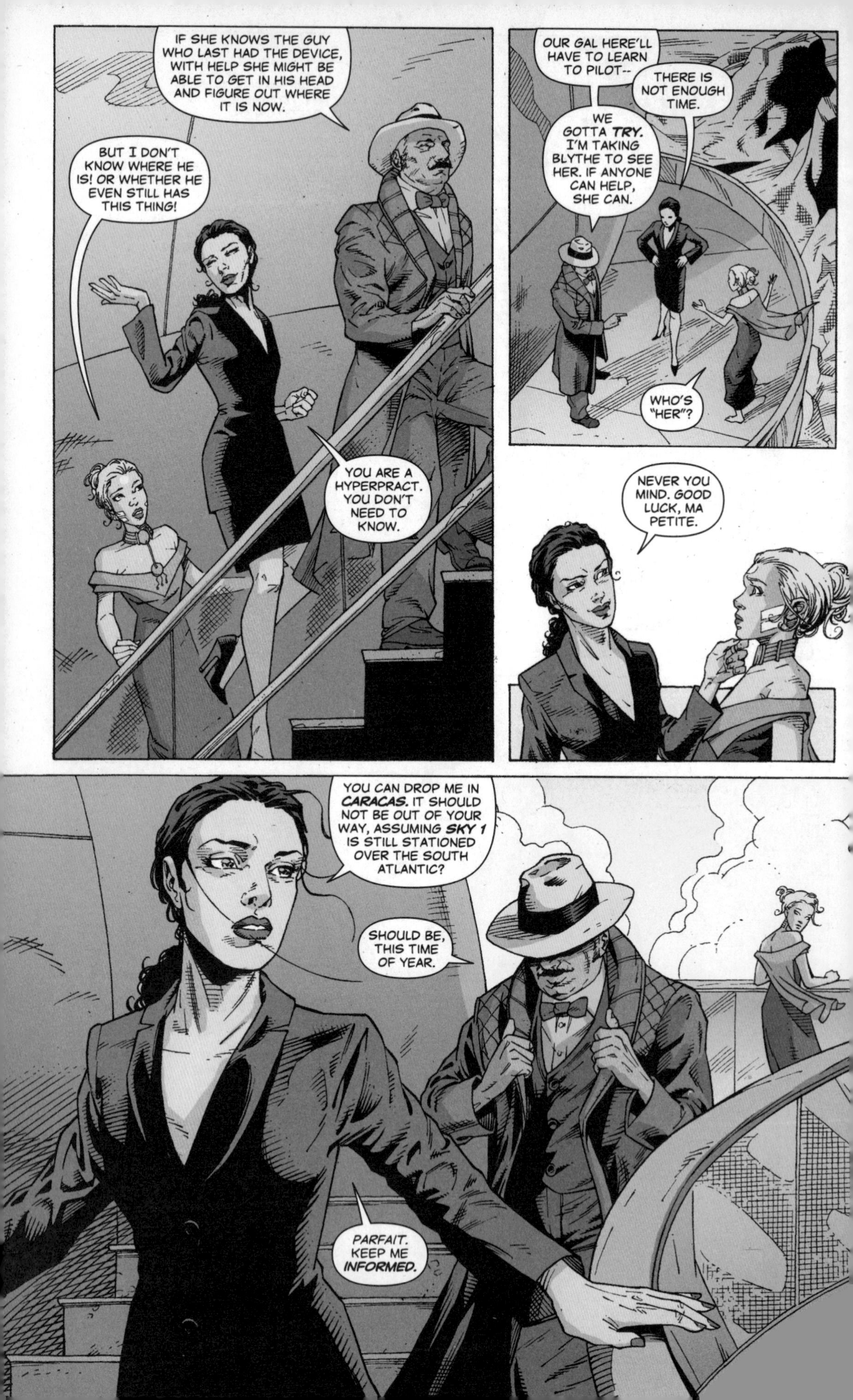
IF SHE KNOWS THE GUY WHO LAST HAD THE DEVICE, WITH HELP SHE MIGHT BE ABLE TO GET IN HIS HEAD AND FIGURE OUT WHERE IT IS NOW.
BUT I DON'T KNOW WHERE HE IS! OR WHETHER HE EVEN STILL HAS THIS THING!
YOU ARE A HYPERPRACT. YOU DON'T NEED TO KNOW.
OUR GAL HERE'LL HAVE TO LEARN TO PILOT--
THERE IS NOT ENOUGH TIME.
WE GOTTA **TRY.** I'M TAKING BLYTHE TO SEE HER. IF ANYONE CAN HELP, SHE CAN.
WHO'S "HER"?
NEVER YOU MIND. GOOD LUCK, MA PETITE.
YOU CAN DROP ME IN **CARACAS.** IT SHOULD NOT BE OUT OF YOUR WAY, ASSUMING **SKY 1** IS STILL STATIONED OVER THE SOUTH ATLANTIC?
SHOULD BE, THIS TIME OF YEAR.
PARFAIT. KEEP ME **INFORMED.**

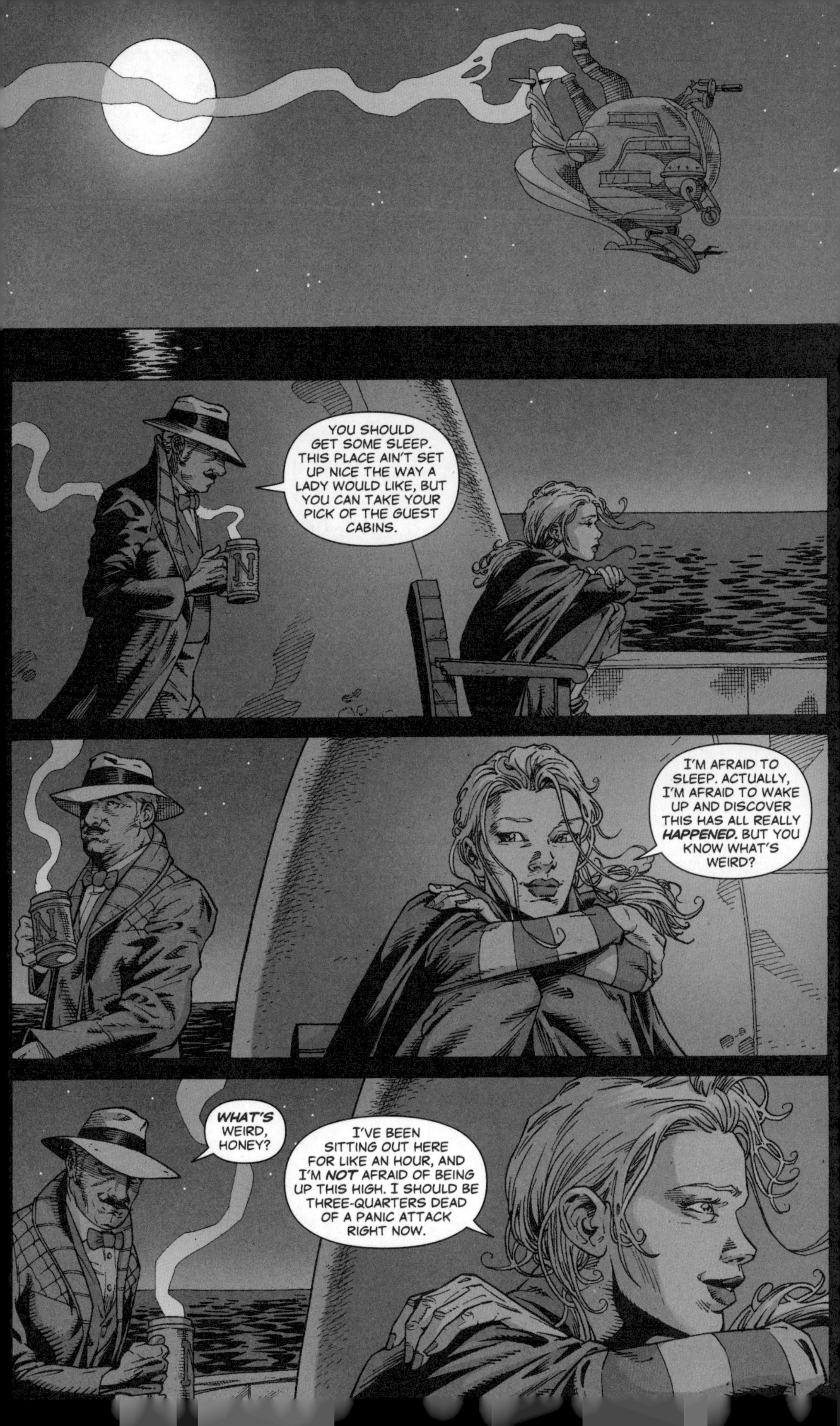
YOU SHOULD GET SOME SLEEP. THIS PLACE AIN'T SET UP NICE THE WAY A LADY WOULD LIKE, BUT YOU CAN TAKE YOUR PICK OF THE GUEST CABINS.
I'M AFRAID TO SLEEP. ACTUALLY, I'M AFRAID TO WAKE UP AND DISCOVER THIS HAS ALL REALLY ***HAPPENED.*** BUT YOU KNOW WHAT'S WEIRD?
WHAT'S WEIRD, HONEY?
I'VE BEEN SITTING OUT HERE FOR LIKE AN HOUR, AND I'M ***NOT*** AFRAID OF BEING UP THIS HIGH. I SHOULD BE THREE-QUARTERS DEAD OF A PANIC ATTACK RIGHT NOW.

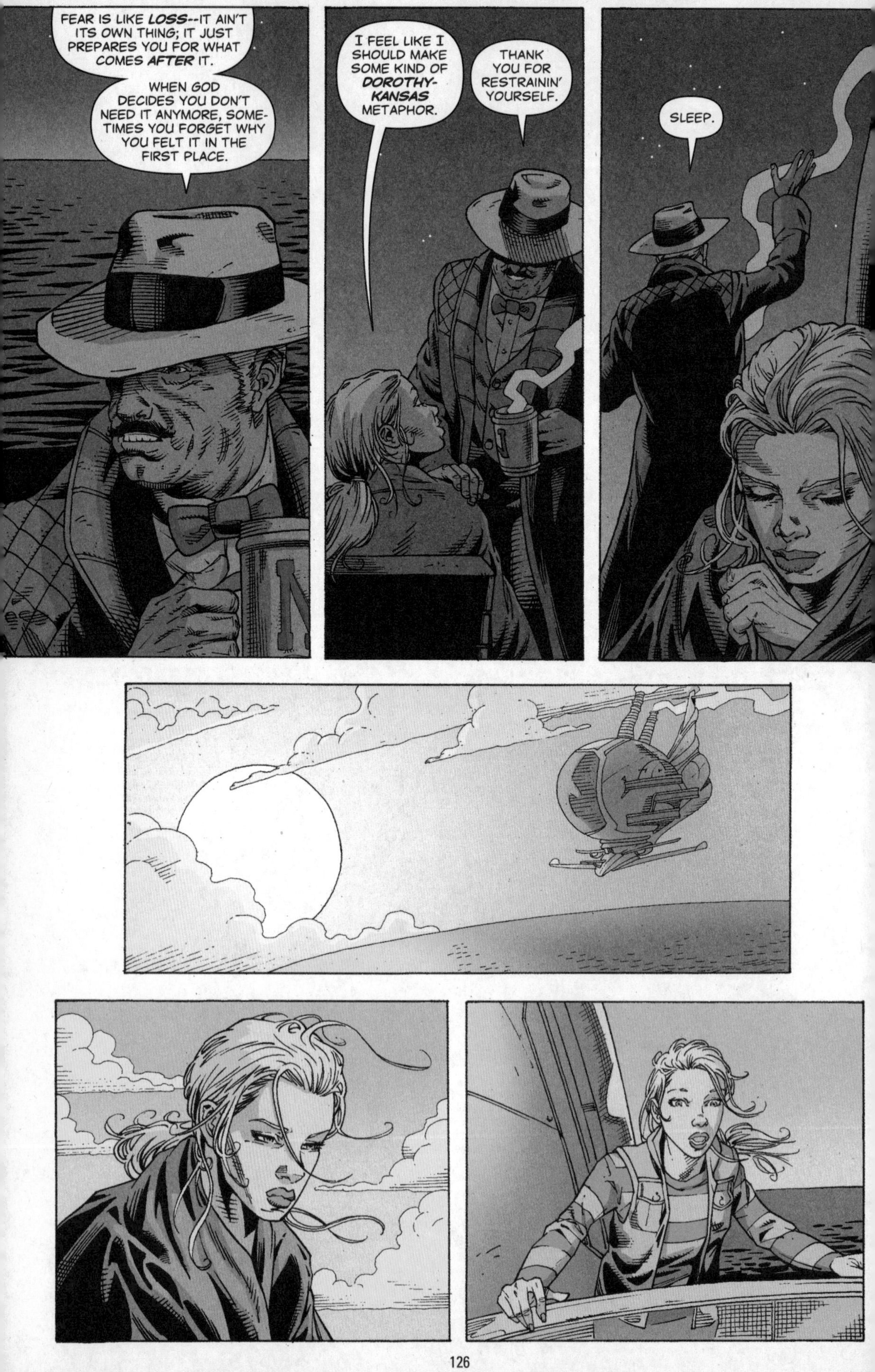
FEAR IS LIKE LOSS--IT AIN'T ITS OWN THING; IT JUST PREPARES YOU FOR WHAT COMES AFTER IT.
WHEN GOD DECIDES YOU DON'T NEED IT ANYMORE, SOMETIMES YOU FORGET WHY YOU FELT IT IN THE FIRST PLACE.
I FEEL LIKE I SHOULD MAKE SOME KIND OF DOROTHY-KANSAS METAPHOR.
THANK YOU FOR RESTRAININ' YOURSELF.
SLEEP.

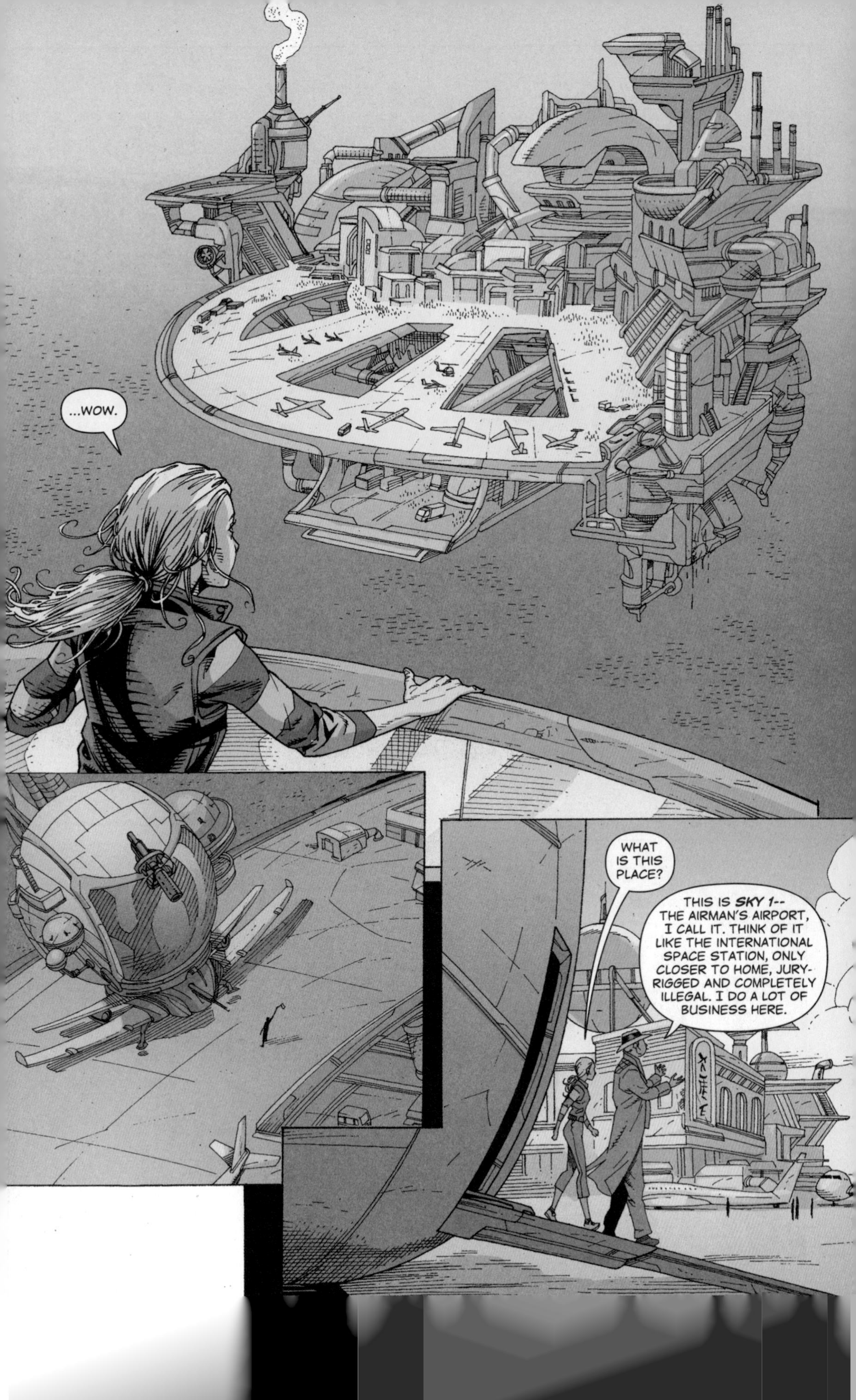
...WOW.
WHAT IS THIS PLACE?
THIS IS **SKY 1**-- THE AIRMAN'S AIRPORT, I CALL IT. THINK OF IT LIKE THE INTERNATIONAL SPACE STATION, ONLY CLOSER TO HOME, JURY-RIGGED AND COMPLETELY ILLEGAL. I DO A LOT OF BUSINESS HERE.

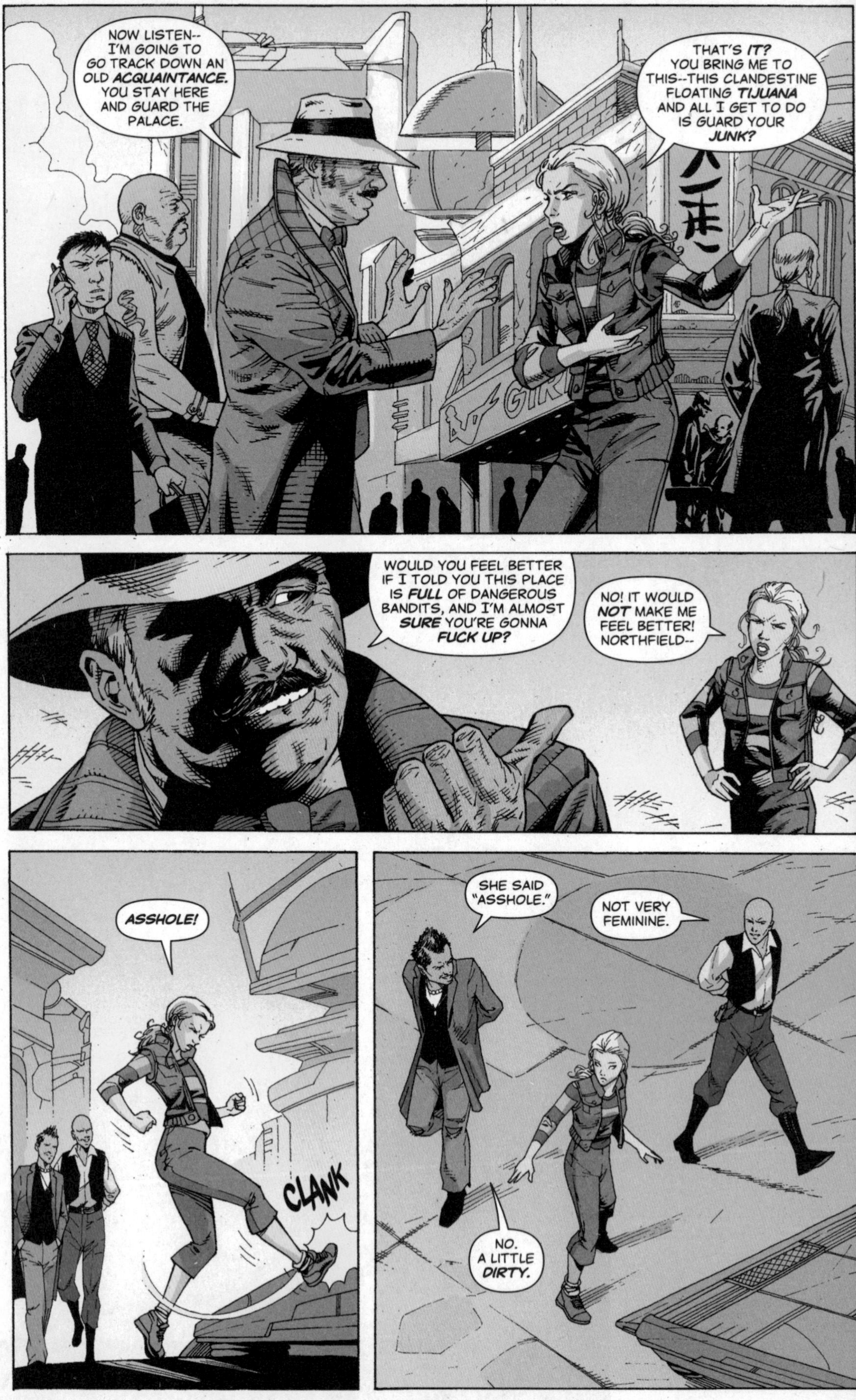
NOW LISTEN-- I'M GOING TO GO TRACK DOWN AN OLD ACQUAINTANCE. YOU STAY HERE AND GUARD THE PALACE.
THAT'S IT? YOU BRING ME TO THIS--THIS CLANDESTINE FLOATING TIJUANA AND ALL I GET TO DO IS GUARD YOUR JUNK?
WOULD YOU FEEL BETTER IF I TOLD YOU THIS PLACE IS FULL OF DANGEROUS BANDITS, AND I'M ALMOST SURE YOU'RE GONNA FUCK UP?
NO! IT WOULD NOT MAKE ME FEEL BETTER! NORTHFIELD--
ASSHOLE!
CLANK
SHE SAID "ASSHOLE."
NOT VERY FEMININE.
NO. A LITTLE DIRTY.

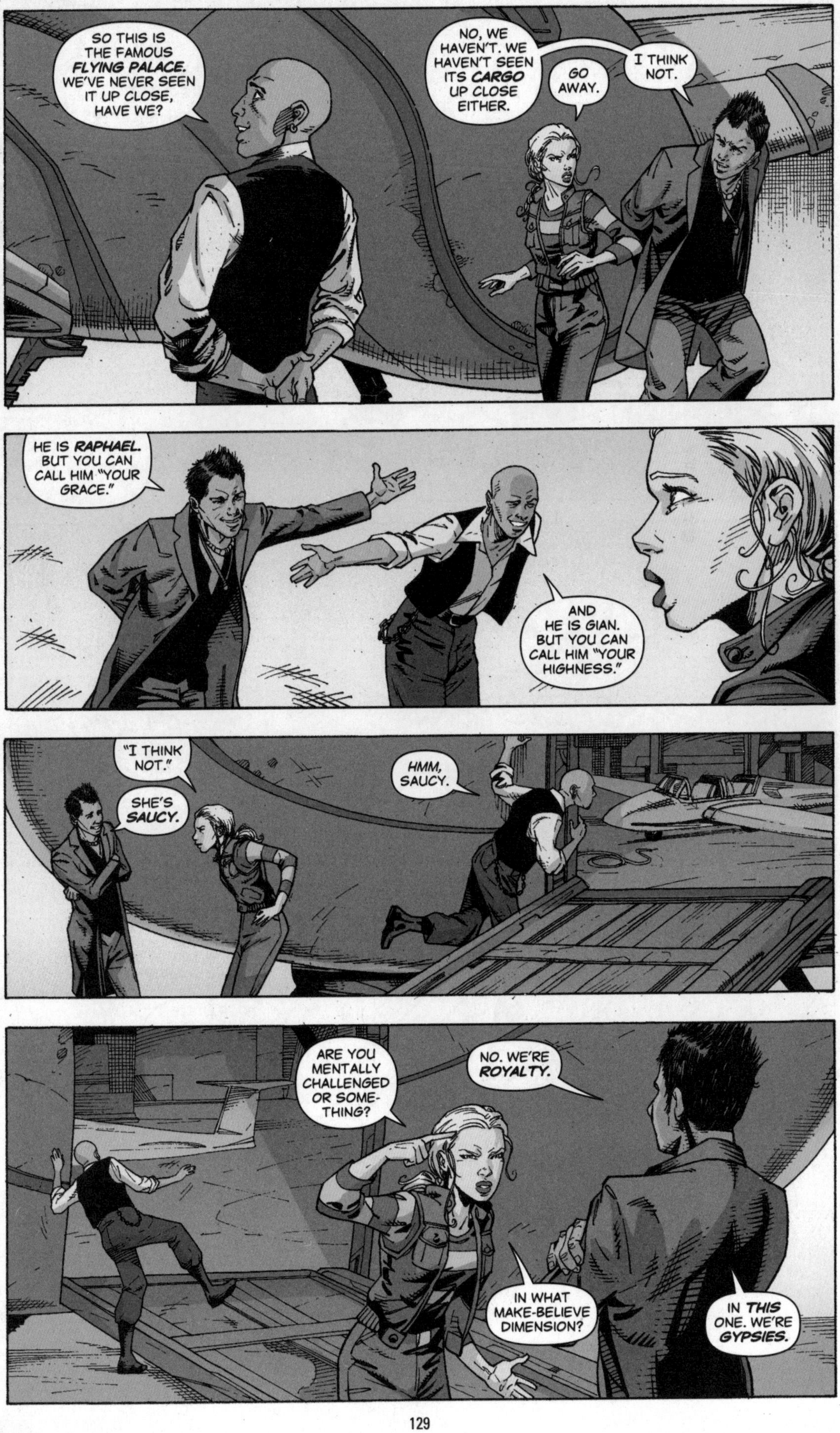
SO THIS IS THE FAMOUS **FLYING PALACE.** WE'VE NEVER SEEN IT UP CLOSE, HAVE WE?
NO, WE HAVEN'T. WE HAVEN'T SEEN ITS **CARGO** UP CLOSE EITHER.
GO AWAY.
I THINK NOT.
HE IS **RAPHAEL.** BUT YOU CAN CALL HIM "YOUR GRACE."
AND HE IS GIAN. BUT YOU CAN CALL HIM "YOUR HIGHNESS."
"I THINK NOT."
SHE'S **SAUCY.**
HMM, SAUCY.
ARE YOU MENTALLY CHALLENGED OR SOME-THING?
NO. WE'RE **ROYALTY.**
IN WHAT MAKE-BELIEVE DIMENSION?
IN **THIS** ONE. WE'RE **GYPSIES.**

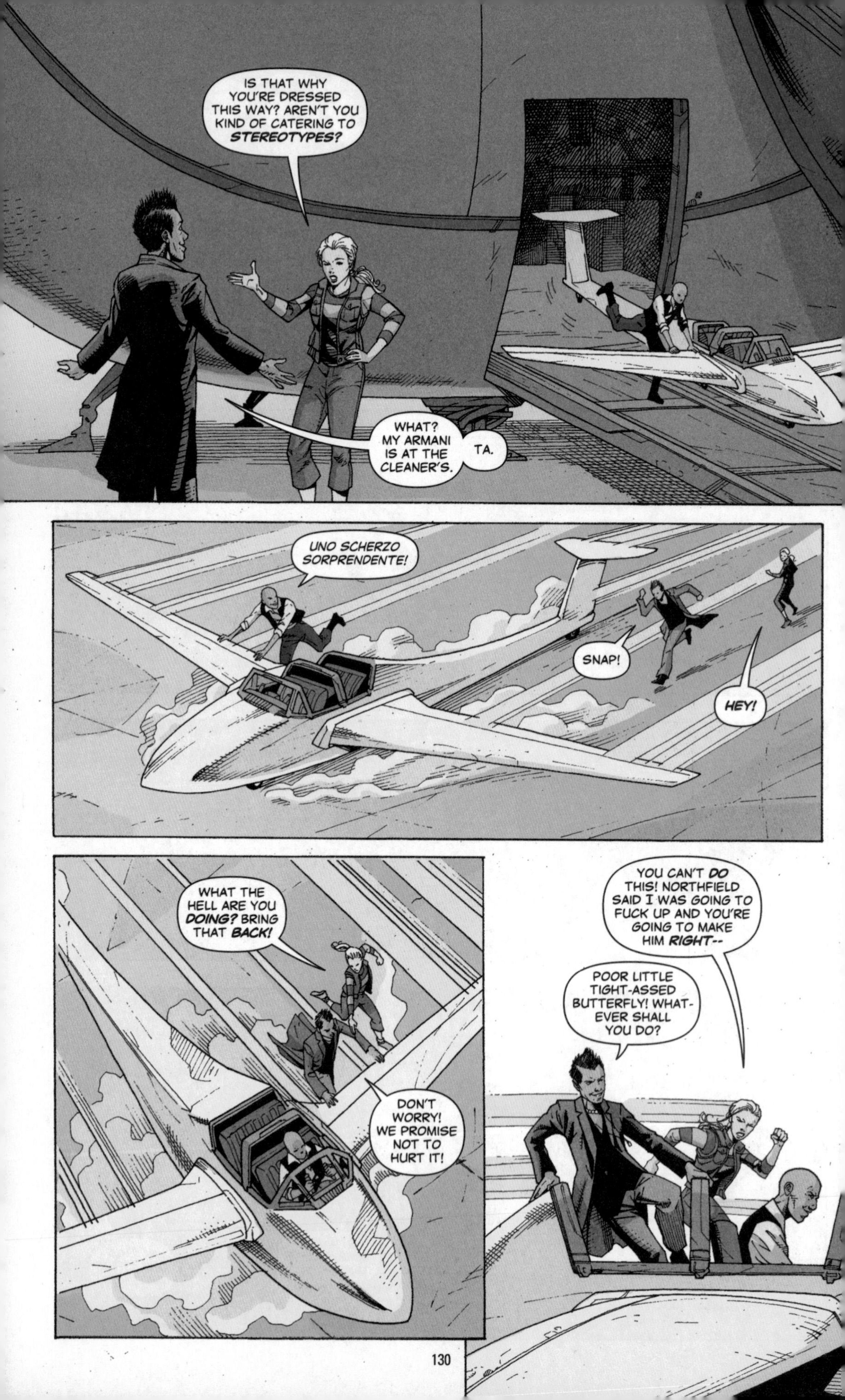
IS THAT WHY YOU'RE DRESSED THIS WAY? AREN'T YOU KIND OF CATERING TO STEREOTYPES?
WHAT? MY ARMANI IS AT THE CLEANER'S.
TA.
UNO SCHERZO SORPRENDENTE!
SNAP!
HEY!
WHAT THE HELL ARE YOU DOING? BRING THAT BACK!
DON'T WORRY! WE PROMISE NOT TO HURT IT!
YOU CAN'T DO THIS! NORTHFIELD SAID I WAS GOING TO FUCK UP AND YOU'RE GOING TO MAKE HIM RIGHT--
POOR LITTLE TIGHT-ASSED BUTTERFLY! WHAT-EVER SHALL YOU DO?

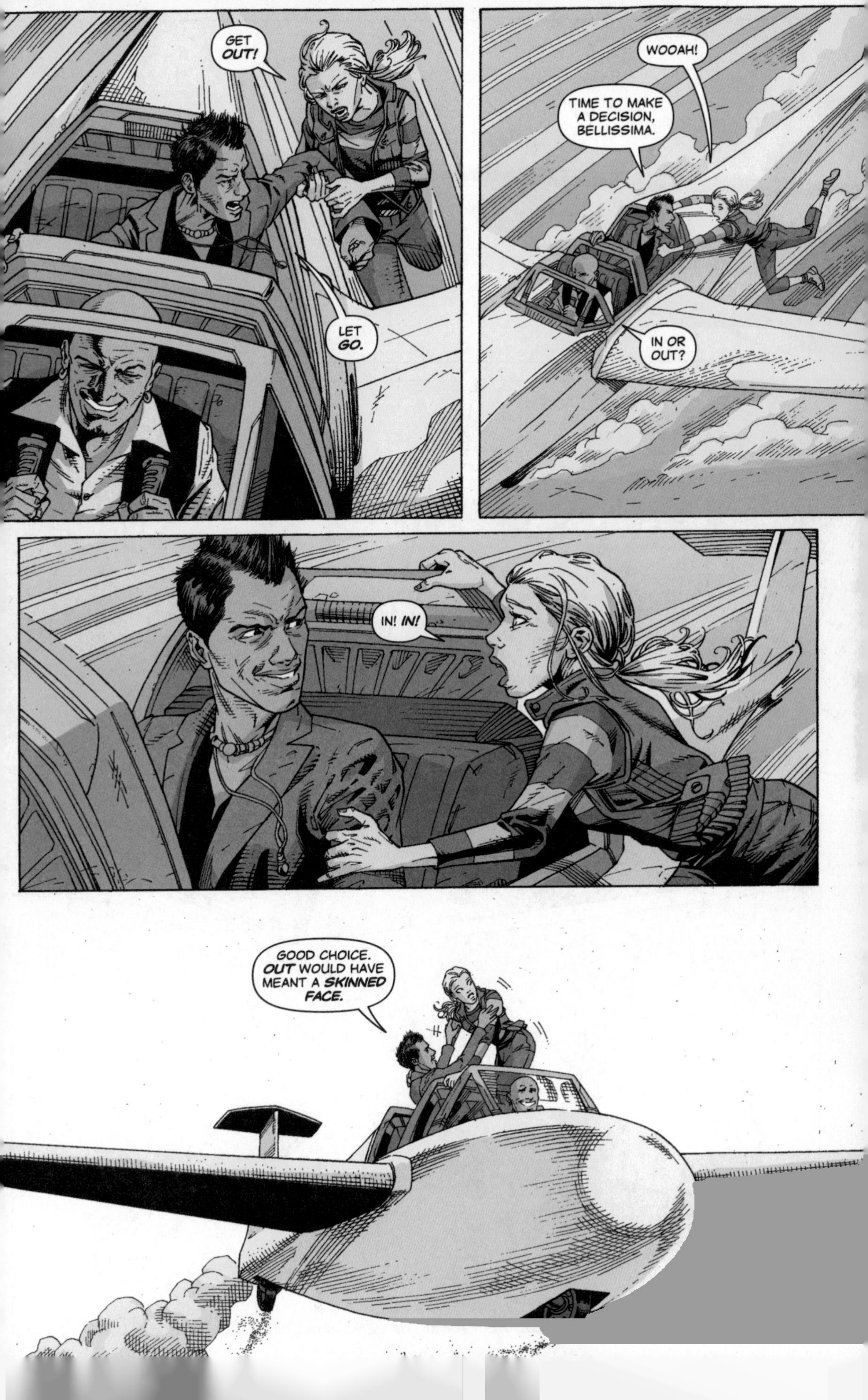

GET OUT!
LET GO.
WOOAH!
TIME TO MAKE A DECISION, BELLISSIMA.
IN OR OUT?
IN! IN!
GOOD CHOICE. OUT WOULD HAVE MEANT A SKINNED FACE.

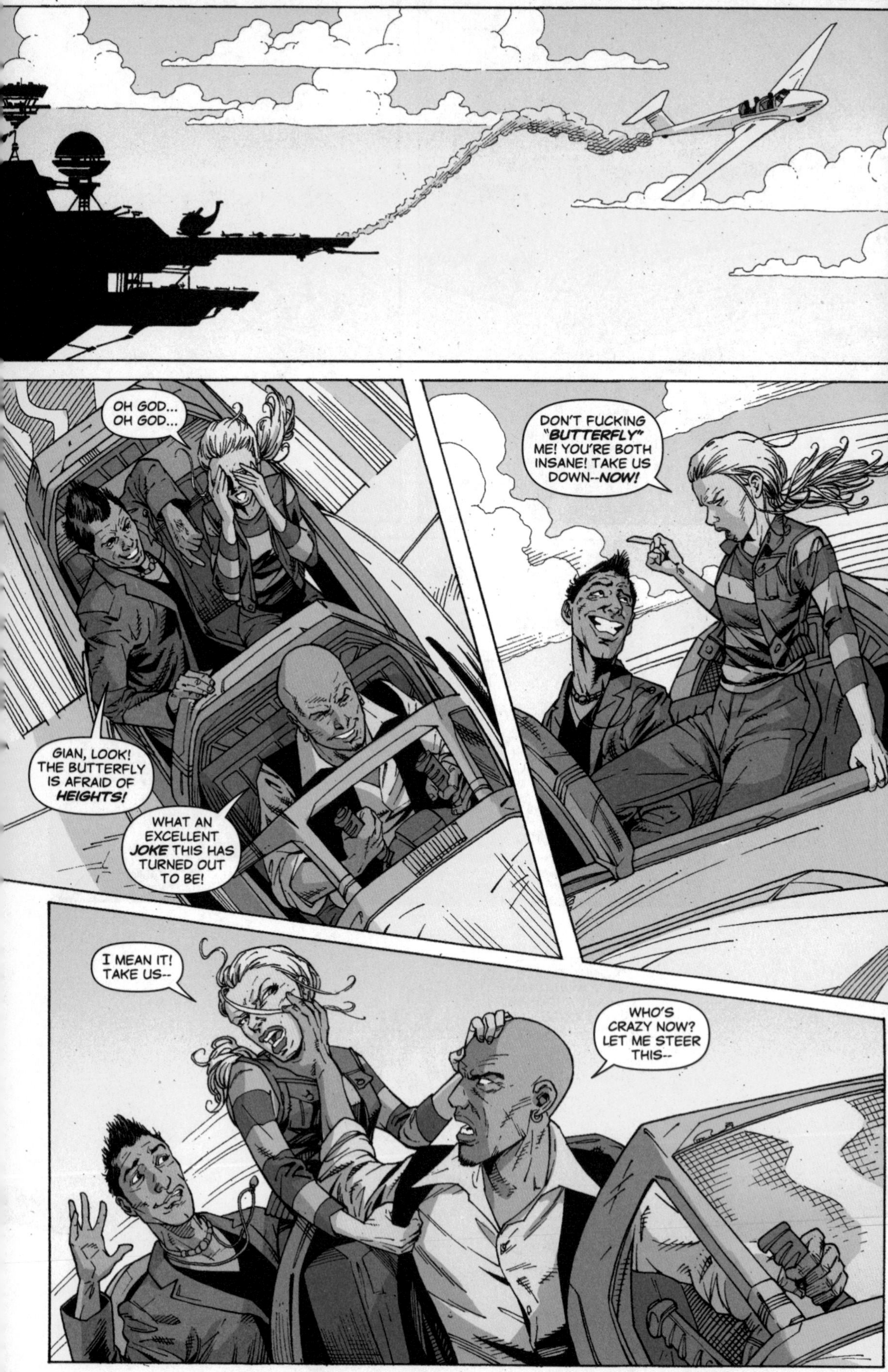
OH GOD... OH GOD...
GIAN, LOOK! THE BUTTERFLY IS AFRAID OF HEIGHTS!
WHAT AN EXCELLENT JOKE THIS HAS TURNED OUT TO BE!
DON'T FUCKING "BUTTERFLY" ME! YOU'RE BOTH INSANE! TAKE US DOWN--NOW!
I MEAN IT! TAKE US--
WHO'S CRAZY NOW? LET ME STEER THIS--

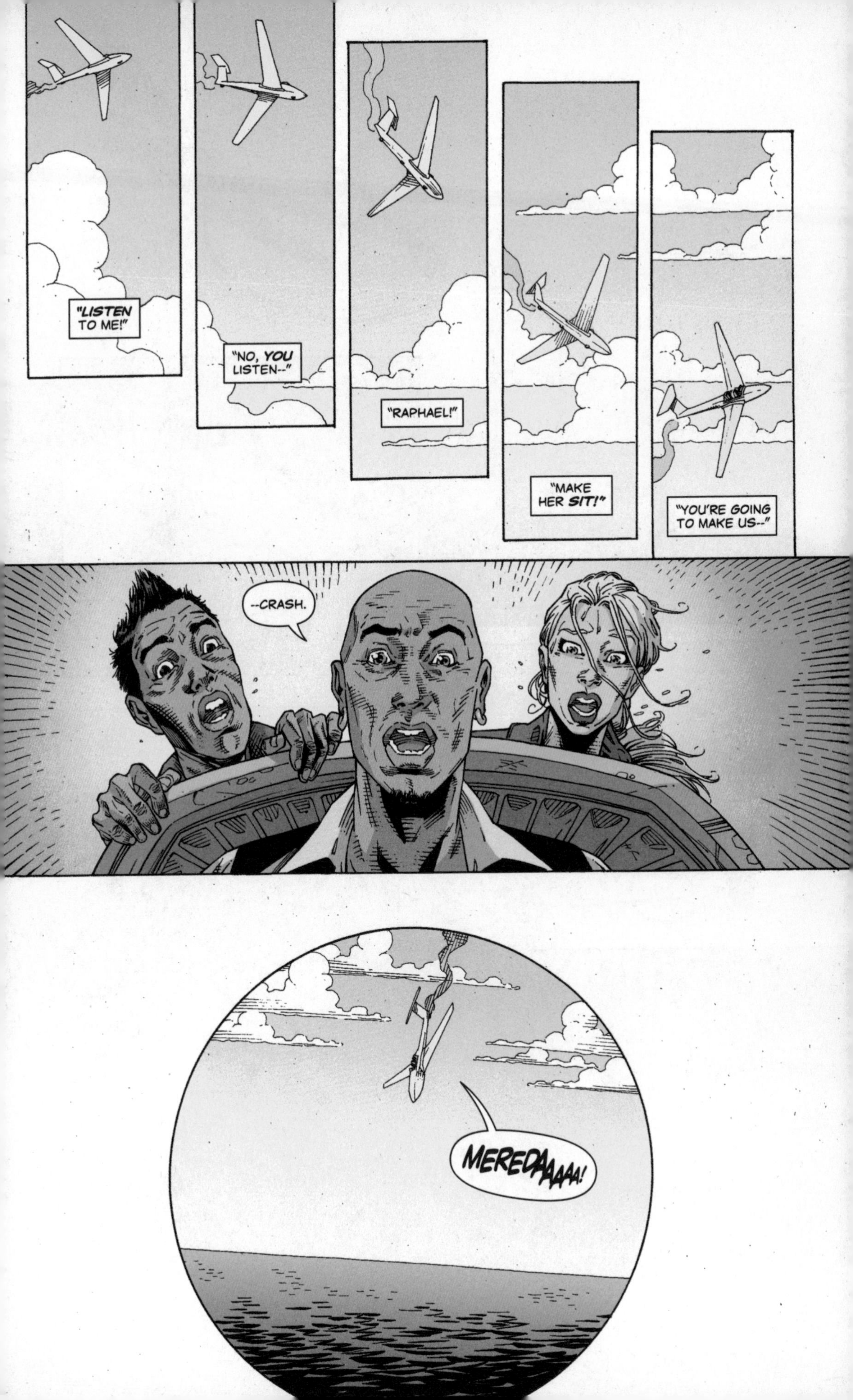
"LISTEN TO ME!"
"NO, YOU LISTEN--"
"RAPHAEL!"
"MAKE HER SIT!"
"YOU'RE GOING TO MAKE US--"
--CRASH.
MEREDAAAAA!

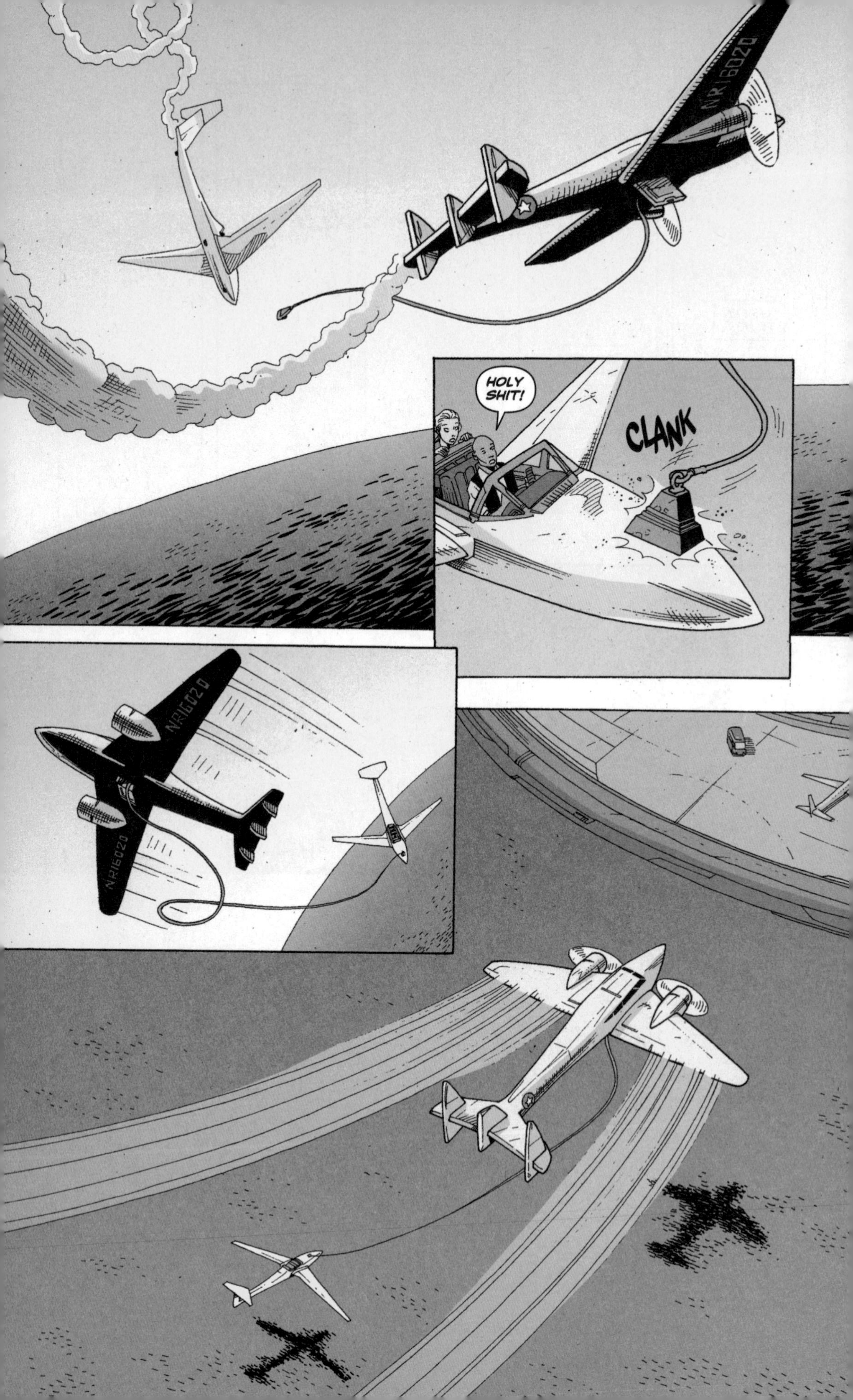
HOLY SHIT!
CLANK

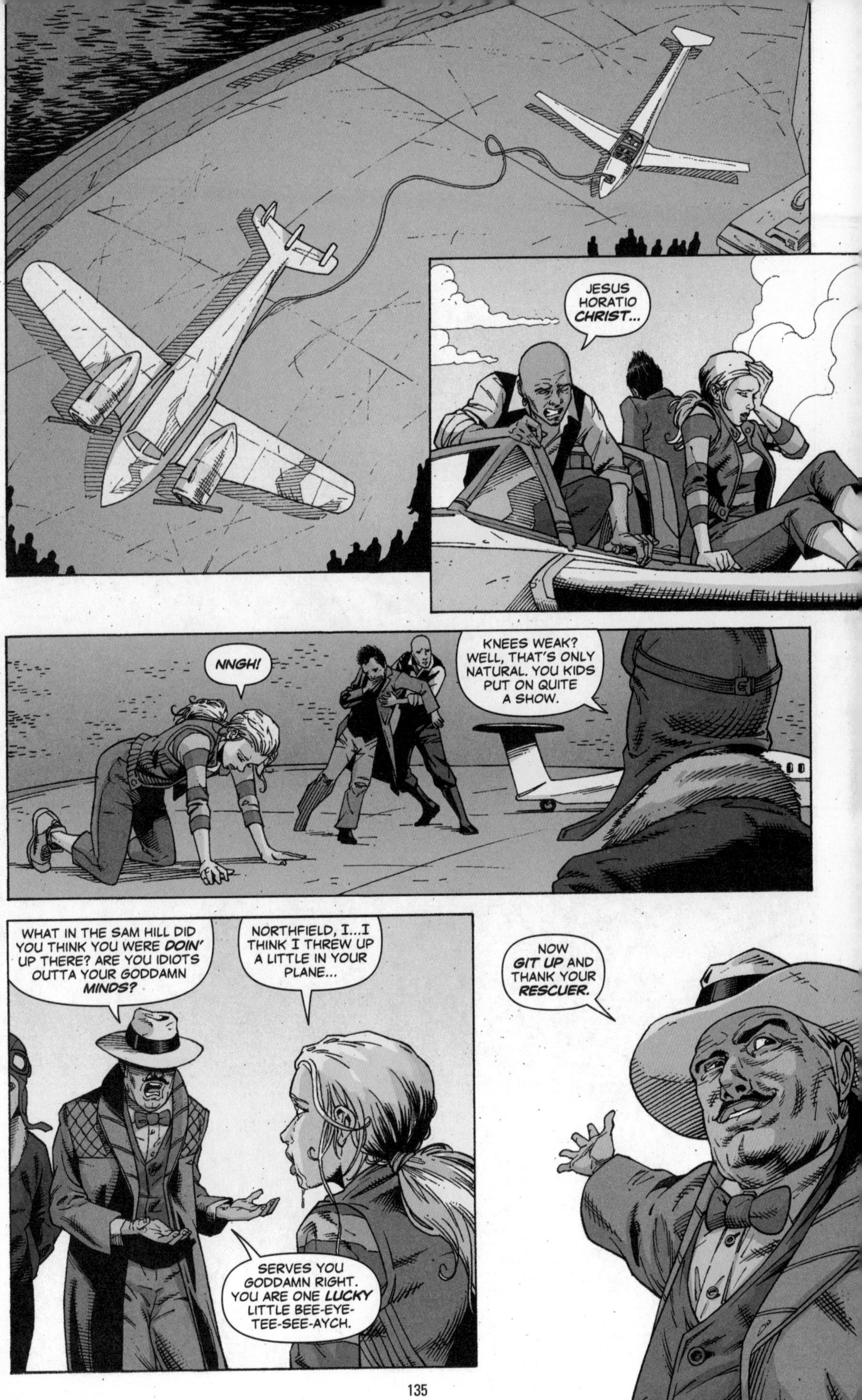
JESUS HORATIO CHRIST...
NNGH!
KNEES WEAK? WELL, THAT'S ONLY NATURAL. YOU KIDS PUT ON QUITE A SHOW.
WHAT IN THE SAM HILL DID YOU THINK YOU WERE DOIN' UP THERE? ARE YOU IDIOTS OUTTA YOUR GODDAMN MINDS?
NORTHFIELD, I...I THINK I THREW UP A LITTLE IN YOUR PLANE...
SERVES YOU GODDAMN RIGHT. YOU ARE ONE LUCKY LITTLE BEE-EYE-TEE-SEE-AYCH.
NOW GIT UP AND THANK YOUR RESCUER.

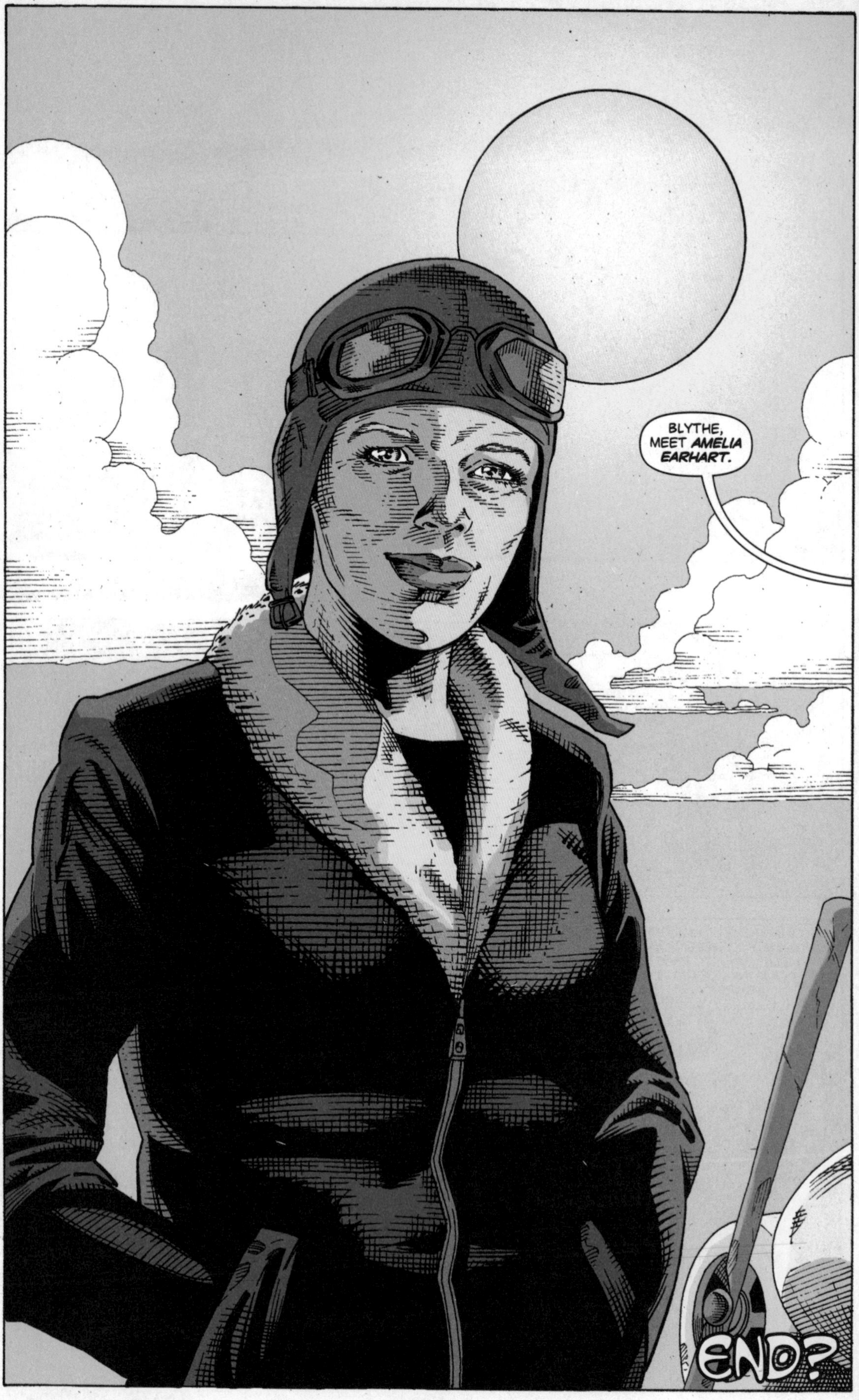
BLYTHE, MEET AMELIA EARHART.
END?

air

sketchbook

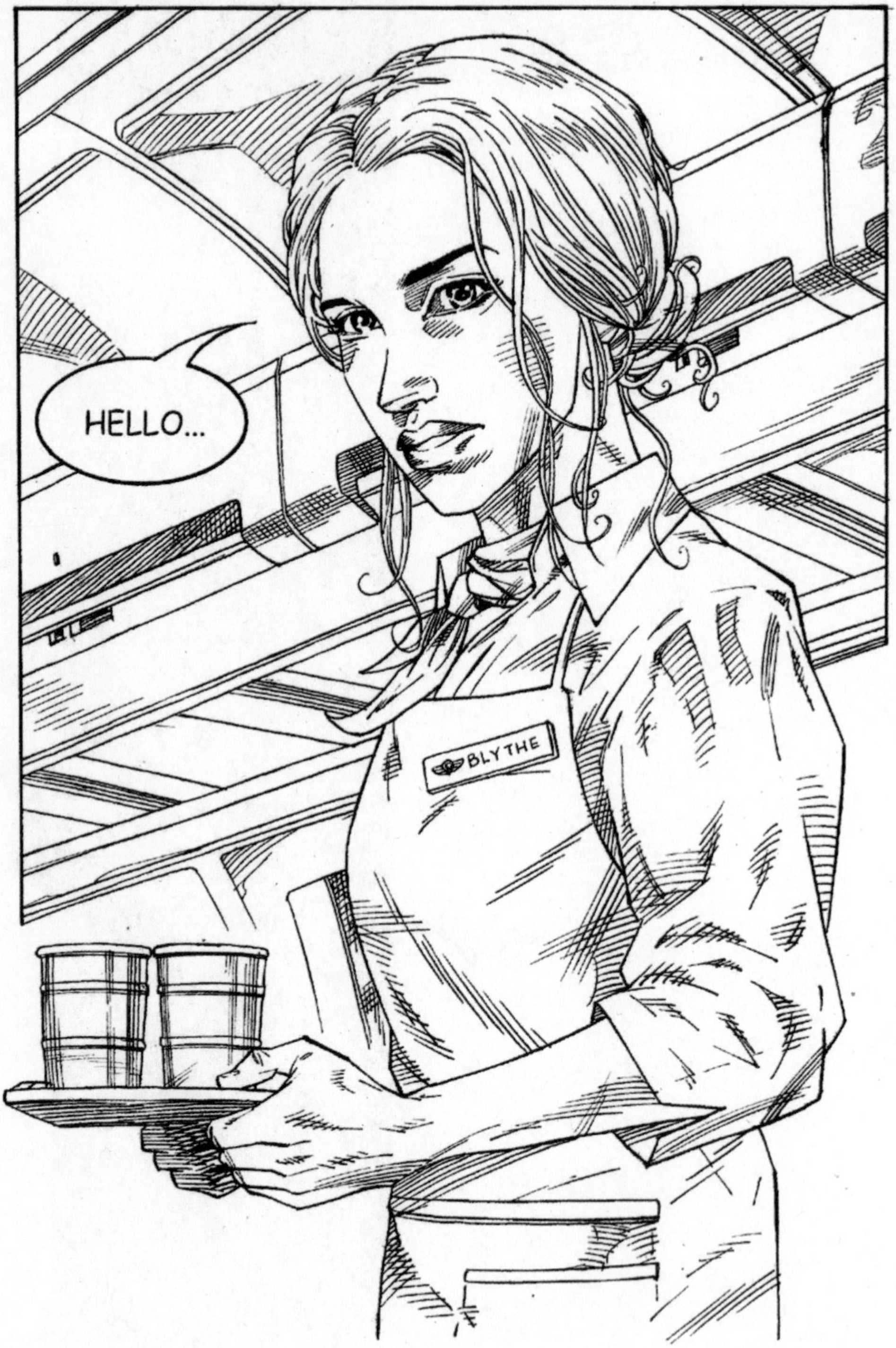
HELLO...
BLYTHE

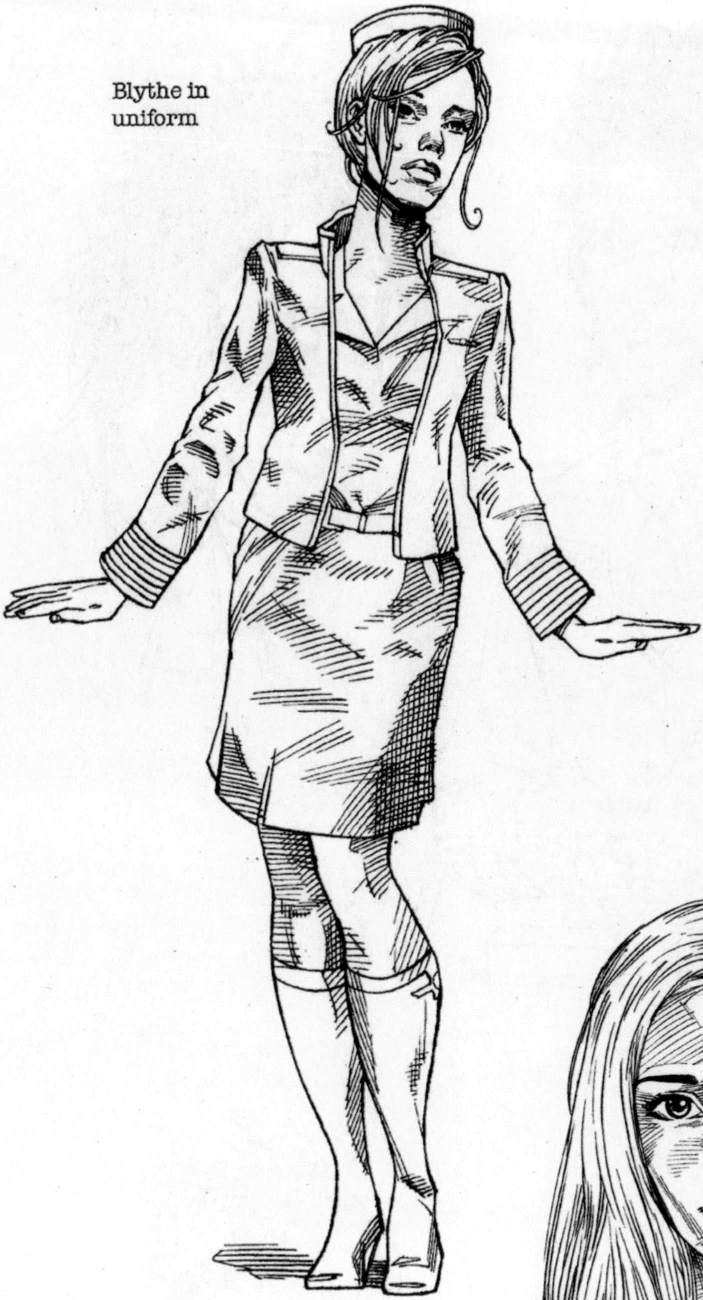

Blythe in uniform

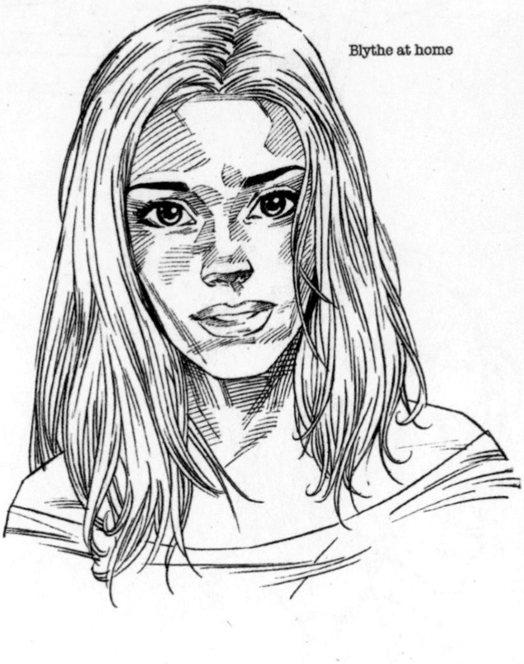

Blythe at home

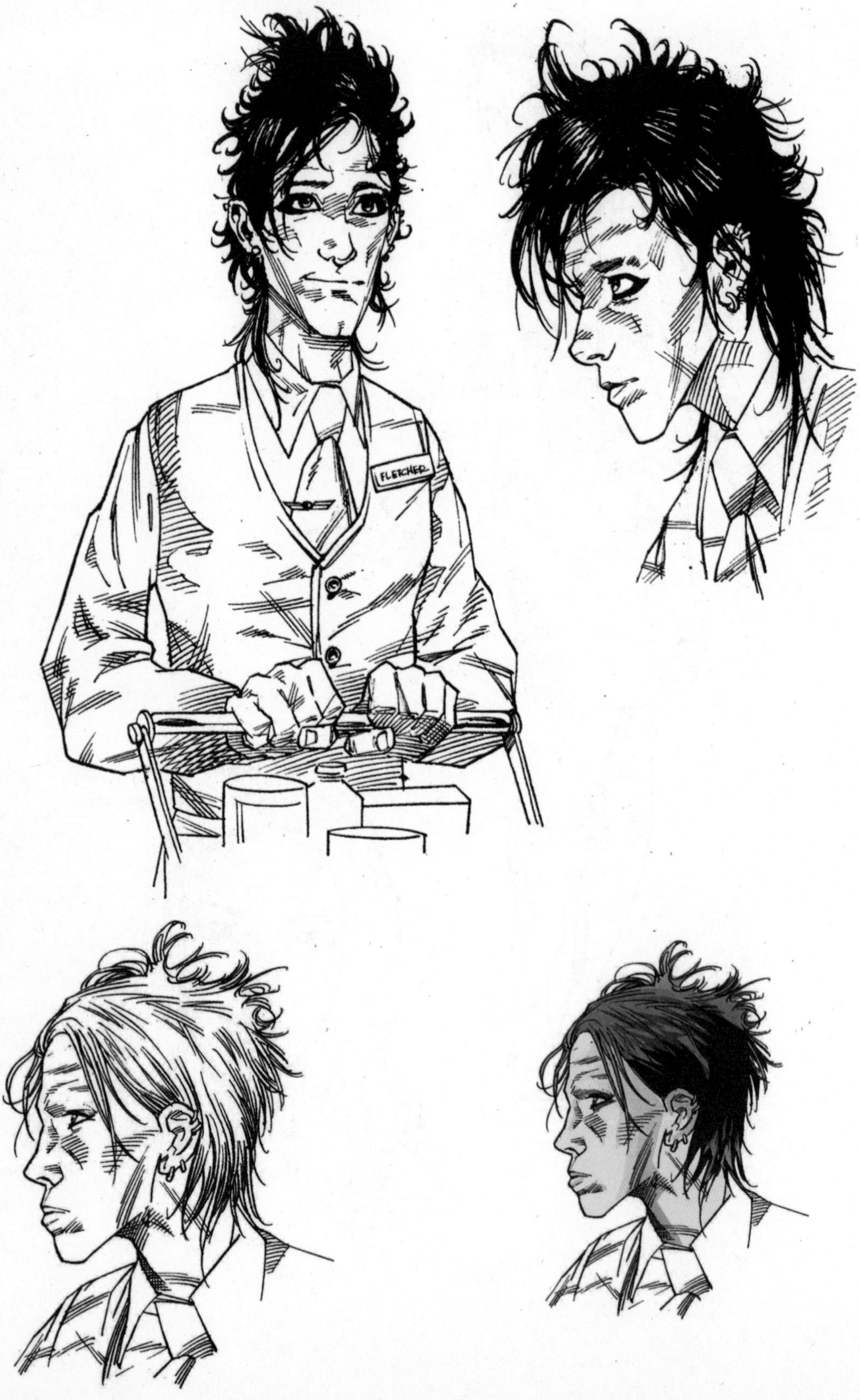
FLETCHER

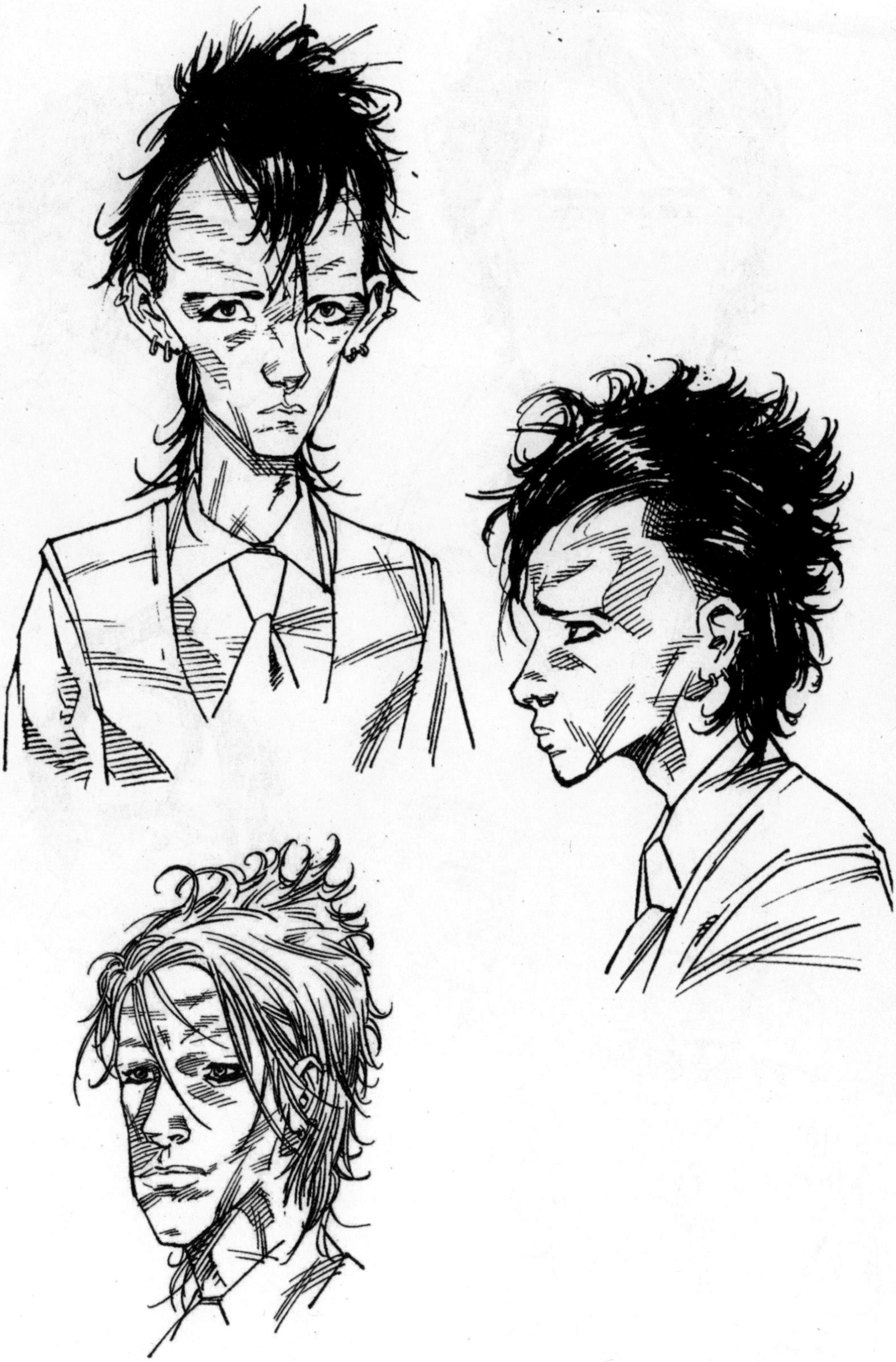

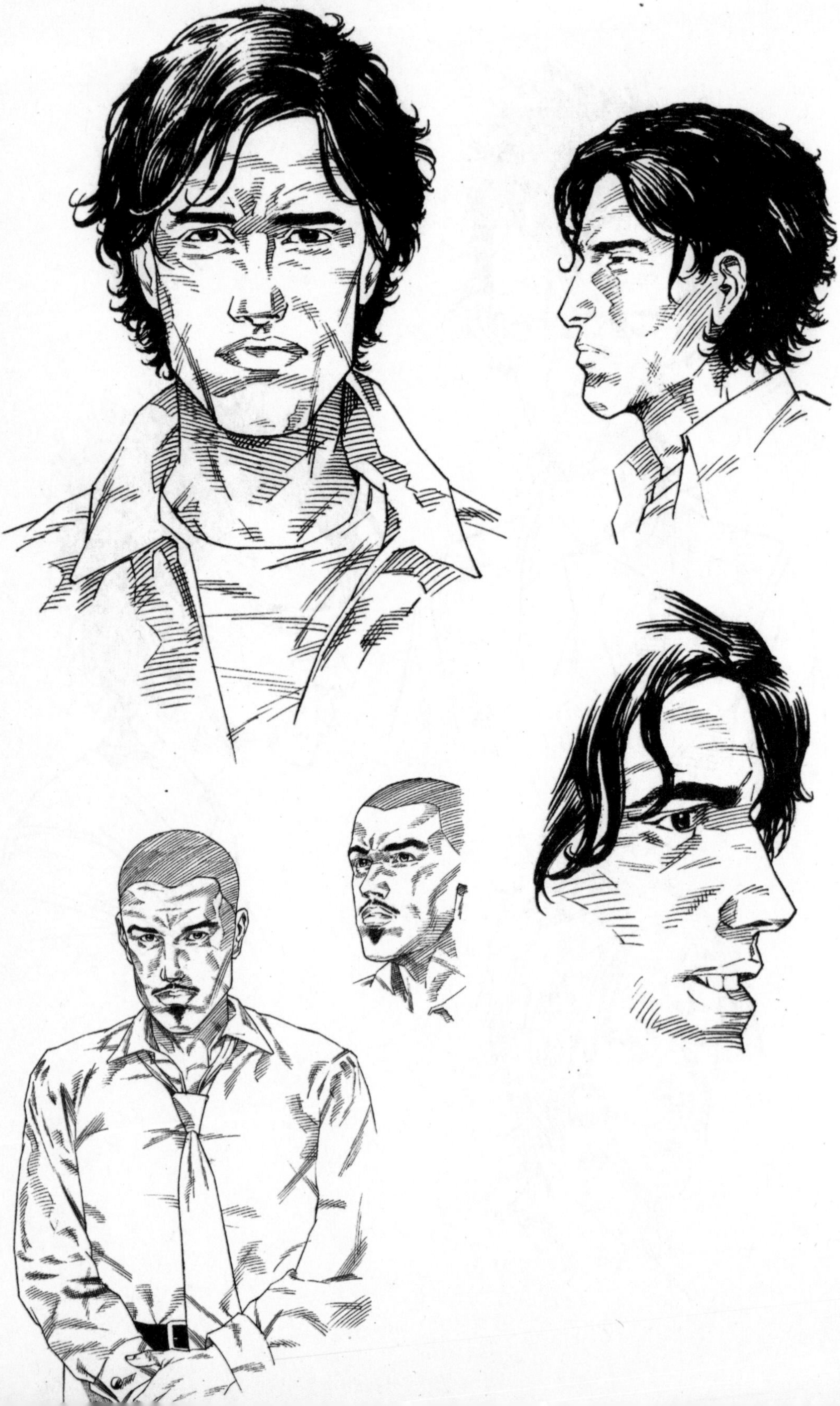

Zayn #2

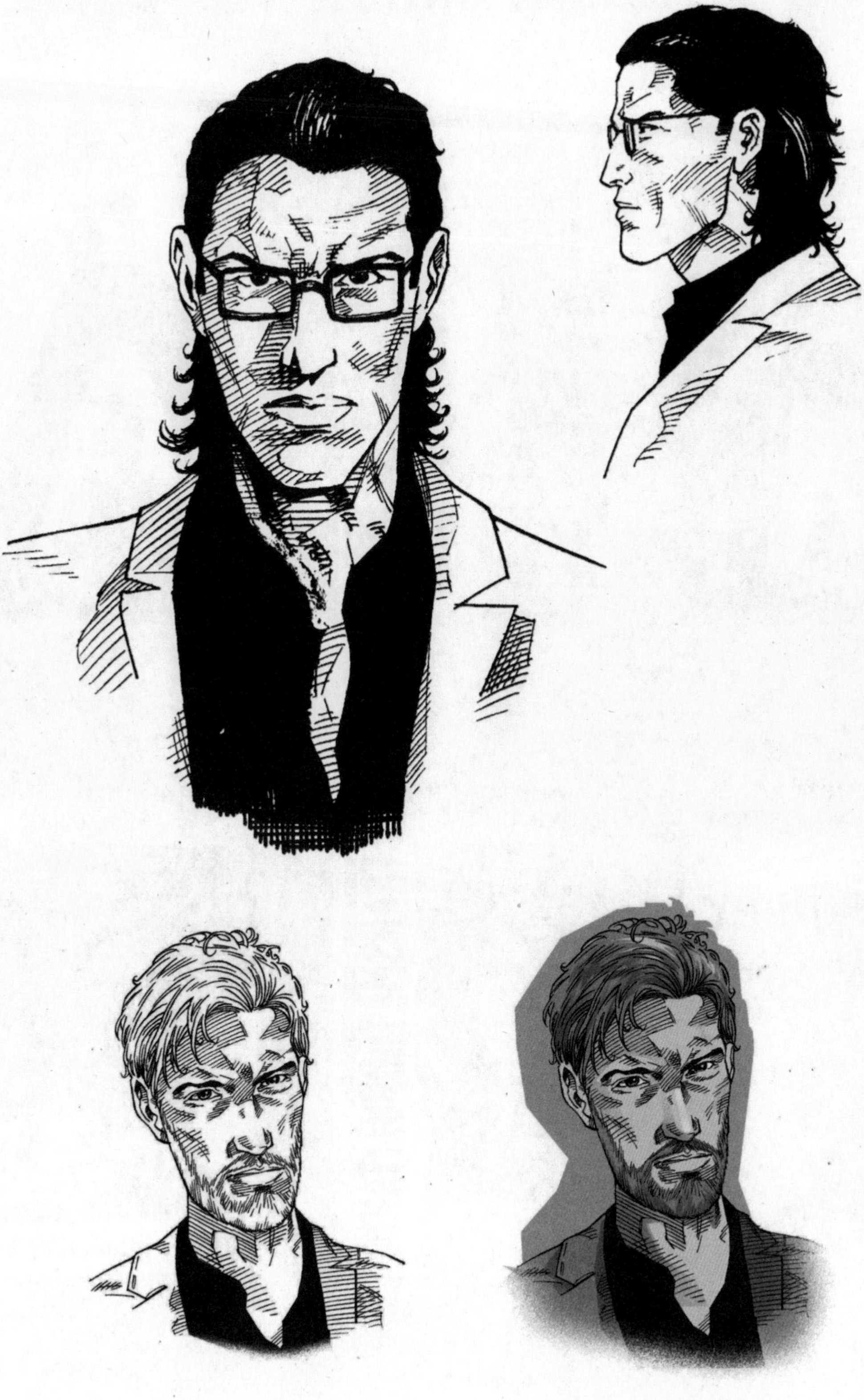

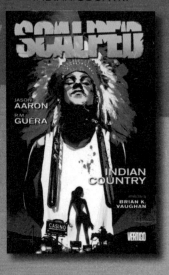

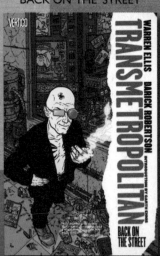